ADVANCE PRAISE
for

in Earth's Company

In Earth's Company is the best book I have seen about the business aspects of sustainable development. Carl Frankel holds up the sustainable development diamond and examines its facets through a business lens. In both praising and criticizing business, the author is insightful. A must-read for people in business and people trying to understand the business world.
— David Buzzelli, ex-co-chair, President's Council on Sustainable Development, ex-chief environmental officer, Dow Chemical Company

— ○ —

In Earth's Company: Business, Environment, and the Challenge of Sustainability is the best-balanced book on business and the environment I've seen. Carl Frankel rightly lays the blame for our current crisis not in any one party's lap, but in the system that has us all talking only 'guild-speak' to each other in our own specialized corners of the world. Frankel transcends the self-righteous conflict between the guilds that has unfortunately dominated the environmental discussion, and presents the issues from a refreshingly broad and positive perspective. He does this by not falling into the 'universalist fallacy' of assuming that one truth fits all. "We now control evolution at least as much as it controls us," according to Frankel, and we have to break down the barriers to discussion and design the future we collectively want. Frankel's book will be an enormous aid in that process, providing both insights and vision in an unfailingly entertaining and inclusive style.
— Robert Costanza, director, Institute for Ecological Economics, University of Maryland .

— ○ —

A very thought-provoking journey from the past of corporate environmentalism into the future of 'corporate sustaincentrism.' This is an extraordinarily energizing book, building creative tension in every chapter as to where (and why) business is now and how it must evolve to become truly ecologically sustainable. Beyond cogent road-mapping, Frankel also weaves into his story a devastating indictment of dualism, reductionism, scientism, rationalism, modernism, technocentrism, and many of the other 'isms' that currently undergird our eco-unfriendly capitalist system. In replacement, he issues a clarion call for a more humanistic, synthetic, and sustainable industrial thinking. This is a progressive *must-read* for any corporate executive wishing to successfully navigate the emergent sustainability industrial revolution. Enjoy, as I did, this mind-shifting ride with Carl Frankel into deep eco- and world-centric consciousness.
— Tom Gladwin, professor and director, Global Environment Program, Leonard N. Stern School of Business, New York University

— ◯ —

A comprehensive, 'state-of-the-art' overview. Indispensable to corporations of the declining, fossil-fueled Industrial Era, as well as to environmentalists, business people, and investors in the cleaner, greener, socially-responsible sectors of the emerging 21st Century economies of the information-rich Solar Age. Frankel identifies many promising pathways to more sustainable societies — and the many 'win-win-win' strategies to get us there while protecting other life forms and Planet Earth.
— Hazel Henderson, author, *Building a Win-Win World*

— ◯ —

Carl Frankel provides a balanced and well-documented exposition of many of the complexities, ambiguities and contradictions of corporate environmentalism.
— David Korten, author, *When Corporations Rule the World*, chair, The Positive Futures Network

— ◯ —

In Earth's Company is a very important book: it will inspire our commerce with hope for a prosperous future for everyone.
— Bill McDonough, sustainable designer and architect and author, Hannover Principles

— ◯ —

In Earth's Company is an outstanding addition to the literature on the role of business as both contributor to the global environmental crisis and as the most powerful sector in moving society on a sustainable path. Frankel's thoughtful and thorough analysis is rich in exploring the historical and deep cultural and societal relationships of business, the environment, and a just and sustainable society and is crucial to devising strategies to move toward a more sustainable path. His accessible style combined with insightful observations and ideas about both current positive steps being taken by industry and the major cultural and technological shifts necessary for the future make the book a must-read for industrial leaders, policymakers, NGOs, and academics from a wide variety of disciplines.

— Anthony D. Cortese, President of Second Nature, former Dean of Environmental Programs at Tufts University, and Commissioner of the Massachusetts Department of Environmental Protection

— ○ —

In western culture, we tend to approach our problems in a compartmentalized fashion with what might be called a frail grasp on the big picture. This is especially true in matters of the environment. Finally, Carl Frankel has presented us with a wise overview which points towards a new paradigm that must be seriously considered if we are to have a livable future on this planet.

— Don Henley, recording artists and environmental activist

— ○ —

This prodigious yet highly readable undertaking shovels through both the 'mom and apple pie' happy face of green business and sustainable development, and the seemingly unbreachable cynicism of greenwash watchers. Frankel diligently and thoughtfully probes both the practical and the philosophical challenges of steering profitable business into harmony with the laws of nature.

— Gil Friend, president, Gil Friend & Associates

— ○ —

Realistic insight into the extraordinary challenges facing us in the 21st century. Both down-to-earth and intensely hopeful. Frankel highlights some indicators that the revolutionary changes necessary to ensuring a sustainable future are actually beginning to happen. A must-read for anyone looking for encouragement and the outline of a pathway.

— Kate Fish, director, sustainable development, Monsanto Co.

— ○ —

in Earth's Company

Business, Environment, and the Challenge of Sustainability

Carl Frankel

Foreword by Paul Hawken

NEW SOCIETY PUBLISHERS

To further the dialogue about business and sustainability,
you can contact Carl Frankel via e-mail at:
Inearthco@aol.com

Cataloguing in Publication Data:
A catalog record for this publication is available from the National Library of
Canada and the Library of Congress.

Cover design by Miriam MacPhail.
Author photograph by Janice Kruger.

Printed in Canada on acid-free, partially recycled (20 percent post-consumer)
paper using soy-based inks by Best Book Manufacturers.

Inquiries regarding requests to reprint all or part of *In Earth's Company:
Business, Environment, and the Challenge of Sustainability* should be
addressed to New Society Publishers at the address below.

Paperback ISBN: 0-86571-380-4

To order directly from the publishers, please add $3.50 to the price of the first
copy, and $1.00 for each additional copy (plus GST in Canada). Send check or
money order to:

New Society Publishers,
P.O. Box 189, Gabriola Island, BC V0R 1X0, Canada.

New Society Publishers aims to publish books for fundamental social change
through nonviolent action. We focus especially on sustainable living, progressive leadership, and educational and parenting resources. Our full list of books
can be browsed on the world wide web at: http://www.newsociety.com

NEW SOCIETY PUBLISHERS
Gabriola Island BC, Canada and Stony Creek CT, U.S.A.

The difficulty lies, not in the new ideas,
but in escaping the old ones, which ramify,
for those brought up as most of us have been,
into every corner of our minds.
— John Maynard Keynes

Table of Contents

Acknowledgments

THIS BOOK BEGAN as a straightforward, rather conservative exercise in business journalism, the aim of which was to provide a status report on the state of corporate environmentalism, with me speaking to business executives from my official business-journalist *persona*. Over time, however, it dawned on me that there was a critically important cultural and philosophical dimension to the domain, and that if I failed to address it – if I limited myself to speaking in my safe professional voice – I would be committing precisely the same error as the many corporations that ignore critical dimensions of experience on the grounds of "professional irrelevancy." Since I wanted business to start thinking more inclusively, I had to do the same, or I would not be, as they say, "walking my talk." And so I set out to write a business book that in addition to touching all the necessary business bases would bring in more humanistically-oriented material on an as-needed basis – psychology, philosophy, and the like. And that is the book, the "business-book-plus," that you hold in your hands.

It has been quite a journey. Along the way, I have had the support of a phalanx of friends and professional associates who have collectively broadened my understanding of the subject matter, kept me on target factually and conceptually, and provided invaluable editorial and moral support.

Dave Buzzelli, Walter Coddington, Ralph Earle, Omar Khalifa, Michael Silverstein, Ross Stevens, and Bryan Thomlison all took time out from their busy lives to respond to a preliminary questionnaire. Brad Allenby, Dan Becker, Beth Beloff, Alan Borner, Joe Cascio, Richard Donovan, Melissa Everett, Ed Gottsman, A.J. Grant, Lois Kaufmann, Rao Kolluru, Bruce Piasecki, Paul Ray, Marty Spitzer, Martin Wright, and Roger Wynne read portions of the manuscript and provided valuable feedback. Eric Booth Miller and Susan Schwarz read many chapters and responded each time with alacrity and intelligence. Tom Gladwin read the entire manuscript and provided a much-needed course correction at a critical juncture.

Others who read the entire manuscript, in various incarnations, include Deborah Bansemer, Molly Barnes, Annie Berthold-Bond, Ralph Earle, Gil Friend, Ann Graham, Jim Nail, and Kate Victory. I am indebted to them all for their advice and support, and of course any errors or flaws are mine, not theirs.

Others to whom I owe a debt of gratitude include Peter Prescott, who provided much-needed encouragement about an early draft; John Willig, my agent, who from his first involvement believed in the book and did a bravura job of communicating its message to the oft-inscrutable world of publishing; Kim Loughran, my editor at *Tomorrow* magazine, who has been more than accommodating in giving me time off to focus on the book; and Chris Plant, my editor at *New Society Publishers,* who has been a delight to work with.

In the event that I have inadvertently left anyone deserving mention off this list, I hope they will accept my apologies. It is my memory, not my gratitude, that is lacking.

I am grateful to AT&T and Church & Dwight, both of which provided modest financial support that helped underwrite early research for this book. The funds were offered, and accepted, on the express condition that they were to have no effect on the editorial content, and they haven't. My answer to anyone inclined to believe otherwise is quite simple: read the book.

Finally, I would like to thank my mother and father, to whose memory this book is dedicated. I am very grateful for who they were and for all they taught me.

Credits

My discussion in Chapter 5 of "John Wayne" and the "Generalissimo" is drawn from an article that I wrote for *Public Relations Journal,* and I have incorporated in Chapters 5, 7, and 11 material I initially wrote for *Tomorrow* magazine. I am grateful to both publications for permission to use those materials here. The *Columbia Dictionary of Quotations* was the source of the quotations by Keynes, Hoffer, Hardy, cummings, Huxley, Orwell, de Tocqueville, Lichtenberg, and Nietzsche. *The*

International Thesaurus of Quotations supplied the quotations by Learned Hand and Whitehead. The Ruskin quotation came from *The Oxford Dictionary of Quotations*. The Proust quotation appeared in *The Viking Book of Aphorisms*, by W.H. Auden and Louis Kronenberger, and the Robert Frost excerpt comes from his poem "Mending Wall," which appears in *The Norton Anthology of Modern Poetry*.

Foreword

by Paul Hawken

C IVILIZATION HAS ARRIVED AT AN EXTRAORDINARY THRESHOLD: all living systems upon which life depend are in decline, and the rate of decline is accelerating as material prosperity increases.

The business philosophies, strategies, and assumptions that have guided commercial conduct for the last century or more are only making matters worse. Corporations routinely ignore the biophysical laws and principles that describe how life sustains itself on the planet. Yet enterprise is wholly and hugely dependent on natural forces and living systems. Are there any living systems it can do without? The atmosphere? The hydrologic cycle? Oceans? What will businesses do if its customers are malnourished, if the topsoil required to produce commodities has a forty-year half-life, if pure water required for manufacturing and consumption diminishes, if the weather becomes so erratic and unstable that it jeopardizes production, investments, and planning? What does business do if it cannot get insurance because climate-related losses have depleted capital reserves, if it no longer can get coverage for product liability because of public health issues, or if the North Atlantic current that maintains the warmth for European agriculture dissipates because of the melting of the Greenland icecap? Then what? Yet these are all real possibilities.

And this throws business-as-usual — all business-as-usual — into question. Our economic and social systems are built on, depend on, the foundation of living systems. If living systems are in decline, then traditional forecasting and business economics — the tools of business-as-usual, in other words — are equivalent to the house rules on a sinking cruise ship. We need more than a new understanding on the part of business about how living systems contribute to economic and human well-being. We also need new barometers for measuring economic and human health.

If one problem is the business community's lack of awareness about the role and importance of living systems, a second is its historically cavalier attitude toward resource utilization. In part this has been based on the assumption that the world's resources are inexhaustible. This may have been understandable in an era when the planet seemed to offer endless frontiers, but today, with the Earth's carrying capacity as stressed as it is, there can be only one explanation for that attitude: denial.

Another reason for industry's eagerness to consume resources has been the assumption that an extravagantly high industrial metabolism was necessary to maintain, if not to improve, our standard of living. While we cannot measure global resource consumption with certainty, e.g., we cannot say whether the rate of worldwide deforestation is proceeding at precisely 35, 37, 40, or 42 million acres per year, there is no arguing the fact that the world's forests are in decline. Yet there persists in some quarters a blank certainty about the necessity, some would call it the right, to use billions of tons per year of natural resources in a system that could not be constructed to be more inefficient. This attitude is anachronistic philosophically — we cannot keep on degrading our living systems — and it is just plain silly from a narrower business perspective. Efficiency is one of the hallmarks of the well-run business, and the gratuitous exploitation of natural resources is wildly inefficient. The modern industrial system is no more than one percent efficient when all material and energy inputs are considered.

In a sense, the business challenge is quite straightforward and no different than it has been since Darwinian time immemorial: adapt, or perish. This requires boldness and creativity on the part of individual companies and, also, more broadly, the inversion of two hundred years of economic thought — what might be called the "next industrial revolution." The core assumption underlying this transformation is that prosperity can no longer be achieved under the historic formulae of the industrial paradigm. Given that industrial growth further removes the capacity of the Earth to support human welfare, future economic progress must be measured by a different relationship, the pursuit of *resource* productivity as opposed to *labor* productivity.

The question is no longer how much timber, soil, minerals, or water are required to create one unit of well-being in society. The new question is: how much prosperity can we create with each board foot of timber, each liter of pure water, each square meter of topsoil, each pound of copper? The answers will not be forthcoming until the validity and central importance of this question, this all-important inversion, are truly understood. Once the move towards resource productivity is underway, it will create the same momentum of Schumpeterian chaos as have past changes in capitalist economies. And as with past waves of innovation, the winners will be in place long before the general public becomes aware of the change.

Already, forward-thinking businesses are seizing the opportunities that are being cast up by our current crisis of unsustainability. Meanwhile other companies hem and haw, while still others do their best to imitate the ostrich.

This is the world — a business world in crisis, a business world in transformation — that Carl Frankel explores in *In Earth's Company*. It is an important and in many ways dramatic story that he tells — a story of hope, denial, innovation and, yes, deception as well. Like all good stories, in the final analysis it is about the human condition, with all the usual frailties firmly in place.

Frankel brings to the story a wealth of knowledge about the business/sustainability domain, having covered the subject as a writer and journalist for a decade or more. His book is blessedly free of doctrinaire ideology. The world is full of people who bash corporations at every opportunity, and of others who blindly sing the glories of free-market capitalism. Frankel's analyses rise above this loud and largely irrelevant shouting match — irrelevant because the economic and social verities move forward, regardless of what this or that person says. If we are to make rapid progress in addressing the current crisis, we need to steer clear of ideology, both *pro* and *contra*, and focus on facts — both simple and subtle — and on solutions. *In Earth's Company* does this, powerfully and persistently. It is post-modern in the sense that, as his introduction notes, it is a "story about stories." But it does not trivialize the drama, as some post-modernists might be inclined to do. The transition to sustainability is, or should be, the central drama of our time. And Frankel treats it as such.

Although the next industrial revolution is about a transformation in our global business practices, sustainable development actually involves more than that. Most importantly, it is also about social justice. The inefficient use of resources is compounded by distributional inequity: the top population quintile, mostly in industrial countries, currently metabolizes 80-85 percent of the world's resources, leaving the balance for the remaining 4.7 billion. If the developing world were to share the same standard of living as the North, and if that living standard were to double over the next forty years, we would have to increase our resource use (and attendant waste) by a factor of sixteen. Publicly, governments, the United Nations, and commerce all work towards this end. Privately, no one believes we can increase industrial throughput by a factor of five, much less sixteen. It simply isn't physically possible. The reality is that we will clearly have to pursue other strategies in order to establish a supportable economic quality-of-life for the ten billion people who are expected to populate the planet by mid-century. This is a matter of basic arithmetic and equity.

Yet, as Frankel points out, the social aspect of sustainable development is not only about a more equitable distribution of resources, important as that is. It is also about a new cultural respect for what he calls the "subjective" dimensions of experience — those aspects that are not readily reducible to raw numbers. In calling for what Frankel dubs a "new humanism," *In Earth's Company* expands the business/sustainability dialogue beyond its usual preoccupation with physical resources and physical well-being.

This is one of several ways in which *In Earth's Company* enriches the business/sustainability dialogue, one of several ways in which it provides a perspective that manages to be both broad and deep. Frankel draws on his years in the journalistic trenches, and on his broader sensibility and sense of cultural directions, to tell a compelling, multi-leveled story of where we are, how we got here, and where we are headed. His insights are fresh, and his vision, when all is said and done, is hopeful. Once you have finished reading *In Earth's Company*, you will have a clear view of the problems and the possibilities, the inhibitions and innovations, in fact the entire panorama of the extraordinary and unfolding story of business and sustainable development. Whether you are a business executive looking to develop a sustainability strategy or a citizen keen on learning more about business and sustainable development, *In Earth's Company* is a book that will illuminate and guide.

Introduction:
A Story about Stories

*Man is eminently a storyteller. His search for a purpose, a cause,
an ideal, a mission and the like is largely a search for a plot and
a pattern in the development of his life story — a story that is
basically without meaning or pattern.*
— Eric Hoffer

IT IS NEW YEAR'S DAY 1997, in the Ambassador Grill downstairs at the
UN Plaza Hotel in New York City. Less than half a block away stands
the imposing facade of the United Nations itself. Built half a century
ago as a symbol of global harmony, it stands now as a monument to
bureaucratic inefficiency and a looming reminder of the suffering of billions worldwide.

Inside the restaurant, where a lavish, $52-a-person brunch is being
served, the poor seem far away. On this 'morning after,' the diners are a
bit subdued, but still celebrating the new year and decked out in their
finery.

I sit at a small table near the bar, chatting with Claes Sjöberg, the
publisher of *Tomorrow* magazine, the publication for which I write. We
have not met there to dine, but to become better acquainted — his base
is Stockholm, mine upstate New York — and to chat about the subject to
which both of us have dedicated our professional lives: business and
sustainable development.

Sjöberg stares thoughtfully into his coffee. "You know, I've been an
environmental journalist since the mid-1980s," he says eventually in his
excellent but lightly-accented English, "and the changes I've witnessed
have been extraordinary. Back then, if I approached a corporation and
said I wanted to speak about the environment, I would be shunted off to
a low-level technical person. Now, if I say the same thing, the doors are

1

opened straightaway and I'm ushered into the highest levels of the executive suite. Environmental issues are much, much more prominent in corporate thinking than they were. We've made enormous progress."

— O —

And now, another story. This one takes place six weeks later and 30 blocks further uptown in Manhattan, in an unpretentious coffee shop. My interlocutor this time is Jed Greer, the co-author with Kenny Bruno of *Greenwash: The Reality Behind Corporate Environmentalism*. We slide into a booth and order breakfast. This is my first encounter with the youngish Greer, and I am a bit surprised by his button-down, rather corporate style — hardly the *persona* I had expected in an ex-Greenpeace researcher whose book is an all-out assault on the corporate Satan.

Greer's careful, precise conversational style matches his physical appearance. "Any apparent changes in corporate attitude or conduct have been insignificant and for the most part hypocritical," he tells me. "Corporations don't exist to help the environment. They exist to make money. Until the basic rules of the games are changed, you will only see 'greenwashing' — corporations pretending to be environmentally concerned — not meaningful change."

— O —

Stories, stories. Everybody's got a story. Before there ever was *homo economicus* (economic man), probably even before *homo habilis* (tool-making man), there was *homo fabulans* — man, the storytelling animal. Claes Sjöberg's story is that things are looking up. Jed Greer's story is that nothing has changed and we're getting the same old corporate runaround.

I too have a story — or, more precisely, a story about stories. It's about what to make of Claes Sjöberg's story, and Jed Greer's story, and the many other ways that people interpret the role of business in the sustainable-development mix. The story I tell is neither pro- nor anti-business. I believe, with the conservative commentator Thomas Sowell, that reality is tricky: the more seamlessly a story holds together, the less likely it is to be true. Unfortunately, people in the sustainable-business world have a penchant for one-dimensional, seamless stories. This is true of the professional business-bashers who tell you that any and all corporate claims of environmental commitment are duplicitous and hollow, and it is also true of the professional apologists who swear by the earnestness of the corporate commitment.

No single analytical system, not mine nor anyone else's, can capture the whole of reality. And so, in setting forth my critique of the corporate response to the challenge of sustainable development, I have done my best to steer as clear as possible of simplistic pro- or anti-corporate ideologies, and to communicate my sense of the richness and variability of the underlying issues. There is a story to be told here, but it cannot be told in black and white.

The story I tell operates on several levels — because it is a story about stories, and in another sense as well. My main goal has been to assess the progress of the corporate community in making the transition to sustainable business practices. To that end, I have compiled a fair amount of data — told the story "by the numbers," as it were — as well as specific examples. Many business books stop there, content to make their case through statistics and case studies, and for a time I was tempted to do the same. Over time, however, I came to realize that were I to follow that course, I would be doing this work, and the reader, a disservice. All too often, business writers separate the performance of business *vis-à-vis* sustainable development from the cultural context in which it occurs. They stay carefully technical, carefully secure within the accepted and relatively narrow mode of discourse for the genre. As a result, critical questions about the framework within which that discourse is being conducted are not addressed. Cultural blinders are not acknowledged, much less challenged. As a result, the analyses are too limited.

Taiichi Ohno, the man credited with inventing just-in-time production, once wrote: "Underneath the 'cause' of a problem, the *real cause* is hidden. In every case, we must dig up the real cause by asking *why, why, why, why, why.*"[1] If we follow Ohno's precept and ask "why?" five times with regard to issues relating to the relationship between business and sustainable development, we find ourselves climbing a ladder, each rung of which takes us away from specific technical questions and toward questions that are ever more abstract and philosophical. This is the path I have followed.

It is in the nature of sustainable development to take us up this ladder. Brad Allenby, AT&T's chief environmental officer, has observed: "The industrial revolution was all Nike: 'Just do it.' Sustainable development adds another dimension: '*Should* we do it?'"[2] The ethical dimension of sustainable development is inescapable, yet as a matter of course is disregarded in the sustainable-business world, which for the most part remains focused on technical issues, and indeed is often dismissive of what it views as all that impractical, pointy-headed theorizing.

— ◯ —

The reader may find how I came to discover and climb the ladder instructive. In the spirit of *homo fabulans*, I will tell it with a story. Imagine a large living room or reception hall, and a cocktail party in full swing. Imagine also that it is quite a gathering: the entire sustainable-business community is assembled. Amidst the clink of glasses, clusters of technical specialists discuss the pros and cons of sustainability strategies like eco-efficiency, green taxes, and pollution credits. There is a surreal aspect to this convocation, however, for seated on some sofas in the middle of the room and minding their own business are some ... *elephants.* They are sitting silently, for all appearances genially, not even feeding on the peanuts that the technical specialists are gobbling down. No one seems to see the creatures: the conversations continue animatedly.

As a writer specializing in business and the environment, I noted some time ago that while there was a quite energetic dialogue in the corporate community about specific environmental-business strategies, a critically important set of oversized, big-picture questions was either not being asked, or being asked solely to pave the way for a pat, self-serving answer. Questions like:

- How much and what sort of progress toward sustainable development has the corporate community made to date?

- In what ways has business veered off target and what course corrections are necessary? To what extent is the corporate interpretation of "sustainable development" aligned with that of the broader sustainability community?

- What does it mean for a corporation to be "environmentally committed" or "sustainable?" Is it even possible for a corporation to be wholeheartedly dedicated to the cause of sustainable development?

- More broadly still: to what extent do corporate failures of vision, such as they are, reflect a cultural myopia?

These and related issues are the elephants in the sustainable-business living room — the critically important navigational and philosophical questions that to date have gone largely unaddressed.

They are also the subject of this book, which in business parlance would be called an "audit and gap analysis." In plain English, that translates into a two-part project: 1) an analysis of the corporate performance to date, and 2) an assessment of where we currently are relative to our long-term destination. All the technical expertise in the world will be of no avail if we should be going to Montreal but are headed to Rome.

Why isn't anyone noticing the elephants? I believe there is a straightforward answer to that question. It has to do with *specialization.* People usually contribute to their chosen field by studying a specific area and coming up with a wrinkle they can call their own. When people get rewarded for having a micro-focus, they tend not to notice the big things — like the elephants in the living room.

Not that it's easy to see the elephants: it took me years to notice them myself. I came to the field of business and the environment as a market researcher, analyzing markets and products. My next stop was a newsletter I founded, *Green MarketAlert,* that provided what the trade calls "actionable information" about corporate environmentalism and green business strategies. I initially conceived of this book project while editing and publishing the newsletter. In large measure because of what at the time was my detail-oriented, rigorously non-theoretical professional focus, I first saw it as a business report of sorts, i.e., as a technical accounting of corporate projects and activities in the business-and-environment arena. It didn't work — the concept was intrinsically flawed. I continued to climb the learning curve, both as a newsletter and then magazine journalist and through independent reading, until eventually I came to see what was missing: a discussion of the elephants in the living room. And so this book has had a journey of its own, in parallel with my own increasing understanding of the field — traveling up a ladder from specific to abstract, from technical to theoretical, from action-oriented to ethical. My context broadened and has kept broadening, until I now have the sense of having climbed up to the mezzanine, from which vantage point I can survey the entire cocktail party: technical specialists, elephants and all. And that is the perspective from which this book has been written.

Specifically, the book consists (in addition to this introduction) of three Parts, divided into 11 chapters.

Part 1 *(The Elephants in the Living Room)* provides an overview of the overall corporate performance to date and analyzes the ways in which it has been lacking. It also provides the theoretical foundation for the more substantive analyses that follow.

• Chapter 1 *(Progress Imperfect)* briefly summarizes the current state of corporate environmentalism and identifies the three main reasons progress has been more halting than desirable.

- Chapter 2 *(Sustainable Development and the New Humanism)*, which is by far the most theoretical chapter in the book, discusses what sustainable development is commonly held to mean and what it needs to mean. The chapter also calls for a "new humanism" — a new appreciation of the qualitative "depth dimension" of experience.

Part 2 *(Where We've Been, Where We're Headed)* examines in greater detail the corporate performance to date with regard to sustainable development:

- Chapter 3 *(A Short History of Corporate Environmentalism)* takes the reader on a historical journey from the earliest days of corporate environmentalism up to its current "Third Era." It provides an historical context for the in-depth analysis of corporate environmentalism that follows and suggests that the business community may be on a sustainability trajectory it isn't quite aware of.

- Chapter 4 *(By the Numbers)* presents statistical evidence of corporate progress with regard to the environment and discusses how those numbers may not tell the whole story.

- Chapter 5 *(Communications and Community)* examines the evolving *ethos* of corporate environmental communications.

- Chapter 6 *(Into the Fourth Era)* identifies some key elements of the emerging era of corporate environmentalism and examines the extent to which they are already beginning to sprout up on the business landscape.

Part 3 *(The Challenge of Change)* examines the critical issues that collectively define the nature of the sustainability challenge and the prospects for meaningful change:

- Chapter 7 *(Mixed Messages)* examines the often ambiguous character of corporate environmental (and sustainability) performance and the constraints that make it so.

- Chapter 8 *(Across the Great Divide)* examines the extent to which corporations are repositioning environmental and sustainability issues internally.

- Chapter 9 *(Whitecaps, Green Consumers, and the Infrastructure-Building Blues)* focuses largely on consumers — on the extent of their commitment to the environment and sustainable development and on the challenge of creating a consumer movement that puts sustained pressure on the corporate community to create meaningful change.

- Chapter 10 *(The Data Game)* discusses the relationship between scientism and environmental (and sustainability) metrics and argues for the need to adopt a new measurement paradigm.
- Chapter 11 *(From Here to Sustainability)* argues that many of the concepts and technologies for creating a sustainable future have already been developed and are in place. It concludes with a summary of the book's main conclusions.

— ◯ —

I have recounted this story about the elephants and me for two reasons. First, to point out the many levels — technical, theoretical, philosophical — that pervade the business/sustainability domain. And second, to launch a brief cautionary discussion about what this book is, and isn't.

First of all, I am not intent on making the case that the environmental crisis — and more broadly the challenge of sustainable development — warrants all the fuss. That is part of what the economist Joseph Schumpeter would have called my "pre-analytic vision," and unfortunately it is confirmed on an almost daily basis by the emerging news and analyses.[3] Here, for instance, is what the 1996 *Global Environment Outlook*, a publication of the United Nations Environment Programme, had to say on the subject:

> The global environment has continued to deteriorate and significant environmental problems remain deeply embedded in the socio-economic fabric of nations in all regions. ... Internationally and nationally the funds and political will remain insufficient to halt further global environmental degradation and to address the most pressing environmental issues — even though the technology and knowledge are available to do so.[4]

And Elizabeth Dowdeswell, UNEP's executive director, lamented, "If we allow these trends to continue, we will ultimately run out of the essential ingredients for life on this planet. We may not know when, but it is clear that we are on an unsustainable trajectory."[5]

The United Nations Development Programme (UNDP) struck a similarly pessimistic note in the 1996 edition of its *Human Development Report,* which concluded that despite a dramatic surge in economic growth in 15 countries over the previous three decades, 1.6 billion people had been "left behind and are worse off than they were 15 years ago. Economic gains have benefited greatly a few countries, at the expense of many."[6] Meanwhile, "the very rich are getting richer. Today, the assets of the world's 358 billionaires exceed the combined annual incomes of countries accounting for nearly half — 45% — of the world's people."[7]

All of which led UNDP Administrator James Gustave Speth to observe in the report's foreword: "The world has become more economically polarized, both between countries and within countries. If present trends continue, economic disparities between industrial and developing nations will move from inequitable to inhuman."[8]

Meanwhile the scientific evidence continues to mount regarding the long-term damage wrought by industrialization. With extreme weather events mounting and the insurance industry buffeted by huge losses, climate change has claimed center stage as a public-policy issue. Even the notoriously cautious President Clinton has come around, declaring in a June 1997 speech that "the science [on climate change] is clear and compelling: We humans are changing the global climate."[9] He went on to detail some of the projected consequences of climate change, including rising seas, increases in vector-borne disease, severe droughts and floods and the disruption of agriculture.

Concern is also mounting about so-called "endocrine disrupters" — chemicals, including chlorine, that affect reproductive capacity. Around the world, scientists are recording high degrees of congenital abnormalities in animal populations. Meanwhile human sperm counts seem to be shrinking. One analysis of the global historical record found that the average sperm count, which half a century ago was 113 million per milliliter, by 1990 had fallen to 66 million. Another study, this one of Parisians, found that sperm counts had dropped by 2% annually over the past 20 years.[10] More recently, after an extensive review of 61 studies, researchers with the California Department of Health Services revealed a steady decline of about 1 million sperm per milliliter per year.[11] Findings like these suggest that our industrial system may be at war with our reproductive capacity — a frightening hypothesis.

These are only a few of the many indicators that point toward a world whose natural and social systems are badly in decline. If a single overarching trendline is to be discovered amidst the great welter of environmental data, it points toward, not away from, confirmation of our fears. And rather than argue this point in detail, I take it as a given.

Nor is this book strictly speaking a technical work. It addresses technical subjects where necessary but it is not specifically about ISO 14001 or Design for Environment or any of the myriad other subjects that collectively comprise a cornerstone of the business/sustainability domain. Subjects like that are the bailiwick of trained specialists, the ones down there on the floor.

It is not a work of cultural criticism either. A certain view of contemporary culture is essential to my argument, but in writing this book I have not been aiming mainly to prove or justify this view, as is the case with more formal works of cultural criticism. I happen to believe that a mechanistic story dominates contemporary western thinking, and that while it has contributed much that is positive, it has also caused, and continues to cause, much environmental, cultural, and spiritual degradation. All that, however, has been trumpeted from Harvard to Hollywood, and I need not belabor it here. The validity of the critique is self-evident to me — like the gravity of the sustainability crisis, it is part of my pre-analytic vision. I suspect that my readers will either cotton to it intuitively, or intuitively find it dubious, and I am content to leave it at that.

Nor do I see myself as speaking through the voice of a particular guild or academic discipline. I do not even see myself writing as a journalist, although I am a member in good standing of the Society of Environmental Journalists and this is indisputably a work of environmental journalism. But Guild-Speak is not the voice I wish to speak in.

Guild-Speak — that's what happens when specialists communicate in their professional voices, reflecting a culturally appropriate tone and corresponding values. The collective *business* Guild-Voice is technical, analytical, bottom line-oriented, and deeply skeptical about matters intellectual ("those academics don't live in the real world") and emotional/spiritual ("those touchy-feely, tree-hugging greens"). The collective *journalistic* Guild-Voice ranges from detached and cynical ("there's only one story — the story of human venality and greed") to mock-neutral ("I just describe and don't take sides — why, I'm hardly even here, simply telling what is and paring my fingernails"). Academics and scientists have their Guild-voices too. So do greens, sort of, although theirs is more loosely ideological and does not reflect formal training or indoctrination.

Guild-Speak has its uses — it provides a sense of identity and belonging, something we all need — but it is troublesome as well. Precisely because it gives us membership in a tribe, it forecloses us from other groups. In addition, to the extent that it defines us in terms of a specific set of biases and predilections, it disposes us to identify less with the larger human tribe to which we all belong. Milton Glaser puts it this way: "It has been said, and I think it's true, that all professional organizations are conspiracies against the public. Beyond that, all professional associations are conspiracies against the self because they basically narrow the context of your investigation and demand a kind of allegiance to certain modes of thought."[12]

Guild-Speak is the voice of differentiation, of specialization. And while sustainable development needs the skills of specialization, it requires something more as well: the recognition that any solutions will also be trans-disciplinary — integrating many disciplines — and humanistic — invoking heart as well as mind, experience as well as objective truth. It requires, in other words, an expansive sense of context. Because of Guild-Speak's tendency to distance us from those awarenesses, i.e., to shrink context, it has been my impulse to steer clear of it and to speak, to the extent possible, in a more universal voice.

Finally, this is not *per se* a "policy book" either. I have read more than a few such books in researching this work. Many are dreary, some are stimulating, and all share a perspective I do not care to emulate. The rules of the "policy book" game, as best I can decipher them, are that the author is to write from the domain of pure mind, as a sort of humanoid supercomputer whose unfailingly logical calculations produce incontestable conclusions. One is to write, in other words, like one logic machine addressing another: hence the often dry and formalistic style of the prose, and the powerfully persuasive arguments of utterly antithetical positions. That is all well and good, but my goal in writing this book has been quite different: to engage my readers in an intimate conversation about a set of issues whose implications are critically important to us in our roles as lovers, as thinkers, as spiritual beings, and as citizens of the planet.

Part 1

THE ELEPHANTS
IN THE LIVING ROOM

Not only is there only one way of doing things rightly,
but there is only one way of seeing them,
and that is, seeing the whole of them.
— John Ruskin

1

Progress Imperfect

*A resolution to avoid an evil is seldom framed 'til the evil
is so far advanced as to make avoidance impossible.*
— Thomas Hardy

OUR CURRENTLY UNSUSTAINABLE LIVING CONDITIONS are everybody's problem. The public sector, civil society, individuals acting as parents and consumers and voters — all have crucial parts to play in the struggle for sustainability. Industry, however, may have the most vital role of all. Not only does it produce much of the world's waste and pollution, but its financial resources and extraordinary capacity for innovation make it the best — if not the only — candidate to lead the rescuing cavalry.

A persuasive argument can be made that it has a moral responsibility as well. Our global economy is largely corporate, as in large measure is our global culture. And so, it can be argued, the duty falls on the corporate community to remedy where we have culturally and economically — and, by extension, environmentally — gone awry. Willis Harman has written, "Business has become, in this last half century, the most powerful institution on the planet. The dominant institution in any society needs to take responsibility for the whole — as the church did in the days of the Holy Roman Empire."[1]

Nor is the argument for business involvement solely ethical. Common sense is also a consideration. More than a few observers of current trends believe we are riding a bullet train toward a world overrun by famine, disease, poverty, and anarchy.[2] That is hardly a healthy environment for business.

How good a job has business done at shouldering this responsibility? Overall — and I address the question in much greater detail in subsequent chapters — the review is mixed. On the plus side, there have been substantial quantitative improvements. Emissions in the U.S. are down as measured by the U.S. Environmental Protection Agency's (EPA's) Toxic Release Inventory (TRI) and other measures, and there are many other positive statistical indicators too. There has also been clear progress in less straightforwardly measurable domains such as technology transfer and public environmental reporting.

There has been a fair amount of forward movement in other areas as well. New markets for certain types of recycled materials have been created, despite the failure of consumers (especially in the United States) to match their avowed enthusiasm for green products with their actual buying behavior. Corporate environmental-management practices are considerably stronger than they used to be, especially at the Fortune 500 level, with more and more companies integrating environmental responsibilities into line operations. Although driven in part by downsizing, this trend also reflects the recognition that unless environmental concerns are integrated into corporations' profit focus, they will necessarily have second-class status. Communication practices with regard to environmental practices are more enlightened than they once were — faint praise, but true. And, not least of all, a few truly forward-thinking companies have begun to grapple in earnest with the full implications of sustainable development.

Unfortunately, however, the negatives outweigh the positives. Companies — including ones with deserved reputations for environmental excellence — continually deliver mixed signals about their environmental commitment. At the great majority of small and mid-sized enterprises (SMEs), eco-responsibility takes a back seat to the day-to-day struggle for survival. To the extent that the environment is on their radar at all, it is seen as an oppressive burden.

Finally, the business attitude toward sustainable development is characterized by a distressing lack of urgency, symptomatic of a parallel lack of vision. The evolution of the financial industry's attitude toward the environment provides a case in point. In the 1980s the environment was essentially a non-issue for banks. Because financial service companies don't extract minerals from the earth or belch particulates into the air, industry executives tended to view the environment as someone else's problem. In May 1990, however, a U.S. Court of Appeals held in the now-notorious Fleet Factors case that a bank which had foreclosed on the assets of a bankrupt company was partly liable for environmental cleanup costs on the grounds that it had been partially involved in the management of the company. This meant that for the first time, banks could lose more than the amount of their investment. A galvanized industry swung into action. In the years since Fleet Factors, banks have refined their liability-containment skills enormously, but their interest in the environment has not extended much beyond that. This is progress of a sort, but only of a sort. They have not crossed the line from reactivity to proactivity, i.e., they are not aggressively seeking to advance the cause of sustainable development.

The commercial building industry provides another example. Human habitat is a leading depleter of our global resource base. Building construction accounts for one-quarter of the world's wood harvest, two-fifths of its material and energy flows, and one-sixth of its fresh water withdrawals.[3]

A fair number of environmentally sensitive buildings have been constructed over the years by owner-occupants, but professional builders, the sort who construct on speculation, have almost without exception shied away. Grim environmental statistics alone cannot inspire commercial real-estate builders to change their ways. If the industry structure were different — if there was a significant centralized R&D or planning capacity — there might be a stronger impulse to innovate, but as things stand, only one thing will persuade real-estate developers to take the plunge into building green: incontrovertible evidence that that they can make as much or more money by following that route than through more traditional procedures. A fair amount of evidence has been compiled indicating that people work faster and smarter inside green buildings, but the professional building community for the most part remains wary. They argue that any existing evidence is circumstantial, and that even if productivity does go up, that doesn't mean they will be able to charge more or rent vacant space faster.

Required are actual buildings whose track records effectively make the business case that commercial real-estate developers require. This in turn requires some pioneers who are willing to go out on a limb, and fortunately they are beginning to appear. In the United States, for instance, the Durst Organization, a prominent New York City-based developer, is building a 1.6 million square foot (150,000 sq. m) multi-tenant environmentally-responsible office building in the heart of Manhattan's venerable Times Square. Chicago developer Kevork Derderian, president of Continental Offices Ltd., is putting together financing for a 307,000 square-foot (28,000 sq. m) environmentally-responsible office tower in the Chicago suburb of Rolling Meadows. A third trailblazer is Barry Dimson, the president of Healthy Properties LLC, a green building consultancy, and a commercial developer in his own right. Dimson is finalizing plans to renovate a 179-room building in Philadelphia into a "green hotel". He is also overseeing the formation of a blind investment pool that will invest in green commercial properties.

The long-term impact of these early initiatives remains to be seen. If they turn a reasonable profit for the pioneers, mainstream developers will probably follow suit. In the meantime, their stance is much like that of the banking community. Conservative. Keep-your-distance. Wait-and-see.

It is not that corporations have missed the boat so much as that they are on a slow one; and on one, moreover, that is off course. Given the corporate community's critically important role in the pursuit of sustainable development, it is essential for it to come to terms with these facts, and to pick up speed and set its sights more accurately.

There are three main reasons for the corporate community's uneven performance. First — and I elaborate on this important point only minimally in later chapters — there are the twin psychological obstacles of *distraction* and *denial*. With the pressures of corporate downsizing compounding those of information overload, managers lack the time to give complex issues the serious, sustained attention they warrant. This is especially true for people working at small- and midsized enterprises (SMEs), but it applies to Fortune 500 executives as well. Under these conditions, it can be difficult *not* to view the environment as a five-minute issue, difficult *not* to transform it into merely one of many topics demanding one's attention, rather than see it for the overarching issue it really is. We (and our minds) inhabit the environment, not the other way around, but the pressures of time and our preoccupation with matters mental make it all too easy to think otherwise. And as we diminish the environment in our minds, we diminish it in our actions too.

As for denial, business executives must be persuaded that the environment — and, more broadly, sustainable development — actually requires their immediate and urgent attention. In a human environment that puts enormous pressure on managers to produce short-term financial returns, it can be very tempting to say, "Damn the natural environment, full speed ahead," and then haul out the anti-sustainability ideologues — of whom there are no small numbers, especially in the United States — in support of one's position.

The second obstacle, and one to which I return in a later chapter, is the more fundamental one of *structural constraints*. Corporations exist to make money, not to help people or to save the world. While this has been the case since public control over corporate charters was loosened in a series of American judicial decisions in the latter half of the 19th century, the decoupling of corporations from the human and natural spheres has been exacerbated by the globalization of commercial and financial markets. In *When Corporations Rule the World*, David Korten makes the point bluntly and dramatically:

> "[T]he global transformation of global institutions has transformed once beneficial corporations and financial institutions into instruments of a market tyranny that is extending its reach across the planet like a cancer, colonizing ever more of the planet's living spaces, destroying livelihoods, displacing people, rendering democratic institutions impotent, and feeding on life in an insatiable quest for money."[4]

As Korten and other critics see it, today's multinational corporations are like ghosts, immensely powerful ghosts, that are drawn irresistibly to wherever costs are lowest and profits are highest.[5] Fiduciary restraints on their behavior are few and far between: for the most part they are owned by pension funds and other massive investors whose managers are interested in short-term price movements, not long-term growth or other long-term issues such as environmental responsibility.

The accounting rules under which companies operate increase their alienation from real-world effects. Corporations routinely disregard the social and environmental costs of their actions, an attitude that is sanctioned and indeed reinforced by the prevailing rules of the game. This reflects a fundamental flaw in neoclassical economics, namely, the assumption that our natural and social environments have no intrinsic economic value because no money changes hands. This is patently false: as Jonathan Rowe writes, "A tree provides air-conditioning services no less than a window unit from Westinghouse. Open spaces provide relief from tension and noise no less than white noise machines and Prozac."[6]

In this rarefied world of capital flows and stock movements, with our prevailing economic systems and accounting practices legitimating the disregard of environmental and other external costs, corporate incentives for making a serious commitment to the environment and sustainable development fall somewhere between limited and non-existent. Indeed, in the light of this harsh portrait of corporate identity, what comes as a surprise is the extent to which many multinational corporations have *exceeded* barebones regulatory requirements in their environmental commitment. This testifies to the power of public pressure and suggests, perhaps, that corporations may not be quite as fully rationalized, not quite as heartless, as critics like Korten make them out to be. Actions to safeguard the environment will invariably be relegated to the periphery when executives perceive them as in conflict with their fiduciary duty to the corporation's shareholders. At the same time, people *do* care about the environment, and corporations *do* care about their public image, and so the business community has taken some quite significant steps that go well beyond the requirements of regulation.

Consider, for instance, Royal Dutch/Shell, the world's second largest petroleum company. In recent years, two widely publicized events have cast the company in an extremely unfavorable light. In Nigeria, operating under contract with the ruling military regime, Shell extracts oil from the land of the Ogoni tribespeople. The company has been accused of moral complicity (and worse) with the government in the oppression of this group, an oppression that culminated in the 1995 execution of Ken Saro-Wiwa, a leading Ogoni civil rights activist. Not to compare it with the plight of the Ogoni, which is genuinely nighmarish, but from a corporate public relations perspective it was a scene straight out of hell, painting as it did the picture of a company indulging in the racist, colonialist oppression of an indigenous people in the blind pursuit of profit.

And then there was the notorious Brent Spar incident. After much careful research, Shell decided that the best way to get rid of one of its North Sea oil rigs was by sinking it. The activist group Greenpeace disagreed, arguing that such a move would be environmentally disastrous. The result: an international barrage of bad publicity, complete with boycotts.

As things turned out, the financial markets proved to be indifferent to all this commotion. Shell's stock price showed nary a blip in response to all this bad press. If Korten's thesis were entirely on target and multinationals were guided solely by financial considerations, Shell management would have heeded the stock price, not the public outcry, and made no adjustments in its course. It did respond, though, revamping its Statement of General Business Principles to include explicit support for human rights.

One can almost hear the voice of Jed Greer, whom we met in the Introduction, whispering "Greenwash, greenwash" — and this concern is certainly legitimate — but if we assume for the moment that Shell's change in formal policy will translate into changes in actual behavior, it suggests that corporations respond to human intervention as well as to strictly economic cues.

The third obstacle to more rapid progress involves the business community's *understanding of the goal itself.* Although the corporate commitment to environmental protection has expanded steadily over the years, the corporate response has fallen consistently short of what actually needs to be achieved. For — and this is a crucially important point — the global challenge is centrally but not solely environmental. It is a *system* problem, not a one-dimensional one, with poverty, population growth, and environmental degradation feeding each other in a self-perpetuating downward spiral.

The contemplated *solution* to what is known in public-policy circles as the "global *problématique* " is much more a matter of common parlance: it is "*sustainable development.*"[7] For years, however, this term did not enter the public discourse about what corporations needed to do: the focus was exclusively on the environment. And, now that sustainable development has finally entered the dialogue — indisputable if belated progress — its meaning still tends to be construed too narrowly and technically, by the sustainability community generally and even more so by corporate executives. Without a broader understanding of the nature and implications of sustainable development, corporate strategies will be misdirected. Given the central role that business has to play in addressing the global *problématique* , that is an inefficiency we can ill afford. So, with this for background, let's examine what is commonly meant by the term "sustainable development," and what it needs to mean.

2

Sustainable Development and the New Humanism

[T]he eco-crisis is in large measure the result of the continued dissociation of ... [objective] nature and [subjective] culture and consciousness; we cannot align nature and morals and mind. We are altogether fragmented in this modernity gone slightly mad.[1]
— Ken Wilber

THE TERM "SUSTAINABLE DEVELOPMENT" describes how we would like the world to be — fair, healthy, and secure. As such, it belongs to a venerable tradition: utopian thinking. But it is utopianism with a twist, the result of two basic changes in our circumstances. Now that the world has been fully colonized, there are no more mysterious "other places" to site an ideal society. We have to do it "here," at home, in the world-space that we know.

Still more fundamentally, we have arrived at a point in history where we control evolution at least as much as it controls us. Our power to transform nature, whether inadvertently — as in the cases of biodiversity loss and global climate change — or intentionally — through genetic engineering — is something utterly new and totally rewrites the social and ethical rules of the game. One consequence is that we can no longer afford to be fanciful in our utopianism. And so, enter sustainable development: it is utopianism gone pragmatic — fueled by urgency and tethered to this world.

Sustainable development is a relatively new concept — its first use dates back to the 1970s — and one still very much under construction. The most frequently cited definition comes from the Brundtland Commission, which in 1987 equated sustainable development with development or progress that "meets the needs of the present without compromising the ability of future generations to meet their own needs."[2] Thus sustainable development implies the integration of economic and environmental planning: wealth continues to be created, but through processes that do not draw down the material resources on which we and future generations depend. We grow without depleting our "natural capital."

Once we get beyond the basic Brundtland Commission definition, sustainable development is most often thought of in terms of a triad, or the "Three E's": Economics, Environment, and Equity. What sustainable development requires, according to this view, is the harmonious balancing of these three elements — growth is to be pursued in a manner consistent with long-term environmental protection and social fairness. (A variant on this is the "three P's" — Poverty, Population, and Pollution.)

A third way to characterize sustainable development is less conventional but also useful. For the past two centuries, the industrial revolution has been transforming the world in ways both good and bad. However, as human population grows and the global "sink" capacity to absorb wastes shrinks, the design principles that guided the industrial revolution are becoming steadily more problematic. From this perspective, sustainable development can be seen as the logical successor to the industrial revolution, i.e., as *the (inevitable) post-industrial revolution.* More specifically, it can be seen as a post-industrial revolution with two purposes, one *conceptual* — to articulate a set of design principles appropriate to a world whose population is expected to top out at 10 billion or more — and the other *practical* — to remedy the unintended negative consequences of industrialization.

All these definitions have merit but are incomplete. True, sustainable development *is* about securing the welfare of future generations, and about balancing the "three E's" (or "three P's"), and about formulating the design principles of the post-industrial revolution. But — and this point is as important as it is customarily overlooked — it has a *vertical* as well as a *horizontal* dimension. Life is not only *technical* and *objective*; it is also *soulful* and *subjective.* Our conception of sustainable development needs to do justice to these "vertical" dimensions of human experience. Sustainable development implies a new and healthier balance in how we conduct our human affairs, one that celebrates depth along with surfaces, community along with individuality, spirituality along with materialism, art along with linear technique.

The ecological economist Herman Daly is mining similar territory when he argues for a

> ...shift in our vision of how the economic activities of human beings are related to the natural world. ...This change in vision involves replacing the economic norm of *quantitative* expansion (growth) with that of *qualitative* improvement (development) as the path of future progress. This shift is resisted by most economic and political institutions, which are founded on traditional quantitative growth and legitimately fear its replacement by something as subtle and challenging as qualitative development.[3] *[italics added]*

Daly's point about the need for a revaluing of *quality* is well taken. Ours is a culture obsessed by quantitative measurement, so much so that what can't be measured empirically is typically viewed as unimportant or even non-existent. This is the error of scientism, and a grievous one it is. According to the contemporary psychologist and philosopher Ken Wilber,

> there are many ways to state the fallacy of scientism. It went from saying, "That which cannot be seen by the eye of flesh cannot be empirically verified" to "That which cannot be seen by the eye of flesh does not exist." It went from saying, "There is an excellent method for gaining knowledge in the realm of the five senses" to "Thus the knowledge gained by mind and contemplation is invalid." As Smith put it: "With science there can be no quarrel. Scientism is another matter. Whereas science is positive, contenting itself with reporting what it discovers, scientism is negative. It goes beyond the actual findings of science to deny that other approaches to knowledge are valid and other truths true."[4]

Classical economics, and conventional sustainable-development thinking, and scientism — in fact, just about all the conceptual frameworks that emerge from the modernist paradigm — suffer from the same shortcoming: they suppress what we might call the *depth dimension* of experience.

This depth dimension has many aspects and can be described in many ways: as soulfulness, as the imaginal (or archetypal) realm, as feelings/emotions (a perspective favored by Al Gore in *Earth in the Balance*), as the intuitive process, as feelings of relatedness, and so on.[5] Regardless of what specific interpretation resonates for us, an essential fact about the "depth dimension" remains: that, without it, the experienced world becomes (relatively speaking) a flat and barren place. For this reason, Wilber refers to the modernist worldview as "flatland."[6]

Consider, for instance, the familiar business concept "value-added." The term, of course, refers to the economic value that is added to a product at each stage of its manufacture or distribution — but whatever happened to the depth dimension of "value"? In this modernist context the word is reduced to a flat, fungible commodity and stripped of its texture and levels of meaning.

Or take another familiar phrase — "quality of life." Typically that's translated into hard numbers — income, size of house, number of cars, what-have-you. But that only tells part of the story, as we are regularly reminded by the tabloid tales that gleefully recount the travails of the Rich and Famous.

The point is that you can measure some aspects of quality, but ultimately quality is more than numerical, more than empirical. It is a tautology, but in our culture it needs saying: *quality is quality, not quantity.*

Our cultural ship is cantilevered, tilted in a way that badly favors quantity over quality. Small wonder, then, that business executives, who spend their time making deals on deck, not worrying about the state of the ship, should mirror this lopsidedness by focusing on technical, exterior issues while undervaluing the human, subjective side of the equation.

But wait, I hear an attentive reader object: doesn't the quality movement that has fairly well colonialized the business world refute this argument? Don't initiatives like Total Quality Management (TQM) and the ISO 9000 quality standard put the lie to the proposition that business has no interest in quality? The answer is an emphatic no. Programs like these actually have zero tolerance for quality as I have defined it here, i.e., as *those subjective aspects of experience that resist quantification.* Soulfulness, connectedness, meaning, artistry — these are the clay of which quality is made, and they furiously resist reduction to raw numbers. What business calls "quality" is actually quantity, renamed. TQM, for instance, measures product quality in terms of the number of defects. That makes sense for products, which don't have much of an inner life, but the approach falls short when the challenge turns to measuring aspects of business performance that don't readily lend themselves to quantification, i.e., that participate more actively in the depth dimension, such as community relations or social responsibility. And indeed this is one reason why such considerations tend to get short shrift in the world of commerce: how much easier it is to measure business performance in terms of profits, which are not and indeed cannot be subjected to an unwieldy translation process because they were never anything but numbers in the first place! "What gets measured gets managed," a TQM maxim has it, without noting the converse: that what isn't measured gets discounted or ignored.

— O —

How has this devaluation of the depth dimension come to pass? I can best answer this question by taking the reader on a brief historical journey — or, more accurately, by telling a story about history, with Stephen Toulmin, a professor at the University of Chicago, as our narrator and guide.[7] During the 16th century, according to Toulmin, an extraordinary humanism flowered: it was the time of Shakespeare, Cervantes, Rabelais, and Montaigne, brilliant writers and thinkers who celebrated life in all its aspects. Far from trying to pull back from their immersion in daily experience, they derived their wisdom from that ongoing participation. For them, truth and knowledge were largely *contextual* — dependent on the circumstances in which they arose.

For largely historical reasons, Toulmin argues, the great thinkers of the next century tried to step back from the embrace of experience that had characterized the 16th-century humanists. They embarked on a search for absolute verities that would take them away from the experience (and experiences) of the human body and enable them to derive truths that would remain valid irrespective of their specific context. "I think, therefore I am," wrote Descartes — but where was his body? Out of this approach emerged rationalism, the scientific method and, more broadly still, the entire spirit of modernism.

This new movement had many strengths, chief among them being science's extraordinary capacity to unfold the laws of nature. But it had weaknesses too, one of which was a persistent distancing from the subjective and transitory truths born of experience. In the hunger for certainty, modernism devalued all that was contextual, i.e., all that came to pass in the great sweep of daily living. It gave priority to the empirical domain of science and technique while simultaneously depreciating the subjective, experiential realm — in other words, the entire "depth dimension."

And that is where we are today, in contemporary culture as a whole and in most sustainability thinking. Clearly we cannot do without science and technique. However, as a culture we need to remember that empirical rigor is necessary, but not sufficient. To use one of Ken Wilber's favorite phrases, we need to "transcend and include" technique in our understanding of sustainable development, specifically by embracing and incorporating the interior, subjective dimensions of human experience.

The times call for a new humanism, one that couples the wisdom of Montaigne and Rabelais with the insights of Descartes and Newton, and that is folded into our collective vision of sustainable development. We need a new synthesis between the wisdoms born of life-in-the-body and those born of the independent operations of the mind. We need to freshly integrate the *objective* and *subjective,* the *interior* and *exterior,* the *ethical* and *empirical,* and the *qualitative* and *quantitative* dimensions of experience. We need, in other words, a new sort of integral thinking.

The now-famous image of the "blue planet" is often cited as a transitional moment in the development of global consciousness, when for the first time Spaceship Earth could be seen as a single and vulnerable whole, but another NASA-inspired image may go even farther in capturing the spirit of the times. That is the image of us — all five billion-plus of us — compressed into a space capsule that is hurtling headlong into the future.

These are unprecedented and extraordinarily stressful circumstances, and in the stress of adapting to them we have lost much — our sense of history, our sense of beauty, our sense of tranquility, our sense of balance, our sense of capaciousness, and (not least of all) our capacity to make enduring ethical connections. In this "modernity gone slightly mad" (to quote Ken Wilber), it is difficult not to devalue the depth dimension, difficult not to resist psychic and intellectual integration, difficult not to be obsessed by the empirical at the expense of the imaginal.[8] And so, when Ted Strong, a native American and member of the President's Council on Sustainable Development, says, "When we think of sustainable development, we think of our ancestors," I understand him to be making a broad statement that honors spirit, honors history, and places the current hurly-burly of activity in healthy perspective.[9] I understand him to be holding two basic principles carefully in mind — *context* and *connections* — and to be taking special pains to hold fast against the motion of the space capsule, to retain the memory of who we really are. And for this reason precisely I see his words as informed by the spirit of the new humanism.

— O —

A more humanistic approach to sustainable development would affect our attitudes and actions in important ways. Most saliently, it would affect what business measures, and how it does so — a subject addressed at length in Chapter 10 (The Data Game). It would affect much else as well — such as, for instance, our understanding of the very term "sustainable development." The current (and understandable) tendency is to treat sustainable development as an objective "thing" — as the Brundtland Commission's development or progress that "meets the needs of the present without compromising the ability of future generations to meet their own needs," or as the "three E's" (Environment, Economy and Equity), or as the design criteria for the post-industrial revolution, and so on. There is another, more humanistic way to view sustainable development, however — not as a reified concept but as an idea that lives inside the mind and that as such is constantly evolving, constantly changing.

Sustainable development, in other words, can be seen as an "emergent," that being the term for a new evolutionary form that appears, in the words of *The American Heritage® Dictionary*, as "a result of an unpredictable rearrangement of the preexisting elements." As such, sustainable development by definition cannot be defined, or rather can be defined only subjectively — we are in the same boat with the concept, so to speak, and cannot know where we (or it) will end up.

The view of sustainability as a sort of work-in-progress seems likely to be embraced by the National Academy of Sciences in the U.S., whose Board on Sustainable Development, as of early 1997, had chosen to focus on the process of making the *transition into sustainability* rather than on attempting to define sustainable development as an end-state. At that time, the Board was favoring the metaphor of a canoe shooting the rapids — a useful image, to the extent that it encourages us to think of sustainability in the context of a real-time series of continuing crises, rather than as a casual stroll toward a distant goal. Inherent in the metaphor are the assumptions that we must paddle furiously and react creatively to keep from capsizing; and that sustainability resists specific definition but is what will emerge from the process.[10]

Should we conclude, then, that sustainable development is not actually an object, but rather a living (and subjective) concept in the mind — a work-in-progress, not a reified concept? Not at all. Remember that the new humanism calls for a fresh integration of the subjective and objective dimensions of experience: were we to re-define sustainable development as subjective, i.e., as solely a work-in-progress, we would merely be replacing the objective with the subjective, not integrating the two. Sustainable development is probably best viewed as both subject and object, as both work-in-progress and specific end-goal. It is, in other words, probably best held in the mind as an idea with many images, all useful in their own way.

— ◯ —

A more integral approach to the challenge of sustainable development would also help counteract the negative effects of specialization which, as I noted in the Introduction, has its uses but alienates us from others and ourselves. Thus the business specialist tends to focus on hard empirical data — on the numbers that make business tick — while turning a deaf ear to the voices that come whispering up from the more subjective realms of the self.

Sustainable development calls for greater integration, or perhaps I should say more seamless communication, both interpersonally and intrapsychically. Unfortunately, specialization pushes us in the opposite direction: away from the integration of the subjective and objective, away from the new humanism.

In early 1997 I attended the DeLange/Woodlands conference, "Sustainable Development: Managing the Transition," at Rice University in Houston. In many ways it was an extraordinary gathering, featuring some of the most prominent thinkers in the sustainable development field. It was, moreover, multi-disciplinary, with participation from business executives, scientists, academics, ethicists, and others.

Despite the exceptional quality of the attendees, however, the gathering left me feeling vaguely disquieted. Eventually I realized that this impression stemmed from my sense that the great majority of speakers had been talking at each other from behind the ramparts of their professional strongholds, rather than from and to a common center. The meeting, in other words, was *multi*-disciplinary rather than *trans*-disciplinary, and that did not feel like enough.

There were exceptions. Brad Allenby, AT&T's chief environmental officer, gave a presentation that effectively interwove ethical, technical ,and business issues. I went up to the lanky, bearded Allenby after his remarks and complimented him, observing that his presentation seemed to have emerged organically, as the expression of a person who has successfully integrated these three distinct modes of perceiving inside his own being. His response surprised me: "You have no idea how many arrows in the back I've taken for precisely that reason."

Later that day, I spoke with Beth Beloff, the then-director of the University of Houston's Institute for Corporate Environmental Management and one of the conference organizers. I praised her for the multi-disciplinary nature of the gathering and then suggested that it needed to be more, that it needed to be trans-disciplinary. She nodded ruefully. "To do that," she said, "you'd have to transform our entire academic structure."

In training people to be specialists, our culture does more than train them to be experts in a specific domain. It also trains them to focus excessively on what Aristotle called the "efficient cause." To explain: for Aristotle, every action had four causes. The *formal* cause is the underlying archetypal principle; the *material* cause is the physical stuff that is worked upon or changed; the *final* cause is the end-product that the actor has in mind; and the *efficient* cause, in the words of the Jungian psychologist James Hillman, is "that which instigates a motion and is the immediate instigator of change."[11] For instance, the formal cause of a statue is the idea of the statue; the material cause is the block of marble; the final cause is the work of art itself; and the efficient cause is the sculptor. "All four causes are necessary; none can be excluded," writes Hillman. Yet that, he argues, is precisely what our dominant culture has done. It has elevated the efficient cause — the actor — and downplayed the other three to the point of disregarding them entirely. "When [the efficient] is singled out as the only cause," Hillman writes, "then it does not matter what happens, to what or whom it happens and for what purpose it happens."[12]

He goes on: "Two insanely dangerous consequences result from raising efficiency to the level of an independent principle. First, it favors short-term thinking — no looking ahead, down the line; and it produces insensitive feeling — no looking around at the life values being lived so efficiently. Second, means become ends; that is, doing something becomes the full justification of doing regardless of what you do."[13]

His conclusion: "The ethical confusions now plaguing business, government and the professions, although having many varied sources, result in part from the pressures of efficiency as a value in and for itself."[14]

Specialization, in other words, strips decisions of their ethical context: it undoes breadth of vision and the sense of balance. It is, in other words, anti-humanistic.

Let me give a specific example of how this plays out in the corporate world. Lockheed Martin Corporation is one of the world's largest defense and aerospace contractors, with annual revenues in excess of $30 billion. It also has what is in many ways a laudable environmental management program: sharp reductions in emissions, membership in all the right voluntary corporate environmental programs, a host of environmental awards, and so on. And yet, in press materials delivered to this writer, the company proudly proclaimed that

> Lockheed Martin Armament Systems in Burlington, Vermont is a leading supporter of the Motor Challenge Program in the New England area. The facility serves as a Motor Challenge showcase facility. Armament Systems upgraded the equipment in their plating and finishing facility in a cost effective manner that reduces energy consumption by approximately 40%. Armament Systems also hosted the 1996 New England area conference, "Plant Engineering in a Green World" in May 1996.

Pronouncements like these are an exercise in the art of overlooking the obvious. Surely Lockheed Martin warrants praise for these environmental initiatives. Still, are the media expected simply not to notice that this particular factory happens to make ... *armaments*? Not that manufacturing armaments is necessarily unethical — in response to a direct question from me, a Martin Marietta environmental manager argued that it is — but wouldn't one expect that fact to be treated as germane to a discussion of whether or not a company is green? Wouldn't it make sense for publicity material to at least acknowledge that the notion of a green conference at an armaments plant might produce a touch of cognitive dissonance? More broadly: what does it say about our culture when a fact as salient as this one is simply disregarded — treated, for all intents and purposes, as if it weren't there? It suggests, at a minimum, a lack of perspective, a measure of unconsciousness about ethical connections. Ours is a culture that privileges efficiency, and efficiency always forgets.[15]

— ◯ —

There are reasonable objections to the call for a new humanism, and this discussion would be incomplete were I not briefly to address them.

The first argument *contra* proposes that philosophical musings about quality, subjective experience and the like are the stuff of ivory towers and have little to do with the real world — little to do with the cold, hard facts of the global *problématique* .

There are two basic responses to this position. The first dismisses it as ideologically tainted. That is, it proposes that it is precisely because speculations like these occupy the depth dimension that the impulse rises to devalue them. Resistance to their relevance, in other words, is a predictable flatland response to a view that diverges from the philosophical materialism that is our dominant ideology.

The second response holds that while these musings may be abstract, consumerism is not, and consumerism is a direct consequence of our culture's dominant philosophical materialism — a highly visible (one is tempted to say, conspicuous) way people act out our collective obsession with the empirical, measurable face of things. And certainly the acquisitive impulse cannot be charged with irrelevance to the global *problématique* , as a metastasizing consumerism stresses the planet up to and beyond its carrying capacity.[16] Problems are best addressed at their source — remember Taiichi Ohno's admonition about asking "why?" five times. Only by attacking the underlying philosophical bias can we hope to address the symptom — consumerism — and its consequence — unsustainability.

A second argument against the new humanism — and an emotionally compelling one at that — holds that the concept is of trivial importance in a world where the levels of straightforward physical abuse and suffering have reached unconscionable and indeed virtually unimaginable proportions. As we sit snugly in our condos, wander the endless aisles of our supermarkets, or bask in the glow of our electronic hearths, it is easy to lose sight of the world's other face. And a tortured one it is, as a brief scan of the sustainability literature attests:

- A billion and a half people — over a quarter of the world population — live in poverty and over half of those poor are malnourished.

- Violence against women is endemic: 60-100 million women are considered "missing," either as a result of selective abortion, infanticide, neglect or abuse during childhood, or domestic violence, with another roughly 100 million women genitally mutilated.

- Since 1990, the number of refugees has more than doubled.[17]

The point is that this is not a world that treats people fairly — for many, life on this planet is a nightmare. Against such a backdrop, it can seem like quite the middle-class conceit to focus on the need to "integrate the depth dimension." Yet crucial it is, for three reasons. First, quality matters. Verities matter. Art and the human spirit matter. Clearly the opportunity to lead a reasonably long life with one's basic survival needs met is of paramount importance. That proposition is axiomatic —

but then, so is people's equally inalienable right to lead lives that are deeply realized emotionally and spiritually. And the one in no way cancels the other out.

Moreover, we inhabit, it has been said, a "culture of objects," which is essentially the same as saying that we live in a flatland world where we experience what we encounter as stripped of its subjective depth dimension.[18] To the extent that we experience the natural world, other people, and ourselves as objects rather than subjects, i.e., as essentially soulless, it becomes that much easier to treat those "others" (including, even, ourselves) as inconsequential. People and the world become commodified. That is certainly the way of our current industrial system, which reflects and reinforces this objectifying view.

The objectivized world is a world without compassion, for compassion is what happens when soul empathizes with soul, and an objectivized world has no soul. We need to embed compassion into the structures of our industrial system, else we all risk being ground up in its machinery. That may seem like a farfetched notion, and perhaps it is; but if it is not, if it is at all practicable, it will only be because we successfully embed compassion in the ground of consciousness from which our industrial system springs. And the way to do that is by re-integrating the subjective and objective, by in this sense "re-membering" the world.

Finally, and perhaps most importantly of all, progress toward sustainable development requires healthy infusions of social capital — and the bedrock of social capital is trust. That is in short supply in western industrialized society, in large measure because people feel, more or less consciously, ontologically off-center. They know something's wrong, and even if they can't quite name it, that doesn't stop them from holding their mainstream institutions of governance and authority responsible for their malaise.

Whole makes whole: we need to feel whole to participate wholeheartedly in the greater society of which we are a part. The sustainability crisis requires all the social capital we can muster. We get it by building trust — and the only way to do that is by returning the depth dimension to its rightful place in our lives.

The third and final argument against the call for a new humanism pleads impracticality: we cannot reasonably expect such a transformation to occur, especially within the limited time frame required by the exigencies of sustainable development. This objection may have merit, and then again it may not. The humanistic upsurge of the 16th century was thrown over in a century: there is no obvious reason why a more modest integration of the humanist and modernist traditions cannot occur within a similar time frame — or even more rapidly, given the extraordinary recent acceleration in information flows.

Moreover, the new-humanistic perspective is building momentum — in sustainable-development thinking generally, and in the corporate community as well. Increasingly, the battle lines are being drawn. Advocates of the new humanism are still very much in the minority, but the number of its partisans is growing.[19] Indeed, it is not implausible to view the new humanism itself as an "emergent." Which is cause for optimism — and also rather surprising, given the extent to which the deck of contemporary culture is stacked against it.

I am not suggesting that the momentum is irresistible: the new humanism is only one of many ideological and emotional cross-currents currently vying for supremacy. There is what Alvin Toffler calls the "infosphere" — the world of electronic communications — which is transformative but peculiarly ungrounded in the natural world. There is also the modernist embrace of technique and exteriors, which is reactionary and quite literally superficial. The infosphere has an extraordinary technological imperative backing it up, while the flatland modernist worldview is buttressed by familiarity, inertia, and unconscious ideological commitment — compelling forces all. But the new humanism holds out the promise of a wholeness that the others lack, and so it too has a powerful appeal.

How the corporate understanding of its obligations *vis-à-vis* the environment and sustainable development has evolved, and the extent to which that evolution points toward the new humanism, are the subjects to which we now turn.

Part 2

Where We've Been, Where We're Headed

We accept the verdict of the past until the need for change cries out loudly enough to force upon us a choice between the comforts of further inertia and the irksomeness of action.
— Judge Learned Hand

3

A Short History of Corporate Environmentalism

Nothing recedes like progress.
— e. e. cummings

B ROADLY SPEAKING, corporate environmentalism can be said to have
passed through three phases, and the stage has been set for a
fourth. The first was launched in 1962 with the publication of
Rachel Carson's *Silent Spring*, which depicted in chilling detail the environmental damage wrought by chemicals. The resulting furor produced
a geyser of environmental laws that flowed for the next 20 years. In the
U.S., the National Environmental Policy Act, the Superfund law, the
Toxic Substances Control Act, the Resource Conservation and Recovery
Act, and the Clean Water Act all belong to the legacy of Carson's work.

Collectively these laws ushered in what might be called the Era of
Compliance. During this period, good corporate citizenship consisted
of simply obeying the law. Corporations routinely proclaimed that it was
company policy to meet all regulatory requirements — an odd pronouncement, considering that the alternative was to declare themselves
outlaws.

The second era of corporate environmentalism came into being on
the night of December 2, 1984, with the accidental release of 15,000
gallons (57,000 liters) of methyl isocyanate from a Union Carbide plant
into the air over Bhopal, India. Over the next three days, 1,500 people
died and many thousands more were blinded or otherwise harmed.
"Bhopal was the environmental equivalent of Pearl Harbor, a violent
wake-up call that shook many nations and many firms," writes Bruce

Piasecki.[1] Earlier eco-catastrophes like Love Canal and Times Beach paled before Bhopal. Literally overnight, it became clear to business executives and the general public that corporate environmental practices had to change.

The chemical industry responded aggressively. The U.S. Chemical Manufacturers Association implemented a program called Responsible Care to improve environmental, health and safety (EH&S) performance. Compliance was made a condition of membership. Union Carbide overhauled its environmental management procedures. Other chemical companies did the same.

In addition to transforming operational procedures, second-era corporate environmentalism put an entirely new slant on external corporate communications. The Bhopal disaster had established just how powerful a stake local communities have in plant activities. To smooth their relationships with locales where their plants were situated, chemical companies introduced Community Action Panels (CAPs), which increased communication between factory managers and concerned citizens. CAPs had no say in corporate decisions but they were more than just window dressing. By encouraging dialogue in a non-confrontational setting, they made corporate managers more sensitive to community concerns.

In 1986, the U.S. Congress moved to protect community interests with the enactment of SARA (Superfund Amendments and Reauthorization Act) Title III, which requires companies to publish annual emission levels of hundreds of chemicals. With the enactment of that law, corporate America abruptly found itself cast into an entirely new relationship with the public. Not all the corporate books were open but important pages were. A new era of public accountability had arrived.

Because of the heightened scrutiny to which they were being subjected, companies began placing more priority on reducing emissions. In 1988, Monsanto Co. announced its intention to voluntarily reduce air emissions by 90%, a goal it met five years later. Other major corporations, including Polaroid and AT&T, followed suit. Thus was launched the third era of corporate environmentalism — the era of Beyond Compliance.

That same year, *Time* magazine declared the environment the media event of the year. In 1989 the supertanker Exxon Valdez ruptured, spilling 11 million gallons (41.6 million liters) of crude oil into Alaska's Prince William Sound, raising the environmental ante once again. This event, coupled with the extraordinary ballyhoo that surrounded the 20th anniversary of Earth Day in 1990, lifted corporate environmentalism to yet a new level. The era of Beyond Compliance was now in full swing: to qualify as forward-thinking, companies had to commit not to meeting but to *exceeding* regulatory emissions requirements. It was no longer enough to obey the law and disclose some information: companies had to set off on their own, into the trackless wilds of what Total Quality Management gurus call "continuous improvement."

This impulse was reinforced by the 33/50 program of the U.S. Environmental Protection Agency, which called for participating companies to voluntarily reduce emissions of 17 high-priority chemicals by 33% by the end of 1992 and by 50% by the end of 1995. At its peak, the 33/50 program, which was not renewed, had over 1,300 participating companies.

Today, "beyond compliance" corporate environmentalism is by no means universal, but it is well on the way to becoming *de rigueur* among the transnational powerhouses that act as role models for the broader corporate community.

— ○ —

Third-era corporate environmentalism brought a new term — eco-efficiency — into the eco-management lexicon. Whereas pollution prevention focuses on reducing environmentally harmful outputs, eco-efficiency considers resource inputs as well. It aims to streamline the full range of corporate metabolic processes — less "stuff" in, less waste out. Eco-efficiency strategies run the gamut from energy-efficiency retrofits to the use of recovered and recoverable materials to what has become known as "de-materialization" (e.g., reducing the amount of materials used, for instance by making packaging thinner and lighter).

In one oft-cited example of eco-efficiency, Lockheed's Building 157 in Sunnyvale, CA, a 600,000 square-foot (56,000 sq. m), $50 million structure, used extensive "daylighting," an architectural strategy for bringing as much sun as possible into the building, to reduce lighting expenditures to one-quarter what they would have been had a standard design been used. The daylighting features cost an additional $2 million, but with savings of close to $500,000 per year, payback was in about four years. In addition, Lockheed reported sharp increases in productivity from workers in Building 157, due not only to the daylighting but to other people-friendly features as well. Lockheed officials have even speculated that this increased productivity led them to win a $1.5 billion defense contract, the profits from which covered the costs of the entire building.[2]

While pollution prevention and eco-efficiency were clearly desirable environmentally, they were less obviously so economically. Business executives tended to view the environment as a cost center assuming that spending money to improve environmental performance would hurt the bottom line. Thus advocates of pollution prevention and eco-efficiency were confronted with a challenge: how to build a business case for their adoption. Their response was what has come to be known as "win-win," another staple of third-era thinking. It argued, successfully in some cases and less so in others, that pollution prevention and eco-efficiency benefited both the environment and the bottom line.

Usually the doctrine of "win-win" is raised in the context of pollution prevention programs, where it is relatively easy to show dollar savings. The classic example comes from 3M, whose Pollution Prevention Pays program since its inception in 1975 has reduced emissions by over one billion pounds (454,000,000 kg) while saving the company more than $750 million.

In its 1993 environmental report, Baxter International captured the essence of win-win in a single sentence. After detailing reductions in non-hazardous waste, hazardous waste, and packaging, the company declared: "The total savings generated from Baxter's environmental program were $48 million in 1993. This added eight cents per share to Baxter's profitability."[3] The communication cut to the chase: eco-efficiency is worthwhile because it creates shareholder value.

Move away from pollution prevention, however, and proving "win-win" becomes much more difficult. Yet it is important to do so, for it is the rare company that will go green out of principle. To that end, Bryan Thomlison developed a business case for the consumer-goods company Church & Dwight, arguing that the company's 1993 investment of $1.9 million in environmental public affairs produced incremental sales of $25 million — a 13:1 ratio. Whatever the merits of this argument — innovative approaches like his are always subject to second-guessing — Thomlison broke important ground simply by attempting to quantify the benefits of environmental public relations.

In the context of pollution prevention, win-win has become so well-established that we are already well into its second generation. During the first generation, "win-win" was accepted on faith. Now, however, it has become a more difficult sell. While there is consensus that substantial savings can be found in what has come to be known as "plucking the low-hanging fruit," it is also becoming increasingly clear that once the obvious steps are taken, win-win grows more problematic, even in the relatively straightforward context of pollution prevention.

Chemical giant Du Pont has even made something of a science out of the fact that win-win has its limitations. It performs a sort of waste-reduction triage based on its "80/20 rule" — "80% of the environmental benefit possible from all initiatives generally derives from the first 20% of costs."[4] The company has developed a sophisticated system for prioritizing projects that allows it to focus on clear winners.[5]

Although "win-win" establishes a business rationale for pursuing environmental improvements, it does not ensure that recommendations will actually be implemented. For instance, the September 1997 issue of *Environmental Science & Technology* magazine cited a case study at a Dow Chemical plant showing that the company would save more than $1 million annually by undertaking certain changes, while also reducing wastes by 500,000 pounds (227,000 kg) and making it possible to shut down a hazardous waste incinerator. The changes were never implemented due to other corporate priorities and concern that shutting down the incinerator might cost the company future business.[6]

In 1994 the subtler levels of win-win were the subject of a controversial *Harvard Business Review* article by Brad Whitehead and Noah Walley, two McKinsey consultants who helped burst the bubble of first-generation win-win by proclaiming:

> We do not argue that win-win situations do not exist; in fact, they do, but they are very rare and will likely be overshadowed by the total cost of a company's environmental program.... We must question the current euphoric environmental rhetoric by asking if win-win solutions should be the foundation of a company's environmental strategy. At the risk of arguing against motherhood (and mother Earth) we must answer no.[7]

Walley and Whitehead make an important point. Environmental planning should not be guided by wishful thinking or feel-good buzzwords. In a response to the Walley/Whitehead article that was also published in the *Harvard Business Review*, Joan Bavaria, President of Franklin Research & Development, took issue with much of their analysis but agreed that "[t]he Pollyanna view that going green is a win-win for all corporations at all times deserves to be refuted."[8]

And make no mistake about it — rhetoric aside, on environmental problems that don't have a "win-win" logic attached to them, businesses will take action slowly, if at all. In the November/December 1996 issue of *Technology Review,* Lester B. Lave, an economics professor at Carnegie-Mellon University, cited research in which he had posed a hypothetical question to 54 large U.S. companies that had expressed environmental concern through actions such as publishing an environmental report:

> Suppose that a material in one of the company's products were found to in some way harm the environment. Further suppose that a non-toxic substitute material were available. The substitute yields exactly the same product quality — but it costs more. How much more would the company be willing to pay for this environmentally non-toxic material?[9]

According to Lave, "Only two-thirds of the respondents answered that they would be willing to make a substitution that raised product costs 0.1%. One-third of firms said they were willing to raise costs 1%. Two companies said they were willing to raise costs 5%. No company was willing to raise costs any further."[10] Lave's conclusion: "Despite their PR, companies will take measures to reduce pollution only as long as they do not involve much effort or cost."[11]

Another characteristic of third-era corporate environmentalism is its continuing emphasis on compliance, albeit sometimes in the more ambitious form of "beyond compliance." Basically, business executives can view environmental management in one of two contexts: as a cost center, or a profit center. Whereas the former is technical and reactive — *compliance-oriented* — the latter is entrepreneurial and proactive — *strategic.* With corporations coming under continuing pressure to demonstrate ever deeper levels of environmental commitment, third-era corporate environmentalism saw the birth of a concept that has come to be known as *strategic environmental management,* or SEM — the notion being that the proper place for environmental management is on the profit side of the fence, i.e., that environmental know-how can be deployed aggressively and creatively to shave costs and create new business opportunities.

The concept has received a great deal of lip service, not least of all from consultants with SEM services to sell. On the whole, however, the practice has been honored mostly in the breach. According to a 1994 survey by Environmental Research Associates, only 18% of companies treat environmental management as a profit center, compared to 82% who view it as a cost center. These findings were consistent with the finding of a 1991 survey by McKinsey & Co. that only 13% of companies take an essentially strategic approach to environmental management. Similarly, in a 1995 survey of 185 environment, health & safety (EH&S) managers, the management consultancy Arthur D. Little found that fully 91% of them believed that significant obstacles were keeping their company from integrating EH&S management into business operations.

As discussed in greater detail in Chapter 8, this is a serious problem. Until environmental management is viewed as part of the profit-making apparatus, as distinguished from "something the lawyers and engineers take care of," it will inevitably have second-class status.

— ◯ —

Meanwhile, as terms like "eco-efficiency" and "win-win" were gaining currency, a parallel set of doctrines was gathering momentum. This was the "socially responsible business" (or "SRB") movement, and unlike mainstream corporate environmentalism, it proposed a fundamental re-ordering of corporate values. Contrary to economists like Milton Friedman, who argue that the sole purpose of corporations is to create shareholder value, the SRB movement holds that economic value is not the only, or even the dominant, corporate *raison d'être*. The mission statement of Ben & Jerry's neatly captures the SRB value system:

> Ben and Jerry's is dedicated to the creation and demonstration of a new corporate concept of linked prosperity. Our mission consists of three interrelated parts:
>
> **Product Mission:** To make, distribute and sell the finest quality [product] ...
>
> **Social Mission:** To operate the company in a way that actively recognizes the central role that business plays in the structure of society by initiating innovative ways to improve the quality of life of a broad community: local, national and international.
>
> **Economic Mission:** To operate the company on a sound financial basis of profitable growth, increasing value for our shareholders and creating career opportunities and financial rewards for our employees.
>
> Underlying the mission of Ben & Jerry's is the determination to seek new and creative ways of addressing all three parts, while holding a deep respect for individuals, inside and outside the company, and for the communities of which they are a part.[12]

Whereas for mainstream corporations, the economic mission is paramount, product, social (and environmental), and economic missions have parity for SRB companies.

The notion that corporations are more than strictly economic entities is not new. Corporate philanthropy, a form of social responsibility that is virtually ubiquitous among transnational companies, was born a century ago when industrialists like Andrew Carnegie and John D. Rockefeller accumulated fortunes and then tried to balance the scales by funding organizations like the YMCA and the Community Chest. Writing in the 1927 *Harvard Business Review* on "The Social Significance of Business," Wallace B. Donham noted that "the social responsibility of the business man ... is inescapable" and went on to bemoan:

> It is peculiarly difficult to make the individual business man understand his opportunities and his responsibilities in harmonizing his economic and social obligations, because there has been inadequate analysis and inadequate statement of the problem.[13]

Fast-forward to the 1960s. It is a time of social turmoil — Vietnam, flower children, the Black Panthers. "You can't do business in a society that's burning," says William Norris, founder of Control Data Corporation, who then sets out to remedy things as best he can by making his own company a model of social responsibility. Against the advice of his staff, he opens a new computer-component plant in inner-city Minneapolis. For largely humanitarian reasons he also launches PLATO, an ambitious (and ultimately doomed) computer-assisted instruction system.

The 1970s saw a predictable reaction to the radicalism of the prior decade. The concept of "social responsibility" was supplanted by "social responsiveness" — the notion that unless businesses show social commitment, they will go down in flames, like the cities of the '60s. This was Friedmanism with a gloss, with economic self-interest, *not* a parallel set of civic responsibilities, as the basis for social engagement. (Indeed, this attitude was one reason the chemical industry responded as strongly as it did to the Bhopal catastrophe — it was concerned it might lose its "social license" to operate.)

In the 1980s, with the entrepreneurial success of counter-culture graduates like Anita Roddick, founder of The Body Shop, and Ben Cohen and Jerry Greenfield, founders of Ben & Jerry's, the pendulum swung back to "social responsibility." A new marketing concept was born: companies whose market appeal was premised wholly or in part on their commitment to alternative values, chief among which was social responsibility. Buying The Body Shop's cosmetics, or Ben & Jerry's ice cream, was a way for shoppers to affirm that they weren't part of "straight" society. Using a similar strategy, Apple Computer, the brainchild of a couple of adolescent computer whizzes, built a hugely successful business as the "un-IBM." The counter-culture had gone commercial, with the occasional great success. Now it is the late 1990s, and the socially responsible business movement continues, with mixed financial and philosophical success, on its niche campaign to forge a new and healthier relationship between money and morals, profits and principles.

— ◯ —

In 1992 there took place in Rio de Janeiro what was, or could have been, a turning point in the struggle for sustainability — the United Nations Conference on the Environment and Development, commonly known as the Earth Summit. An extravaganza of remarkable dimensions, it brought together leaders from government and industry along with some 30,000 representatives of non-governmental organizations (NGOs). The goal was hugely ambitious: to develop a world-wide plan of action for addressing the global *problématique*.

As was perhaps inevitable, the conference produced mixed results. Among the positives, it focused worldwide attention on sustainable development, and it catalyzed the creation of new international treaties on climate change, biological diversity, desertification, and high-seas fishing. In addition, in the years since Rio thousands of cities and towns worldwide have developed sustainability plans based on Agenda 21, the global blueprint for sustainable development that was the conference's main work product. That the document should have come into being at all was a remarkable acchievement: it was signed by delegates from more than 130 states, ranging from heads of state to representatives of NGOs to prominent scientists, and has been praised by one fairly progressive policy group as "a prototype of a global contract of great symbolic and potential political relevance."[14]

Overall, however, the Earth Summit fell well short of its goals. It had two main objectives: to create a united front in the battle to achieve sustainability, and to raise the international sense of urgency about the global *problématique* to a new pitch. It largely failed on both counts, victim to two powerful opponents: the vagaries of politics-as-usual, and the fickleness of a global citizenry that, more audience than community, is constantly switching to the next event. In the 1997 edition of its annual *State of the World* publication, the Worldwatch Institute acknowledged that "[i]n the five years since the Earth Summit, the international community has begun to embrace the concept of sustainable development and to use that notion to shift the priorities of existing agencies and programs."[15] On balance, however, the organization condemned the "failure to fulfill the legacy of Rio in the past five years" and concluded: "[O]ne lesson is clear: Although substantial progress has been made on specific environmental problems, the world has so far failed to meet the broader challenge of integrating environmental strategies into economic policy."[16] Maurice Strong, who was the Earth Summit's Secretary-General, has also been critical, declaring in one speech that while "fundamental change does not come quickly or easily, nevertheless it has to be said that the process of following up and implementing the results of the Earth Summit by governments has been disappointing in many respects."[17]

Two summonses to business emerged from the Earth Summit. One was Agenda 21. Chapter 30 sets out a charter for business, but it is extremely broadly formulated, hardly the sort of document to serve as a practical road map for industry. Nor do the other chapters of Agenda 21 provide the sort of specific guidance that lends itself to concrete action at the single-company level.[18]

The second call to arms came from a book that appeared in 1992, hard on the heels of the Earth Summit. Entitled *Changing Course: A Global Business Perspective on Development and the Environment,* it was nothing if not bold, calling for "profound changes in the goals and assumptions that drive corporate activities, and change in the daily practices and tools used to reach them. This means a break with business-as-usual mentalities and conventional wisdom that sidelines environmental and human concerns."[19]

Changing Course did not mince words, targeting senior-level corporate executives in a directly *ad hominem* assault:

> The painful truth is that the present is a relatively comfortable place for those who have reached positions of mainstream political or business leadership.
>
> This is the crux of the problem of sustainable development, and perhaps the main reason why there has been great acceptance of it in principle, but less concrete actions to put it into practice: many of those with the power to effect the necessary changes have the least motivation to alter the status quo that gave them power.[20]

These are incendiary words, the sort one might reasonably expect to have come from a harsh critic of corporate capitalism. But no: the author was Stephan Schmidheiny, a Swiss billionaire industrialist, writing on behalf of the Business Council for Sustainable Development, a group of executives from major multinationals such as Dow Chemical, Du Pont, and Royal Dutch/Shell. It was big business that was issuing this call for change, big business that was pointing an accusing finger at itself.

In hindsight, the publication of *Changing Course* emerges as a defining moment in the history of corporate environmentalism. It bespoke a genuine sense of urgency about the environmental crisis at the highest levels of the transnational corporations that in David Korten's formulation "rule the world." It also communicated a clear readiness — on paper, at any rate — to break with conventional values and ways of doing business. This was that rarest of events in mainstream business circles: subversion from within. As such, it spoke to the dawning of a new set of intuitions about the nature of corporate responsibility in a world under siege.

It also expressed, elegantly and articulately, all that was best about third-era corporate environmentalism. *Changing Course* emphasized the need for pollution prevention and eco-efficiency. It also came out strongly for another third-era staple: "stakeholder partnerships," i.e., collaborating with environmental groups, regulators, employees, suppliers, and other interested parties. More provocatively, it argued for full-cost pricing: making corporations account in their financial bookkeeping for any natural capital they draw down.

For all its earnestness, however, *Changing Course* was lacking in important ways. For one thing, it failed to pose critical questions about the limitations imposed by underlying structural constraints, i.e., about the degree to which corporate self-interest, as mandated by the current rules of market-economy capitalism, puts a cap on the extent to which companies actually *can* "break with business-as-usual mentalities and conventional wisdom"; the unfortunate fact is that sustainable development and the current market-economy rules of engagement just may be incompatible. For companies to break the negative feedback loop that fuels the current global *problématique,* it may be necessary to judiciously apply a stick or two of dynamite to some of the bedrock principles and systems of late 20th century corporate capitalism. Despite its bold tone, *Changing Course* did not address this possibility.

Not only that, but the Business Council for Sustainable Development

(BCSD, since renamed the World Business Council for Sustainable Development) has itself been taken to task for precisely the sort of self-serving behavior that has had people up in arms about corporate heavy-handedness for years. Prior to the 1992 Earth Summit, the United Nation's Centre for Transnational Corporations had recommended the imposition of a set of mandatory rules regulating the environmental conduct of companies overseas. BCSD, Paul Hawken writes, "had the recommendations of the UN agency shelved during the conference, and substituted for them a voluntary code of conduct drawn up by the corporations themselves."[21] He continues:

> Besides the official delegates to the UNCED conference, some 30,000 other delegates met in Rio, representatives of indigenous cultures, academic institutions, churches and religions, environmental and women's groups, and non-governmental organizations (NGOs) working on behalf of the environment and the disenfranchised. Virtually none of the 30,000 NGO delegates supported the proposals put forth by the Business Council on Sustainable Development. It is precisely with these stark refusals to acknowledge the democratic process that business must come to terms."[22]

Nor is Hawken alone in condemning the BCSD. The organization also had the dubious privilege of being included in the 1993 *Greenpeace Guide to Anti-Environmental Organizations.*

Changing Course came up short in another way as well. Precisely through its ardent espousal of conventional third-era strategies, it failed to confront a greater issue: the reality that pollution prevention, eco-efficiency and other third-era strategies, indispensable though they are, fall woefully short of meeting the challenge. Whereas pollution prevention and eco-efficiency are local problems that can be addressed internally and often linearly, sustainable development is a global problem, and a massively complex one at that: it demands a much broader, deeper, and ultimately more creative level of engagement. This is a step corporations have been loath to take, and from one perspective understandably so. Sustainable development is abstract, unwieldy, and subversive, and business resists all three.

At the same time, however, the global *problématique* clearly warrants addressing. How could business feel good about its role, yet dodge the sustainable-development bullet? The solution that emerged over the years — and it emerged organically, not as the result of a specific conscious process — was to cut sustainable development down to a more manageable size. Third-era corporate environmentalism sent "sustain-able development" through a semantic and conceptual sausage-grinder, whence it emerged as the more palatable "eco-efficiency." And that, for the most part, is how it continues to be viewed to this day.

4

By the Numbers

Facts are ventriloquists' dummies.
Sitting on a wise man's knee, they
may be made to utter words of wisdom;
elsewhere, they say nothing, or talk
nonsense, or indulge in sheer diabolism.
— Aldous Huxley

IN THE PREVIOUS CHAPTER, we surveyed how corporate environmentalism has evolved, and the general contours and character of third-era corporate environmentalism. I see ourselves as having flown in a time machine over a landscape, with me as tour guide pointing out general patterns over the past 30 years. In this chapter, I land the time machine and take you on a walking tour of the present, in order to provide a more detailed understanding of third-era corporate environmental impacts and practices.

So here we are, afoot in the land of current *praxis.* Not surprisingly, we will encounter both good and bad news. To start with the positive: the vast majority of large manufacturing companies have a formal, written environmental policy — fully 97%, according to a 1997 survey of Standard & Poor's 500 (S&P 500) companies by the Investor Responsibility Research Center (IRRC). (In the same survey, 79% of service companies indicated they had a formal environmental policy.) Similarly, 97% of S&P 500 companies conducted audits for environmental performance, again according to IRRC.[1]

Another positive indicator is the popularity of Total Quality Environmental Management (TQEM), a set of practices based on the hugely popular Total Quality Management (TQM) philosophy that is widely associated with the name of W. Edwards Deming. In IRRC's 1997 survey, 66% of manufacturing companies said they apply TQM principles and practices to the environmental aspects of their business.

Nor are these by any means the only favorable indicators. According to a 1994 Price Waterhouse survey, more than 40% of midsized and large companies have elevated the oversight of environmental compliance to the corporate board level. From one perspective this is low, but it was also nearly double the finding of a similar 1992 Price Waterhouse survey, and almost three times the result of its 1990 survey. Thus the clear trend is toward formalizing environmental oversight at the board level.

Another positive sign is that more and more companies are encouraging their suppliers to be environmentally responsible. In a 1991 survey by McKinsey & Co., 22% of respondents said they evaluated the environmental performance of suppliers.[2] By 1994 the numbers were sharply higher, with 45% of respondents to an American Opinion Research survey indicating that they "currently have environmental requirements or standards in place."[3] Nor does this trend show any sign of abating. Thirty-one percent of respondents to the survey said their organization was "considering expanding or adopting...environmental requirements or standards for its vendors."

The trend also looks positive in terms of pollution emissions data. In the U.S., the best-known measure of environmental performance is the EPA's Toxic Release Inventory (TRI) data, which are published pursuant to the SARA Title III Emergency Planning and Community Right-to-Know Act of 1986.[4] From 1988 through 1995 (the last year for which data are available), TRI releases dropped by about 46%, with a 4.9% decrease for core chemicals from 1994 to 1995.

Other useful corporate performance measures come from IRRC, with its Spill and Emissions Efficiency Indexes©.[5] The Spill Index© reflects the combined total volume of oil and chemical spills per billion dollars in revenue, while the Emissions Efficiency Index© measures the total reported volume of toxic chemicals released or transferred off-site for disposal per thousand dollars in annual revenue. Thus in both cases a trend toward smaller values indicates improvement — a company has reduced its spills and emissions per unit of revenue.

For non-financial companies in the S&P 500, IRRC's Spill Index© declined from an average 2.30 in 1987 to 0.82 in 1995, the last year for which data are available. A similar pattern emerges for emissions: a sharp and steady decline in IRRC's Emissions Efficiency Index© for the S&P 500 generally, from 2.09 in 1988 to 1.0 in 1992 to 0.66 in 1994, the last year for which data are available.

— ○ —

There are softer signs of progress as well. Earlier we saw that environmental policy statements are very common at the Fortune 500 level, with more than 80% of companies having one. Not only that, but over time they have steadily gained more substance. Early versions tended to be brief declarations of noble intentions, the sort of document that could easily be dismissed as puffery. However, more and more companies are upgrading their mission statements as they come to understand that an environmental mission statement is an expression of corporate will and as such warrants depth and seriousness. Thus Digital Equipment articulated its environmental agenda in a 3-4 page *Earth Vision* statement, Apple Computer transformed its mission statement from a short, general declaration into ten specific principles premised on the ICC Business Charter for Sustainable Development, and Bristol-Myers Squibb updated its mission statement to include commitments to biodiversity and greening up the supply chain, to name just three examples.

In addition, more and more corporate programs are rewarding employees for superior environmental performance, either through awards programs or by the more powerful strategy of integrating environmental considerations into managers' compensation.

Du Pont annually honors employee teams for their environmental accomplishments by donating funds in their name to environmental organizations of their choosing. Baxter Healthcare positively showers employees with rewards — for the best program, for the best packaging, for waste minimization, for the best all-around division, for the best pollution prevention program within a division, and for the best environmental management system within a division. The company also confers environmental merit awards on non-environmental employees.

And in a dramatic gesture, Monsanto has taken the award concept outside the corporate walls by offering separate $1 million grants to support the development of commercially practicable technologies that address specific wastewater purification challenges. The company has also announced a $100,000 annual award to support the development of new technologies that promote sustainability.

Offering financial rewards to employees for superior environmental performance by building them directly into their compensation packages is also an increasingly popular strategy. In its 1994 survey, IRRC found that over 60% of S&P 500 manufacturing companies had established environmental performance as a component of senior management compensation, while a Price Waterhouse study conducted in the same year placed the figure at 38%.

Hoechst-Celanese includes environmental performance in a bundle of other performance criteria that collectively comprise 25% of managers' compensation packages. Another leader is the waste-management services company Browning-Ferris, which uses an environmental performance index as a multiplier for bonuses. Fall short on the index, and no bonus.

There are other positive signs as well. In recent years, over 40 corporate codes of environmental conduct have sprouted up worldwide. Among the more noteworthy are the International Chamber of Commerce's 16-point Business Charter for Sustainable Development, which has attracted roughly 2,000 signatories; the chemical industry's Responsible Care program, which was launched in Canada and has been replicated in approximately 35 countries; and the 10-point CERES Principles, which was developed by the Coalition for Environmentally Responsible Economies and has about 80 signatories, including ten Fortune 500 companies.

Most of these codes of conduct encourage but do not mandate environmentally responsible behavior, an approach that invites charges of greenwashing. To date, these initiatives have enjoyed something of a honeymoon, but they are beginning to be subjected to closer scrutiny, both from the usual corporate watchdogs and from analysts who, while less adversarially inclined, are eager to see the corporate community develop policies that actually make a difference.

Meanwhile another set of environmental-management standards has been launched that promises to have more teeth. Sponsored by the International Organization for Standardization (known by the inverted acronym of ISO), these voluntary environmental-management standards, known collectively as ISO 14000, have the potential to do for environmental management what ISO 9000 has done for quality — make an in-place environmental management system premised on the TQM model of "continuous improvement" a virtual prerequisite for doing business globally.

ISO 14000 standards are being developed under the auspices of what in the daunting bureaucratese of the international standard-setting community is known as a "technical committee" (ISO TC 207). ISO TC 207 in turn oversees sub-committees on such topics as environmental auditing, environmental labeling, environmental performance evaluation, life-cycle assessment, and environmental aspects of product standards. ISO 14001, which covers environmental management systems, was finalized in 1996.

Asian companies are extremely gung-ho about ISO 14001, as are many North American businesses. In a 1995 Arthur D. Little survey, 62% of responding environmental managers said that third-party certification to the ISO standard would be important to the future business success of their companies, while 86% said it was important that their environmental management systems be as good or better than the ISO standard.[6]

However, the attitude in North America is tempered by a measure of skepticism. Some business executives have taken a wait-and-see attitude, unpersuaded that the not insubstantial investment will produce an adequate payback. Others view the ISO standard as another in a long line of schemes to siphon money from the pockets of front-line business into the coffers of hungry consultants. The mixed response of North American companies notwithstanding, ISO 14001 may have a considerable impact on corporate environmental-management policies and practices.

Precisely how much that will translate into actual improvements in environmental performance is a matter of some debate. The standard is not prescriptive: while it requires companies to have a formal environmental management system in place, to conduct regular audits, and to commit to continuous improvement, it does not require specific performance levels to be met. Some argue that this will add up to little more than a gloss. Some companies may fraudulently pursue certification, and from companies that do rigorously conform to the spirit and letter of the standard, significant progress is not assured. It is one thing to have an environmental management system in place and to commit to continuous improvement, and another actually to achieve it.

Is ISO 14001 ideal? No. But it is just as surely better than nothing. The effectiveness of ISO 14001 will vary depending on the will and intentions of each company. As applied by some companies, it will be next to meaningless. For other companies, it will be a steppingstone to substantial progress. Would a prescriptive standard be more effective at bringing about improvements in corporate environmental performance? Yes — but in the current business environment a worldwide standard of that sort is not going to be designed, much less accepted. That being the unfortunate reality, ISO 14001 represents a step in the right direction, despite its various shortcomings. And, over time, it should make a difference.

Thus, the list of positives is not inconsiderable. But what do they all add up to? To answer this question, let's create a composite portrait of an imaginary corporation whose environmental attitudes and policies are representative of S&P 500 manufacturing companies generally. This company

- has made consistent progress in reducing spills and emissions;
- has an environmental mission statement, with the increasing likelihood that it has some real substance;
- conducts regular environmental audits (but for compliance, not for excellence);
- has an active TQEM program;
- is seeking ISO 14000 registration or is giving thought to doing so;
- recently implemented a program evaluating suppliers' environmental performance, or is considering doing so;
- publishes an environmental report or has plans to do so;
- has an environmental awards program and is also beginning to integrate eco-performance into its managers' compensation packages;
- is a signatory to one or more industry codes of environmental conduct;
- is pursuing eco-efficiency, at least to some degree —
- and yet, as discussed in Chapter 3, still treats environmental management as a cost center.

The great majority of these are positive indicators, and collectively they go a good way toward rebutting the argument raised by people like *Greenwash* author Jed Greer that corporations never really change their stripes. Corporate environmental conduct *has* changed, and in important ways.

However, we must take care not to read too much into the above catalog of positive developments. The problem, in a nutshell, lies with *what* and *who* is being watched and measured; or, to put the same notion somewhat differently, how the indicators play out at the macro level. Consider, for instance, the TRI data (EPA's Toxic Release Inventory). Earlier we noted sharp reductions in levels of TRI chemicals over time. Encouraging as these data are, they only tell part of the story. For one thing, SARA Title III requires only manufacturing companies with 10 or more employees to file TRI reports. That leaves out a great many small companies. The logic for excluding them is perfectly understandable: small enterprises have enough trouble making a go of it without being subjected to onerous and expensive reporting requirements like TRI. Still, the public-policy consequence of this exception is that these small companies are left free to go about their merry polluting way without being publicly accountable. And the measurement consequence is that their considerable TRI emissions go unreported.

In addition, the TRI inventory covers only a small percentage of industrial chemicals, the health effects of many of which are pernicious or unknown. More than 72,000 industrial chemicals are used in commerce in the United States — and that figure *excludes* foods, drugs, cosmetics, and pesticides. According to the environmental group INFORM, "almost none of these chemicals have been fully characterized for their ability to cause environmental and health effects."[7] TRI requires companies to report on emissions of 643 toxic chemicals. This is not to suggest that TRI tracks less than 1% of the problem — the TRI roster is the toxic equivalent of the FBI's Most Wanted List. Still, subtract 643 from over 72,000, and you're left with an awful lot of chemicals, and chemical emissions, that go untracked.

Furthermore, the TRI data apply only to plants within the U.S. When a company moves a factory overseas – a commonplace occurrence in this age of globalization – TRI emissions decline, but not worldwide pollution emissions. And of course this problem is compounded when companies move extremely polluting factories overseas, as has been known to happen.

There are other problems as well. For instance: the volume of toxic waste being generated remains enormous — over 35 billion pounds (16 billion kg) in 1995. What's more, overall levels generated are actually increasing: the 1995 total is close to 7% higher than the figure for 1991. The explanation for the apparent contradiction between decreased emissions and increased generation is that while fewer toxic chemicals are being released into the environment, more are being transferred off-site for recycling, incineration, treatment, or disposal. What this tells us is that although source reduction is the first priority in the EPA's waste management hierarchy, progress is being made more slowly on that front than in the management of toxic chemicals once they have become waste. Toxic wastes are being managed more effectively, but no headway is being made toward the larger goals of reducing or eliminating their use.

In other words, we are doing fairly well at implementing end-of-pipe solutions, and less well at moving the solutions to the front end of the pipe, which is where they belong. And the TRI data, in part because they seem to paint such a glowing picture of progress, tend to obscure that all-important fact.

— ◯ —

Thus we find that while the TRI data initially seem quite positive, the findings become more troublesome when you dig a bit deeper. The situation is similar for the non-emissions-related indicators of progress — both qualitative and quantitative — that I outlined above. Almost all the research on corporate environmental performance focuses on S&P 500-level companies. While these companies for the most part have sharply strengthened their environmental-management practices, that leaves a huge segment of the industrial populace unaccounted for — the so-called "small and midsized enterprises," or SMEs. Pull back the big-company curtain and you'll find one of sustainable business's dirty little secrets: SMEs are barely in the game. With small businesses accounting for about 50% of private-sector economic output in the U.S., this is a serious and indeed potentially disastrous problem.

To get a sense of the disparity in environmental performance between large companies and SMEs, consider that as of 1993 only 17% of middle-market manufacturers had a written environmental policy statement, compared to over 80% for Fortune 500 companies. Not only that, but only 12% of middle-market manufacturers had a formal environmental program, and a mere 2% had both an environmental policy statement and an environmental program.[8]

There is a straightforward reason for the SMEs' relative backwardness: inadequate resources. Fortune 500 executives may be badly strapped for time, but at least they have the funds to meet environmental goals. SME managers have neither time nor money, so matters of seemingly secondary importance like environmental proactivity get short shrift.[9]

In fact, so do more obviously high-priority items like compliance. Alan Borner, executive director of EHMI, a non-profit organization that works with business on environmental issues, puts the matter bluntly: "Regulations in the U.S. are so tortured, so patchwork and sometimes so contradictory, that compliance has become literally impossible. That's true at big companies and even more so at smaller ones. Environmental managers at small companies who tell you they're on top of compliance are lying."[10]

With environmental regulations weighing on them like an anvil, many SME executives view the environment as an enemy. So how do you break through SME executives' chronic case of *agita* and implant a new and more generous notion of what the environment can mean and do for them? That's the challenge, and it's a stumper.

To a significant degree, the issue is one of logistics. Over five million establishments in the U.S. have under 100 employees, and close to 90% of these companies have fewer than 20 people working for them. There is no simple way to reach them all. Still, the situation is not entirely hopeless. For one thing, government agencies are starting to turn their attention to the problem. For instance, in 1996 the U.S. Environmental Protection Agency launched Energy Star Small Business, designed to encourage the adoption of energy-efficient products and technologies by SMEs. The agency is supporting a host of other initiatives as well, such as a Small Business Ombudsman office that advises SMEs on compliance issues. Also attracting attention of late is the possibility of using large-to-small business mentoring as a way to improve SMEs' environmental performance.

In addition, three departures from business-as-usual are in the offing that may eventually make a difference. The first of these is ISO 14001. Many SMEs that want to supply Fortune 500 companies or compete on their own will be encouraged to seek certification. Presumably this will also induce them to get their environmental houses in order.[11]

For many SMEs, this will not be easy. Whereas companies with active environment, health and safety (EH&S) programs already in place will probably find that ISO 14001 either confirms what they've been doing or at most demands a modest stretch, the many SMEs without formal EH&S management systems will find ISO 14001 much more imposing. This creates a real danger that ISO 14000 will create a competitive advantage for bigger and wealthier companies that can afford effective EH&S programs. But fairness issues aside, it is also clear that ISO 14001 will improve the environmental performance of many SMEs.

The second promising change-in-the-making is regulatory reform. At present, the oppressive nature of environmental regulation discourages environmental proactivity. The solution: make environmental regulation more SME-friendly — and do so without lowering performance standards. Reduce the raw tonnage of environmental regulations that need to be complied with. Simplify the remaining paperwork. Provide a helping hand for the work that needs to be done. In the words of environmental-management consultant Gil Friend, "Move from cop to coach."[12]

And indeed this is starting to happen. The influential President's Council on Sustainable Development recently declared that "the current regulatory system should be improved to deliver required results at lower costs. In addition, the system should provide enhanced flexibility in return for superior environmental performance."[13] The U.S. EPA has many initiatives in this area, including sector-specific Compliance Assistance Centers that help SMEs stay on top of the latest environmental requirements and technologies. At the state level, California has experimented with "one-stop permitting," which aims to let businesses get all their permits in a single transaction rather than subjecting them to the regulatory Chinese water torture of innumerable separate procedures. California has also begun to provide on-site compliance assistance, with a cap of $500 on charges to small businesses.

This trend is significant theoretically as well as practically, suggesting as it does an entirely new attitude toward compliance on the part of regulatory authorities. Writing in *The Green Business Letter*, a trade newsletter, Joel Makower commented,

> Regular readers of this newsletter may take pause at this seemingly sudden coverage of the regulatory world. Our self-imposed mandate, after all, is to cover beyond-compliance issues. But suddenly, the two worlds seem to be colliding. Federal and state agencies are making "beyond compliance" a key part of their regulatory strategies. After all, the more that companies move out front of the government's inspectors, litigators, and paper-pushers, the fewer resources these agencies will need to do their jobs.
>
> In short, "beyond compliance" is becoming the law of the land.[14]

Last but not least, there is the electronic information revolution. The Internet and related media such as CD-ROM hold out the promise of simplifying SME executives' lives by delivering them precisely the information they need, when they need it, and in the form they require. In the digital age, the knights of eco-efficiency won't come riding in on horseback. They'll come driving down the information superhighway.

ISO 14000, regulatory reform, and the Internet are all steps in the right direction, but they are only a beginning, especially in view of the fact that many observers are skeptical that the public sector has the will or the resources to successfully tackle the Herculean challenge of bringing the SMEs up to speed environmentally, despite the recent rash of new programs. For the foreseeable future, the eco-backwardness of the SMEs will continue to be a serious problem. Not the only problem, to be sure — substantial progress is required at the Fortune 500 level as well — but without a doubt the most often overlooked. The media tend to focus on large companies and their successes and shortcomings, while allowing the SMEs to pass beneath their radar. This is a problem in its own right. Meanwhile, the numbers tracking environmental progress will continue to mislead.

— ◯ —

Now that we have come to the end of this brief tour of the technical and operational state of the art, we are left with the classic image of the glass that is half full or half empty, depending on one's perspective. If we consider the progress that has been made over the past three-plus decades, the transformation is truly remarkable. Just as clearly, however, the work has only begun.

In the next chapter, we continue our review of the current state of the environmental-management art with an analysis of a quite separate (and equally important) domain: environmental communications.

Communications
and Community

Something there is that doesn't love a wall,
That wants it down.
— Robert Frost

I N THE PREVIOUS CHAPTER, we reviewed the internal technical steps that
companies are taking to improve their environmental performance,
with an emphasis on eco-efficiency and pollution prevention. But
organizations are more than aggregates of policies and procedures.
They also have a social aspect. At the heart of the social domain is
communication which is the subject of this chapter.

Here, too, we are in a process of transition. By and large, two corporate *personas* have been dominant in this century. The first was the
"Generalissimo." This early model for corporate behavior, which can be
traced to the robber baron era of the late 19th and early 20th centuries,
is largely a thing of the past but still crops up occasionally — for
instance, in Exxon's mishandling of the 1989 Exxon Valdez oil spill.
Arrogant and willful, the Generalissimo lets power speak for itself. At
most, he (and it most assuredly *is* a he!) gives only token explanations
for his behavior. As befits a dictator, he dictates: why should a
Generalissimo bother to negotiate or explain? The origins of this attitude can be traced to social Darwinism. In a survival-of-the-fittest
world, why not grab what you can?

After the Generalissimo came "John Wayne" (aka the Duke), which is
the *persona* most mainstream corporations present today. Unlike the
Generalissimo, John Wayne is not arrogant, but he *is* very private. John
Wayne corporations present themselves to the world as self-assured,
self-contained, and stand-alone. They are very selective in what they
choose to divulge. The strong, silent, self-sufficient, male achiever of

great things is a heroic model with a long and honorable lineage, and so it is only natural for the (largely male) corporate world to have admired and adopted it. From a certain psychological perspective it makes sense practically, too. It's a cowboy world the Duke lives in, a frontier where it's every man for himself (the women are in the kitchen, being protected...). In this fundamentally hostile environment, a cautious, guarded stance makes sense. "Trust no one," the popular television show *The X-Files* cautions us. The Duke says the same thing too, only powerfully and without that paranoid edge.

The era that bred John Wayne is passing, however. The Duke has mounted his horse and is riding off into the sunset. Important changes are overtaking corporate communications in general and corporate environmental communications in particular. Call it, with only a small dose of overstatement, the greening of corporate communications. It's not that corporations don't still spin the truth as a matter of course — they do, sometimes outlandishly — or that they never indulge in green-washing about their overall environmental commitment — there are all too many instances of that. Still, an environmental communications *ethos* is emerging that places a heightened emphasis on collaboration, communication, and consensus-building. *Discourse is being valorized,* is how academics would put it. Or, more straightforwardly: corporations are placing greater value on communication techniques that aim to build trust. That's not the stuff Dukes are made of.

In large measure this change represents an evolutionary response to a broad spectrum of changing business and cultural conditions. There are six major drivers in all.

The first factor, and the broadest of all, is that "discourse is being valorized" in our culture generally. It was the French cultural historian Michel Foucault who detailed the extent to which sex has been brought into the domain of public discourse, i.e., been made an act of telling as much as doing. The evidence that he was right pervades our popular culture. Watch Geraldo, or Jenny Jones, or any of the myriad other television talk shows, and you will meet person after person being exuberantly public about their private lives. There is only one way to make sense of their behavior — they're experiencing emotional gratification through the act of telling.

These electronic exhibitionists are not alone. New Agers get a similar rush from "sharing." Therapy patients are persuaded they'll be healed if they can only "express" enough. From stem to stern, our popular culture, or rather popular cultures, have a strong bias toward divulging.

And predictably a surfeit of media — talk radio, the Internet — has emerged, offering anyone with the requisite *chutzpah* a platform from which to hold forth. Ours is a culture of telling, and so it is small wonder that corporations should have gotten a bit of the bug as well.

A second driver of the greening of corporate communications, and an especially powerful one, is the emergence of the global marketplace, which requires extreme adaptability in the face of super-rapid change, a readiness to work closely and collegially with outside partners, and a willingness to distribute authority internally to teams of employees in order to improve response times. To meet these needs, a new corporate *persona* is emerging that is one part shapeshifter, one part communicator, and one part corporate democrat. Much about the new corporate environmental communications *ethos* reflects this more adaptable, more accessible identity.

A third driver is Total Quality Management (TQM), which locates a primary source of corporate power, as well as potential competitive advantage, in the creativity of a company's employees. Just as atoms release extraordinary amounts of energy when properly "encouraged," so according to TQM do humans — *creative* energy. TQM facilitates this process by implementing structures and policies that "de-hassle" and empower employees. Whereas the traditional concept of leadership involves giving orders, TQM-trained managers take a different approach. They lead by getting out of the way — and then listening.

TQM also re-defines the meaning of "customer." In TQM-speak, the term no longer applies only to purchasers of a company's products or services: it covers every person and organization affected by the company's activities. External customers consist, among others, of regulators, citizen groups, corporate suppliers, the media, and residents of communities where company plants are located. Internal customers include employees in other departments and at higher levels of management.

As we saw earlier, TQM defines quality as "zero defects." And what precisely is a "defect?" According to TQM, it is defined by reference to what the customer wants. And how do companies learn what their customers want? The answer: by getting close to them. By developing relationships of trust with them. Again, by listening.

Thus in multiple ways TQM points the way to a communications *ethos* that emphasizes open dialogue and active listening. TQM-trained managers work to tear down walls and to build long-term relationships — and not just with purchasers of their products, but with the full array of their company's "customers." And of course they apply the doctrine across-the-board to the full range of corporate activities, including the management of environmental issues.

The next three drivers of the greening of communication are more directly environmental. First (or, rather, fourth), there is a growing perception that corporations should be held responsible for their environmental impacts — and where there is accountability, there will inevitably be disclosure. As we saw in Chapter 2, the doctrine of environmental accountability has its roots in the Bhopal disaster and subsequent legislation requiring the disclosure of toxic emissions. But it reflects a larger imperative as well. With each passing day, the global *problématique* and the information revolution make it more difficult to disregard the extent to which the world's social and economic systems are interconnected. And this sense of a web, i.e., of a complex system of causes and effects, is having an effect of its own: it is forcing a re-evaluation of the meaning of "product." Historically, the term has been associated with goods and services that are deliberately offered for sale, and that remains its everyday definition. But systems thinking is driving a broader definition of the term: "product" becomes all of a corporation's *outputs* — including, for instance, waste — and, more radically still, all its *consequences* — for instance, the social consequences of a massive downsizing or the impacts on human health of an inadvertent toxic chemical emission.

A fifth driver is the quite practical realization that collaboration is an effective, efficient way to address environmental problems. Business executives are beginning to realize that whereas conflict drains resources, pooling resources creates synergies. For instance, when a company and an environmental group join forces, the business gains access to scientific and technical expertise that it may not possess in-house, while the advocacy group gets the benefits of tough bottom-line thinking.

Finally, the emerging environmental communications philosophy represents a new approach to an old and grievous public-relations problem. Rightly or wrongly, corporations have come by many to be perceived as the executive arm of an industrial society that willfully and indifferently wreaks environmental havoc. Polls typically find that a mere 10-15% of U.S. adults view corporations' eco-claims as trustworthy.[1] Both corporations and the environment occupy a prominent place on people's symbolic landscape: they have become diametrically opposed yet inextricably connected characters in a morality play that paints good and evil in starkly black-and-white images — on one side the innocent environment, on the other the ruthless corporation.

This puts corporate environmental communicators in a difficult position, to put it mildly. When corporations speak out for the environment, they are asking people to believe that they have switched sides — that they have traded their black hats for white ones. In a country where almost nine out of ten adults deeply distrust corporations, this is not an easy sell, and the shopworn strategy of lobbing public-relations missives over the corporate ramparts has only made matters worse. The new, more open approach to environmental communications represents an attempt to build a new foundation of trust with a deeply dubious public.

Taken together, all this adds up to a fundamentally new approach to corporate environmental communications. Not that corporate culture doesn't give mixed signals: for many corporations, it's still old-style communications-as-usual. Still, the general direction is unmistakable. Stonewalling is out and communication is in.

— ◯ —

One way the new environmental communications *ethos* is reflected is by a greater willingness to enter into formal and informal strategic partnerships. Businesses are forming environmental collaborations with partners from many different sectors, including industry, environmental groups, and government.

Business-to-Business Partnerships. Businesses are increasingly linking up, often across sectors, to address environmental issues. The Geneva-based World Business Council on Sustainable Development is one such organization; another prominent one is the Global Environmental Management Initiative (GEMI), a group of over 20 U.S.-based Fortune 500 companies. A 1994 survey by *Tomorrow* magazine and the British eco-consultancy SustainAbility identified over 20 such entities and commented: "[T]hey represent only the very tip of a rapidly growing iceberg of industry associations, coalitions, federations and networks that have set themselves new environmental objectives."[2]

Currently, most of these green business networks focus on information and technology transfer. While these activities are likely to intensify as electronic communications systems such as the Internet become more universal, in time an entirely new role may emerge. SustainAbility speculates that these organizations will evolve into what it calls "Sustainable Development Consortia" (SDCs), which it likens to the

Japanese *keiretsu*, loosely linked companies that share expertise, technology, capital, and other resources. SDCs, SustainAbility opines, will function as "green *keiretsu*," joining forces not only to swap information but to drive pro-sustainability market-based initiatives. There is a compelling logic to this vision: as the pressure to pursue sustainable-development strategies intensifies, a ramping up from technology-based initiatives to more intensely collaborative market-building activities seems a likely direction.

Businesses are linking up vertically as well. In the last chapter, we touched on the increasing popularity of what has come to be known as "greening the supply chain." Among the leaders in this area are S.C. Johnson & Son, which held environmental conferences in 1991 and 1994 for its suppliers and publishes a regular eco-newsletter for them; McDonald's, which is purchasing over $350 million annually in recycled products under its *McRecycle* program; the British retailer B&Q, which requires its 450 suppliers to have an environmental policy backed by a full environmental audit and to comply with B&Q's own environmental policy; The Body Shop, which has a supplier accreditation program that awards ratings of zero to five stars and publishes a list of suppliers who have reached a certain rating level; and General Motors which, through its trademarked PICOS program, is helping its thousands of suppliers cut costs by becoming more eco-efficient. Also worthy of special mention is the U.S. apparel industry, which is working with the trade association Businesses for Social Responsibility to develop and impose pollution discharge standards on their textile suppliers worldwide.

Greening the supply chain, which is arguably the most dynamic trend in the entire environmental-business movement, may get a boost from ISO 14001, the international environmental-management standard that requires companies to have a serious environmental-management system in place. So far, Daimler-Benz is the only company to require its suppliers to be ISO 14001-certified, but the ranks will probably increase over time.

Strategies for greening the supply chain run the gamut from gentle suggestion to rigid requirement. A corporate policy can be hortatory or mandatory; it can spell out suppliers' environmental duties in detail or only sketchily; it can require minimal or extensive substantiation. Whatever the tactic, the underlying principle is the same: collaboration in the name of improved eco-performance.

Business/Environmental-Group Partnerships. In recent years, businesses and environmental groups have shown a greater willingness to enter into partnerships with each other. Consider, for instance, CERES, or the Coalition for Environmentally Responsible Economies, which is a coalition of social investment professionals, environmental groups, religious organizations, public pension trustees, and public interest groups. In 1989, the group challenged corporations to endorse a rigorous 10-point code of corporate environmental conduct that it had developed. Small companies signed on but the Valdez Principles, as they were then called, made no headway whatsoever in the Fortune 500. Executives were concerned that signing them would subject their companies to legal liability, and they also resented CERES' attitude — they felt they were being dictated to.

Realizing that it was getting nowhere with its most important constituency, CERES somewhat softened its principles (since renamed the CERES Principles) — and its preaching. The strategy paid off in 1993, when the Sun Company became the first Fortune 500 company to sign the CERES Principles. Since then, nine more Fortune 500 companies — H.B. Fuller, Arizona Public Service, Polaroid, General Motors, Bethlehem Steel, Bank of America, ITT, Bank of Boston, and Coca Cola USA — have signed on, and others are reportedly circling the CERES runway.

In many ways, the CERES Principles are rather tame. The document does not create legally binding obligations, nor do many of its principles ask corporations to commit to anything more than what responsible companies are already doing. Yet some of the principles have real substance. One provision, for instance, calls for signatories to "go voluntarily beyond the requirements of the law," i.e., to publicly commit to going beyond compliance. Another commits them to "consider demonstrated environmental commitment as a factor" in selecting the Board of Directors.

Most telling of all is the principle calling for "an annual self-examination of … progress in implementing these Principles" and the publication of an annual "CERES Report, which will be made available to the public." This is the pledge that gives the CERES Principles their teeth. On the disclosure side, the CERES Principles are something of a modern-day Magna Carta, proclaiming the citizenry's inalienable right to corporate accountability. Companies that sign the CERES Principles are promising to lower their drawbridges and raise their gateways — if not always and for all occasions, at least some of the time. That's an important concession to changing cultural expectations. And while the handful of Fortune 500 companies that have endorsed the CERES

Principles are well ahead of the pack, their willingness to endorse a document drafted by environmentalists bespeaks a fundamental change in corporate/advocacy-group relations.

Companies are also proving somewhat more willing to work directly with environmental groups, despite their reputation as the "enemy." The most renowned partnership to date was the landmark 1991 agreement between the Environmental Defense Fund and McDonald's to jointly develop waste reduction strategies for the fast-food giant. In McDonald's case, the proof has been in the pudding, or more precisely in the pudding's packaging: the company now has in place almost 100 initiatives to reduce, reuse, and recycle or compost waste. Over the four years prior to 1995, these efforts succeeded in eliminating 10,500 tons of packaging annually, increasing the average recycled content of corporate packaging from 17% to 45%, and raising the consumption of recycled packaging to 220,000 tons per year.

The EDF/McDonald's collaboration was at least as important for the precedent it set as for the waste-reduction progress it has produced at McDonald's. The EDF move legitimized in-depth collaborations between environmental groups and industry (although at some cost to EDF, which was heavily criticized for "selling out" to industry). Virtually overnight, corporations lost their status as arch-enemies and began to be seen as potential allies.

Following up on its success with McDonald's, EDF later teamed with the Pew Charitable Trusts to form the Alliance for Environmental Innovation, with the express goal of developing programs along the EDF/McDonald's model. In 1996, the initiative bore fruit with the announcement of a partnership with consumer products company S.C. Johnson & Son to jointly weave environmental considerations into new product design by developing new tools, metrics, policies, and practices. Later that same year, the Alliance teamed up with Starbucks to reduce the environmental impacts of coffee cups through increased use of reusable cups and by redesigning single-use cups.

Another important alliance was forged in 1996, when the giant multinational Unilever, with global fish sales of $900 million and a 20% share of the U.S. and European frozen fish market, teamed with the World Wide Fund for Nature to form the Marine Stewardship Council. Their aim was ambitious: to ensure the long-term viability of global fish populations and the health of the marine ecosystems on which they depend. They hope to do this by establishing a certification program for fisheries and by getting fish processors and retailers to commit to buy product solely from sources certified as sustainably managed.

Whether this noble goal can be achieved remains to be seen. Many practical obstacles stand in the way, such as, for instance, the Marine Stewardship Council's lack of influence in the Pacific Rim. Still, for our purposes the important point is that the initiative brings together a major global corporation and a major global environmental group — suits and sandals — to protect a common interest.

Even Greenpeace, which has long been hostile to collaboration, has reassessed its position. Not that it is abandoning its no-compromises, direct-action stance, but the organization has announced its willingness to work with companies that have an acceptable product and mindset.

As a rule, partnerships between corporations and environmental groups are quite constrained. After all, it's one thing for a business to work with an advocacy group on one specific issue, and quite another to let the whole camel into the tent. Dow Chemical has a Corporate Environmental Advisory Council consisting of nine outside environmental experts (including a representative from an environmental group) who advise Dow on environmental issues, but they are the only major corporation with such a group. Companies have also been reluctant to put out-and-out environmentalists on their boards. Scarcely two dozen environmentalists currently serve on corporate boards, and these tend to be high-profile figures — four are former EPA Administrators — who do not necessarily bring a sharply different viewpoint to the dialogue.

Public/Private Partnerships. At the federal, state, and local levels, regulatory agencies are abandoning the stick of command-and-control for the public/private carrot. Some of the U.S. Environmental Protection Agency's more prominent public/private programs include

- *Green Lights,* which promotes energy conservation by providing on-site technical guidance and other resources that help companies switch to more energy-efficient lighting
- *Energy Star Computers,* which encourages computer makers to produce equipment that "powers down" when not in use. The EPA has signed partnership agreements with participating manufacturers to develop the products
- *WasteWi$e,* which promotes cost-effective steps to reduce the amount of solid waste generated by businesses. Participants commit to cutting back on the trash they generate, stepping up their recycling efforts, and buying or making recycled products. WasteWi$e has approximately 300 participating companies, of

which close to one-half come from the Fortune 500.

At the local government level, regulators are starting publicly to reward businesses for meeting or exceeding local regulations. In Sonoma County, California, businesses in selected industries that comply with local environmental, health, and safety laws receive a seal of approval from a local green-business program. "Beyond compliance" this most assuredly is not: the program recognizes companies for simply obeying the law — quite a statement about the current state of environmental compliance. Still, it does provide another example of the public/private partnership in practice.

Nor is this sort of activity limited to the U.S. In 1996, 81 organizations representing industry, government, and NGOs joined forces in Japan to launch a Green Purchasing Network to promote the purchase of environmentally superior products, especially ones containing recycled content. The participants include close to 40 major companies, over a dozen consumer and environmental groups, the Japan Environment Association, and the Japan Environment Agency. The U.S.-based Buy Recycled Business Alliance, a project of the Washington-based National Recycling Coalition, seems to have been a model for the Japanese initiative.[3]

The Multi-Stakeholder Partnership. Bryan Thomlison, formerly of Church & Dwight, is an ardent advocate of what he calls "multi-stakeholder partnerships" — initiatives that unite people from separate sectors and with widely disparate interests around a single cause or activity.

Church & Dwight's En-Graffiti program, which was developed under Thomlison's tutelage, provides an impressive example of such a partnership in action. The project addresses one of the country's most urgent problems: our blighted inner cities, where broken homes are the rule and drugs and crime are rampant. Despair is pervasive in these areas, and this isolates people and drives them inward. The sense of community fades and what social scientists call "incivilities" — increasing noise, trash, vandalism, graffiti, loitering and the like — proliferate, accelerating the demoralization process and perpetuating the downward spiral.

Although En-Graffiti addresses the "incivility" of graffiti, it was initially conceived of for business, not social reasons. Church & Dwight was looking for new markets for ARMEX Blast Media, an environmentally benign, baking soda-based alternative to harsh chemical cleaners and solvents. Graffiti removal was a logical application: however, the company could not persuade municipalities to switch over to ARMEX, not because the product was inadequate but because graffiti was too low on the urban totem pole to warrant serious expenditures of time or money.

The graffiti application would probably have died, but for a fortuitous conversation Thomlison had with Emory Jackson, president of We Care About New York, a local litter prevention organization and a long-time Church & Dwight stakeholder. In passing, Jackson mentioned the desirability of employing homeless or otherwise disadvantaged people to clean up business improvement areas. That thought, coupled with Thomlison's desire to apply Church & Dwight's product to graffiti removal, led to the birth of En-Graffiti.

Over the next months, Church & Dwight and We Care About New York expanded their partnership to include the Queens County Overall Economic Development Corp., the Salvation Army, and the Queens Borough President's Office. All the partners had a strong interest in seeing the venture succeed: Church & Dwight because En-Graffiti represented a wedge into a new market; the Queens County Overall Economic Development Corp. because it was a business-development project; the Salvation Army because it wanted to help residents of their homeless shelters build new lives; the Queens Borough President's Office because En-Graffiti promised Borough President Claire Shulman a wealth of favorable publicity; and We Care About New York because, well, they cared about New York.

As a proof of its commitment, Church & Dwight donated a graffiti removal system to the venture. The company also engaged Coddington Management, a professional business and project-management firm, to structure and help manage the partnership as well as to provide ongoing human resources, sales, marketing, and financial-management support. The Salvation Army recruited employees from the 400 occupants of its Borden Avenue Veterans Residence and after a screening process came up with 14 candidates, which was eventually winnowed down to six.

En-Graffiti was officially launched in February 1994. By the time a press conference including such luminaries as New York City Mayor Rudolph Giuliani was held some two months later, the business was already operating at roughly break-even.

In this multi-stakeholder partnership, everyone won: the borough and the city, which achieved reductions in the "incivility" of graffiti at no cost to the taxpayer; local businesses, which got a more attractive commercial environment; Church & Dwight, which got favorable publicity plus a new market for an important product line; and the homeless veterans, who got a new lease on life.

After two years of operation, the Salvation Army hailed the program as the most successful "runway" program it had ever been involved with. Every person who entered the En-Graffiti program found gainful employment, either with the program or because of the program's ancillary benefits in skill-development and confidence-building. However, En-Graffiti ran into operational difficulties because of administrative bottlenecks in finance and bookkeeping. Eventually, Coddington Management found a new home for En-Graffiti with the New York City Police Athletic League, where it will be used to train and employ youth as well as formerly homeless veterans.

— ◯ —

The changing environmental communications *ethos* is also reflected by an increased willingness to engage in less formal types of dialogue and collaboration. For instance, companies are paying more and more attention to the communities where their plants are located. This is especially true in the chemical industry, whose Responsible Care program recommends the formation of Citizen Advisory Councils, or CAPs — organizations made up of volunteers who serve as the eyes, ears, and voice of the community. As noted in Chapter 3, CAPs have proven to be an effective mechanism for building trust by encouraging dialogue and letting members of the community know the corporation is listening.

The awakening of interest in community relations has both practical and theoretical underpinnings. At the practical level, communities where facilities operate can block companies from obtaining required permits. More abstractly, the rising interest in communities reflects a shift in traditional notions of corporate power and information flow. Historically, the corporate model has been feudal: information and directives traveled from corporate headquarters down to the divisions and the plants. The flattening of corporate hierarchies and distribution of responsibilities out into the ranks is changing that. Information is now perceived as flowing from the "extremities" to the "head," not vice-versa. This new respect for the grassroots extends to local communities, which are increasingly being viewed as sources of valuable information. Once again, a basic TQM principle is at work: listen to your customers.

Another significant area of change is public environmental reporting, a hot enough topic in environmental-management circles for three separate green business networks — the World Industry Council for the Environment (WICE), the Global Environmental Management Initiative (GEMI), and the Public Environmental Reporting Initiative (PERI) — to have issued guidelines and primers.[4]

Why the fuss? In its primer, WICE gives three sets of reasons why environmental reports "can be an effective tool to manage and improve the way you do business":

- *Business benefits* (help meet the increasing expectations of existing customers and win new business; assist in identifying efficiencies and cost savings, and in reducing future environmental liabilities; allow for easier access to capital/investment markets)

- *Improved performance* (encourages measurement, collection and collation of data and information to be put into a more manageable form, providing better management information; strengthens management systems and processes and ensures that procedures are based on good management practice; motivates employees and others on whom your business depends; encourages continuous improvement)

- *Enhanced reputation* (helps maintain the confidence of different audiences and your "license to operate;" responds to shareholder and public concerns; provides tangible evidence of your environmental commitment; gives credibility to your contributions to the public debate).[5]

Omitted from the WICE list are two important public policy rationales for environmental reporting. The first of these is *accountability*. Environmental reports — objective, data-rich, warts-and-all environmental reports — testify to a company's readiness to put its environmental performance to the test of public opinion. The second is *benchmarking*. Environmental reports allow the public to track corporate environmental performance over time. Talk about progress is cheap. Environmental reporting moors that talk to the *terra firma* of hard numbers.

The number of companies publishing an annual environmental report is growing rapidly. The first annual environmental report in the U.S. containing extensive environmental performance data was published by Monsanto in 1991. By 1994, according to SustainAbility, more than 100 companies worldwide were producing some sort of annual environmental report in book form, and by year-end 1996 the figure had grown to an estimated 450–500.

This is rapid growth but there is still a long way to go, both in terms of the number of companies publishing corporate environmental reports and the quality of those reports. SustainAbility has identified five stages in environmental reporting:

- *Stage 1.* "Green glossies, newsletters, videos. Short statement in annual report."

- *Stage 2.* "One-off environmental report, often linked to first formal policy statement."

- *Stage 3.* "Annual reporting linked to environmental management system, but more text than figures."

- *Stage 4.* "Provision of full TRI-style performance data on annual basis. Input/output data for service companies. Corporate and site reports. Available on diskette or on-line. Environmental report referred to in annual report."

- *Stage 5.* "Sustainable development reporting. Aim: no net loss of carrying capacity. Linking of environmental, economic, and social aspects of corporate performance, supported by indicators of sustainability. Integration of full-cost accounting."[6]

SustainAbility's research indicates that the number of companies producing Stage 4 reports is increasing. However, Stage 5 continues to be largely unexplored territory. In an analysis of 1995 corporate environmental reports published by large publicly-held U.S. companies, Douglas J. Lober, a business professor at Duke University, found that only a few directly addressed the extent to which corporate activities were sustainable.[7] But the leading edge *is* moving forward: British Telecom's environmental report for 1996/97 explored the relationship between telecommunications and sustainability, and also pledged to implement social reporting. The bottom line is that momentum is building but environmental reporting is still in its infancy.

As the cultural winds shift to favor increased dialogue and disclosure, corporate environmental communicators are finding themselves confronting a new and difficult set of challenges. Traditional business interests still must be protected, yet in a manner consistent with the emerging *ethos.* That calls for new thinking — and a delicate sense of balance on the tightrope.

How does an environmentally progressive company respond when eco-considerations directly threaten a core line of business? That is the situation Dow Chemical has found itself in of late, and its response vividly demonstrates the delicate line companies must walk as they strive to balance environmental responsibility against their short-term financial interests.

Dow (yes, the same Dow that brought you napalm and Agent Orange) has earned an excellent environmental reputation in recent years. Until his recent retirement, David Buzzelli, the company's chief environmental officer, served as co-chair of the influential President's Council on Sustainable Development. Also, as noted earlier, Dow is the only major U.S. company with an environmental advisory council of independent environmental experts. It has also been a leader in the area of environmental reporting — in 1991, Dow Europe's annual environmental reports began including emissions on a site-by-site basis for every facility in Europe, establishing a precedent that didn't exactly thrill the rest of the industry.

But chlorine is where the rubber (or maybe dioxin) really meets the road. It is one thing to be an enlightened environmental communicator when it gives you good publicity and perhaps some competitive advantage, and another when it exposes you to the possible destruction of a core business. Dow derives about 40% of its revenue from chlorine-based products: the growing alarm over chlorine directly threatens its existence.

With such a grave danger confronting the company, it would have been easy for Dow to abandon its environmental commitment, throw up the barricades and start denying, stalling, and hiding in the good old-fashioned way. But it hasn't. Instead it created a new position — Director, Chlorine Issues — and started putting its energy into finding a middle ground that protects at least some of its interests.

The company's basic argument is that the broadbased attack on chlorine, which is to say on chlorinated organic compounds generally, is misguided. Joe Stearns, Dow's chlorine issues manager, says, "All our science tells us that it is inaccurate to say that chlorine associated with a molecule leads to health concerns."[8]

Dow's position is that the focus should be on categories of health and environmental problems, rather than on chlorine, chlorine, chlorine. For example, persistent toxics that bioaccumulate should be scrutinized as a class. If some chlorinated compounds happen to get nabbed in the process, well, that's one for the environment: as an environmentally responsible company, Dow won't object. Meanwhile chlorinated compounds generally — and a substantial portion of Dow's business — will be out of the line of fire.

Is this enlightened environmental communications or simply sophisticated obstructionism? Frankly, it can be seen either way. Greenpeace, for one, is persuaded that it is the latter. In a 1996 report, the organization charged Dow with obscuring the sources of dioxin, denying their connection to industrial chlorine chemistry, and working through corporate front groups and political action committees to delay meaningful progress. Greenpeace's position has merit to the extent that it's not just an irrational fringe that is attacking chlorinated organic compounds: many reputable scientists have expressed serious concern.[9] Dow's threshold position — that sound science clearly supports its position — has wobbly moorings. With old-style stonewalling out of fashion, it may be that Dow simply has chosen the best of all possible business responses.

Still, something important has changed. Says David Buzzelli, "We're seeking common ground. Five to ten years ago, these dialogues wouldn't even have taken place."[10] And Buzzelli is right. Although the conflicts haven't gone away, a new and more flexible strategy for dealing with them has emerged.

— ○ —

Dow is not alone in being caught between a traditional interest and an emerging ethic. The entire environmental public relations industry is in the same predicament.

With adversarial positioning *vis-à-vis* a corporation's stakeholders falling out of fashion, much of the "new" environmental public relations is about mediation — spinning communication webs, opening lines of interaction with a company's stakeholders. It is also about working *collectively*, i.e., for the benefit of the environment. The sentiment that "we're all in this together" is often expressed by the current crop of environmental PR executives, and it is meant sincerely.

But it is also true that the basic rationale for public relations — putting clients' companies and products in the best possible light — remains unchanged. That's an *advocacy* role, pure and simple, and advocacy is the same old song public-relations firms have been singing for years.

And so we have a clash of paradigms. On the one hand, there is the emerging model of environmental public relations, in which central roles are played by collaboration and mediation, and the environment is a *de facto* client. On the other, there is the traditional advocacy role, in which environmental public relations executives serve as hired guns to create the best possible public image for their clients.

There are built-in conflicts here; rhetoric aside, the two missions sometimes clash. Coming up with strategies that enable the public relations industry effectively to serve its traditional customers as well as its new one — the environment — is no easy matter.

For A.J. Grant, President of Colorado-based Environmental Communication Associates, much of the problem can be traced to the reputation of the public-relations industry: "In today's world, you can't get away with saying 'environment' and 'PR' in the same breath. Public relations is widely viewed as surface-oriented, as a one-way communication telling the world what you want them to be believe. It's viewed as intrinsically manipulative. 'Environmental PR' is a ship with a giant hole in it."[11]

Grant is calling attention to a real problem — the ineffectiveness of outdated communication strategies in a world of changing values and expectations. Is the solution to do away with public relations? Not according to Grant — instead, you reinvent the genre. What is called for is a new model of public relations. Grant calls it "stakeholder relations," but whatever name you give it, the basic principles are the same: more listening, less spinning; more dialogue, less dictating.

Implicit in this model is the assumption that more than talk happens. In the final analysis, dialogue without action — even sophisticated dialogue featuring empathetic listening and all the rest — is just another type of spin, another way to curry favor without actually doing anything. Grant emphasizes that the dialogue must lead to meaningful changes in corporate behavior, else it is all a sham. Thus, in her role as a public-relations executive, or rather a communications specialist, she also sees herself as an agent for change inside the corporation. "If a company isn't ready to respond proactively in terms of its actual behavior, I won't work with them," she says.[12]

Environmental communication professionals like Grant are trying to steer the industry away from its traditional role as corporate mouthpiece toward a more centrist function featuring increased mediation and facilitation. It's one way to resolve, or begin to resolve, the conflicts that result from having two clients — corporations and the environment — with sometimes antithetical interests, one way to help build a more seamless cultural fabric. Like Dow's response to the chlorine crisis, it's a tightrope act fraught with conflicts and ambiguities. But it's also a logical direction for an industry that is groping for a new identity as the dominant paradigm moves away from posturing and toward more substantive communication.

Into the Fourth Era

*In every age of well-marked transition there is the pattern
of habitual dumb practice and emotion which is passing,
and there is oncoming a new complex of habit.*
— Alfred North Whitehead

To DATE, IN OUR SUMMARY of third-era corporate environmentalism, we have seen that while the business community has made considerable progress in addressing environmental issues, it is animated by a vision that remains altogether too narrow and inturned. For the most part, companies have focused on improving their internal environmental performance. That is both understandable and appropriate: environmentalism begins at home. However, even if corporations around the world were to vastly improve their environmental performance, that would hardly make a dent in the global *problématique*, whose dimensions burst the boundaries of what local, technical, linear fixes can ever hope to accomplish. More — much more — is required. And so we come to the matter of a guiding vision, and a crucial set of questions. In what ways must the dominant vision be amended? How can corporations target sustainable development in its fullness rather than in a watered-down version? What are or will be the characteristics of fourth-era corporate environmentalism?

The following set of four interrelated principles represents a first step toward answering these questions. I am not suggesting that the implementation of these principles alone will be enough to bring about the transition into sustainable development — still more improvements and more eras will surely be required — but they do represent a natural progression (and in some respects a quantum leap) beyond current practices.

Principle #1: *Toward zero waste.* The more we keep fouling our air and water, the less able they are to sustain life in a maximally diverse and vital form — and it is our industrial processes and products that are doing most of the fouling. For this reason, the pursuit of sustainability calls for a radical transformation of how corporations manage their metabolic inputs and outputs. We need dramatic reductions in emissions, not just incremental ones. In the final analysis, the challenge boils down to this: rather than settle for *reducing* waste, companies need to come as close as possible to *eliminating it completely*. This reality calls for wholesale changes at both the individual corporate and broader industrial levels. This is not all that is required — companies need to address sustainability challenges that exist outside their doors as well — but, as a core strategy, the aggressive pursuit of resource productivity is essential.

Principle #2: *Whole-system thinking.* How are dramatic changes like the transition to a close to zero-waste industrial economy to be achieved? Surely not via linear strategies that work within the basic *status quo*. A broader approach, one that allows strategists to re-conceptualize their industrial processes *ab novo*, is required. This *design* approach, which is "higher-level" in the sense that it affords greater freedom of action, is intrinsically radical: unlike more constrained engineering strategies, it looks to "reinvent" rather than to "fix" or "improve."

When we start addressing problems at the level of the entire system rather than at the level of the individual parts of the system, a very interesting fact emerges: the relationship between cause and effect stops being linear. No longer does A cause B which causes C and so on, down the line. Things are no longer that simple: A may still cause B which causes C, but we also find that C has an effect on A, which affects what happens to B, which alters the impact on C, and so on. We find ourselves, in other words, operating in complex systems of negative and positive feedback loops. At the system level, the design process becomes very holistic. This approach isn't superior for New Age reasons of moral or mystical superiority, but because of the very down-to-earth fact that optimal design requires us to account from the beginning for feedback loops — and to do that, we must understand how the system works as a single integrated unit.

It is only at the holistic system level that the challenge of sustainable development can effectively be addressed. Why? Because the global *problématique* is itself the quintessential system problem, one in which a set of once-appropriate, now-outdated constructs keep reinforcing each other in a web of mutually reinforcing, socially and environmentally destructive feedback loops.

There is nothing wrong with linear thinking — it is good, and necessary, and has its place — but we can no more rely on linear problem-solving to address the challenge of sustainable development than we can expect a child to lift a 300-pound weight. "Is it progress if a cannibal uses a knife and a fork?" the writer Stanislaus Lec once mused. The formulation is harsh to the point of unfairness — eco-efficiency and the other advances brought about by linear thinking have been much, much more than trivial — but the basic point holds. Bigger, more creative, higher-level thinking — *systems-level thinking* — is required.

Principle #3: *Look outward.* Corporations need to attack unsustainability externally as well as internally. To date, they have focused largely on cleaning their own houses. Which makes sense, and is perfectly understandable. But the world's house also needs cleaning, and business, as the sector with the most resources, absolutely must chip in and help. To adopt the world's problems as their own — that is one of the great leaps forward of fourth-era corporate environmentalism.

Companies can do this in three basic ways. The first is *technology transfer* — providing smaller companies and developing countries with the equipment and expertise that will help them address their environmental problems. The second is *industrial ecology*. This approach takes a systems approach to eco-efficiency and applies it to multiple corporations working in concert, such that one company's wastes become another's raw materials. The best-known example of industrial ecology comes from Kalundborg, Sweden, where a group of local companies — a refinery, a power plant, a pharmaceutical company, and a fish farm, among others — found that they could reduce costs and increase efficiency by using each other's waste as resource inputs.

The third external strategy calls for corporations to actively seek to exploit the opportunities created by the need for sustainable development. Instead of being viewed as "too big to handle" or "somebody else's problem," sustainable development is re-conceptualized as a *business opportunity*. This was the thrust of an award-winning *Harvard Business Review* article by Stuart Hart, in which he summarizes the situation as follows:

> It is easy to state the case in the negative: faced with impoverished customers, degraded environments, failing political systems, and unraveling societies, it will be increasingly difficult for corporations to do business. But the positive case is even more powerful. The more we learn about the challenges of sustainability, the clearer it is that we are poised at the threshold of a historic moment in which many of the world's industries may be transformed.

To date, the business logic for greening up has been largely operational or technical: bottom-up pollution-prevention programs have saved companies billions of dollars. However, few executives realize that environmental opportunities might actually become a major source of revenue growth. Greening has been framed in terms of risk reduction, reengineering, or cost cutting. Rarely is greening linked to strategy or technology development, and as a result, most companies fail to recognize opportunities of potentially staggering proportions.[1]

Principle #4: *Remember sustainable development!* As we saw in Chapter 3, corporations for perfectly understandable reasons have been overly focused on environmental issues. Corporate strategists need to expand their field of vision from "the environment" to "sustainable development." And not just to its objective, technical aspects, but to its subjective, social aspects as well.

— ○ —

Are these guiding principles mere ephemera — dreams of a brighter tomorrow that may never come to pass? Not necessarily. To some degree, all are already being implemented — some more, some less.

Zero Waste. Major corporations that have committed to reaching zero emissions include Du Pont in the U.S. and EBARA, Chichibu Onoda Cement and Ogihara in Japan, where the Environment Agency concluded in a white paper sanctioned by the powerful Ministry of Trade and Industry (MITI) that zero emissions was an appropriate standard for industry.

Internationally, the concept has gotten a significant boost from the Zero Emissions Research Initiative (ZERI), an initiative launched in 1995 by eco-entrepreneur Gunter Pauli under the umbrella of the Tokyo-based United Nations University. ZERI has set out to prove that zero-waste industrial ecology — the clustering of businesses so that one company's waste becomes another company's input, resulting in the 100% capture and reuse of resources — is scientifically and commercially feasible. The organization has cast its net wide: early programs include a research initiative on materials separation technologies, the development of a zero waste curriculum, and pilot projects to recover brewery waste. In Ann Arbor, Michigan, for instance, the Ann Arbor Brewing Company and an adjacent restaurant have developed plans in conjunction with ZERI to deploy a wide range of "loop-closing" and waste-elimination strategies, including using solid wastes to cultivate mushrooms for sale in the restaurant and using wastewater from the restaurant in the brewery.[2]

Systems Thinking. Many companies have incorporated whole-system thinking into the product-design process in the form of "design for environment," or DFE. This strategy, which is discussed at greater length in Chapter 8, seeks to minimize environmental impacts by taking into consideration all aspects of the product life-cycle, up to and including product takeback, during the up-front design process. A complex and fascinating area, DFE leads to lines of inquiry such as: In what ways can the product be designed so that (immaterial) information replaces (physical) material? And (especially important in an environment where manufacturing is often a collective effort involving multiple suppliers) how can we ensure that our manufacturing partners will cooperate wholeheartedly to help us meet our environmental goals? DFE has been respectfully received throughout industry, but it has enjoyed a particularly warm reception from electronics companies, whose accelerated product-development cycle — 18 months — makes them particularly receptive to aggressive design-level interventions.

Looking Outward (Technology Transfer). Transnational companies have had a visible commitment to technology transfer for some time. Until recently, the mission of the Industry Cooperative for Ozone Layer Protection (ICOLP, since renamed the International Cooperative for Environmental Leadership) was to promote and coordinate the worldwide exchange of non-proprietary information on alternative technologies, processes, and substances for CFCs and other ozone-depleting substances. ICOLP produced technical manuals capturing the best available information on alternatives to ozone-depleting substances and provided technology assistance in the form of workshops, primarily in developing countries. It also created *OzoNet*™, which is housed with the United Nations Environment Programme and lists alternatives to and technical research on ozone-depleting substances. The World Business Council on Sustainable Development has also been actively involved in technology transfer.

Looking Outward (Industrial Ecology). In June 1993, President Clinton created the President's Council on Sustainable Development (PCSD), a group of prominent industrialists, environmentalists, government executives, and activists, and charged it with creating a consensus document on sustainable development. The final report, published in 1996, came out strongly in favor of the so-called "eco-industrial park," which it defined as

... an environmentally efficient version of industrial parks. They follow a systems design in which one facility's waste becomes another facility's feedstock, and they ensure that raw materials are recycled or disposed of efficiently and safely.[3]

In addition to this explicit endorsement of inter-corporate collaboration in the form of industrial ecology, the PCSD supported demonstrations relating to industrial ecology and eco-industrial parks in Baltimore, Maryland; Port of Cape Charles, Virginia; Chattanooga, Tennessee; and Brownsville, Texas.

Clustering green companies at a single location without seeking to link their outputs and inputs is a relatively straightforward operation. However, as soon as one adds the industrial-ecology waste-exchange vision to the mix, implementation becomes much more difficult. Not only is a delicate technical balance required, but participating companies lose a measure of their operating freedom. If Company B depends on Company A's wastes and A goes under, B's future is jeopardized too.

Given these challenges, the likeliest implementers of industrial-ecology style eco-industrial parks may not be private developers or public economic-development institutions, but thriving businesses with land to spare and a commitment to reduced or zero waste. And indeed, some forward-thinking companies are beginning to tiptoe in this direction. At Pewaukee, Wisconsin-based Quad Graphics, a $1 billion printing company, environmental manager John Imes has pitched an eco-industrial park to top management. He has proposed siting one of the company's printing plants next to a zero-effluent paper mill, feedstock for which would come from Quad's corporate waste and what Imes calls the "urban forest." Power would come from a cogenerating facility, and waste heat could be used for a fish farm and greenhouse.

Stonyfield Farms, a Londonderry, New Hampshire-based yogurt manufacturer, has similar plans. It is working with the town to develop a 95-acre (39 hectare) site adjacent to its main factory and hopes at some point to attract a cluster of eco-compatible enterprises to it.

Regardless of whether eco-industrial parks aim to eliminate waste or have a less ambitious orientation, they are indicative of the growing interest on the part of business executives and other members of the sustainable-business community in having companies "look outward" and work for sustainable development within a system larger than that of the single corporation or the broader corporation/supplier enterprise.

Looking Outward (Sustainable Development as a Strategic Opportunity). In 1995, Monsanto Company unleashed a strategic initiative that represented a quantum advance beyond standard third-era corporate environmentalism. Rather than focus solely on eco-efficiency, the company announced that it would pursue broad new lines of business based on their ability to address the global *problématique*. One can't accuse Monsanto of thinking small: areas under investigation include water resources and world hunger.

Actually, Monsanto is doing little more than following a time-honored company tradition. In the early part of this century, the company's founder, John Queeny, bet that automobiles would be important in the future and invested in rubber chemical companies. He was right. In the 1930s the new CEO, the founder's son, saw a newfangled washing machine that agitated clothes, and wagered that phosphates, which lower the bubble rate, would be in high demand. He was right. Now the company is banking on sustainability solutions as a key to future growth. In a 1997 speech, Kate Fish, a sustainability specialist and the company's director of public policy, put the company's strategy this way:

> We are betting that as global pressures continue to build, the market will increasingly "select" products and services that are dramatically more efficient, provide much more value with much less throughput, and, in the future, have a net restorative impact at all levels — social, ecological, and economic.[4]

This isn't emotionalism at work; it isn't even "ethicalism," particularly. Monsanto's strategic gambit is best viewed as sound, sensible, creative, long-term business planning.

Monsanto's initiative is not without controversy, largely because biotechnology is at the heart of the company's vision. For Monsanto, biotech is not only consistent with sustainable development: it is perhaps the only way to boost agricultural productivity while dramatically reducing material throughput. "I would like to replace the stuff of pesticides with the information of biotechnology," Monsanto CEO Robert Shapiro told *Tomorrow* magazine in a 1997 interview. "When we put a gene, which is essentially coded information, into cotton and reduce insecticide use by 30 percent, that's a major step towards sustainability."[5] Opponents of biotech, however, view Monsanto's sustainability initiative as misguided if not hypocritical.

Another example of a strategic commitment to sustainability — and one that dates back decades — comes from Aracruz Cellulose, a $2 billion Brazilian producer of eucalyptus pulp. Starting in the late 1960s, Aracruz Cellulose took advantage of a tax incentive to acquire and reforest badly degraded land. By the early 1990s, the company had planted 320,000 acres (130,000 hectares) with managed eucalyptus, while restoring an additional 170,000-plus acres (70,000-plus hectares) as conservation land, thereby providing a direct environmental benefit. The company also directly addressed local social issues by annually distributing millions of seedlings to farmers, thereby reducing their need to harvest wood from local forests, and by investing heavily in the creation of schools, housing, hospitals, and a training center for employees. In fact, reports Stuart Hart, "[u]ntil recently, Aracruz spent more on its social investments than it did on wages [about $1.20 for every $1 in wages]."[6] As a result, "[t]he standard of living has improved dramatically, as has productivity. The company no longer needs to invest so heavily in social infrastructure."[7]

The Aracruz Cellulose example provides a compelling reminder of the extent to which corporations are positioned to fill the governance gap created by the public sector's increasing inability to meet people's survival and security needs. Some business executives may view that as an onerous responsibility; others as simply irrelevant. But for Aracruz Cellulose it has been an effective business strategy.

Another company that has made a similar adjustment, although much more visibly in the U.S., is Nike, whose community support programs in America's inner cities have given the company a sort of *de facto in loco parentis* status. Now, a sustainability strategy this most surely isn't. Still, it *is* a form of social engagement, and an effective one at that: it is in large part because of the company's community involvement that many young people proudly sport the company's ubiquitous "swoosh" emblem. (In fact, as companies increasingly move to fill the "governance gap," it may make sense to start thinking in terms of corporate "flags" instead of "logos," and of "brand patriotism" instead of "brand loyalty." In effect, it's Nike's flag and not its logo that inner-city kids are wearing on their chests.)[8]

Remembering Sustainable Development. The emergence of sustainable development as a business strategy is one of several indications that companies are beginning to bring sustainability (as distinguished from eco-efficiency) into their sights. As an environmental-business journalist who is constantly interviewing corporate environmental executives, I have found more and more executives and committees cropping up with some variation of "sustainable" in their title. And on a more formal note, as of several years ago the consultancy Roy F. Weston had identified some 43 companies, including major transnationals like Mitsubishi, Honeywell, Ford, General Motors, and Procter & Gamble, that had publicly embraced sustainable development, as distinguished from environmental protection. Whether these companies have meaningfully expanded their activities along with their terminology is, of course, another question, but the mere fact that sustainability now falls within their field of vision points to the eventual (if not necessarily immediate) incorporation of a broad range of sustainability issues into their planning.

Noranda Inc., a $13 billion company with operations in three sectors — mining and metals, forest products, and oil and gas — is one of several companies that is developing a set of corporate sustainability principles. A corporate document developed by an internal task force calls for the company to implement "practices and policies which allow us to meet the current and future needs of our customers, suppliers, shareholders, employees, the communities in which we operate, and the public, while simultaneously contributing to the well-being of the environment, economy and" — here's where it gets interesting — *"society"* [italics added]. It enumerates six specific sustainable development principles, among which are commitments to "foster constructive dialogue with interested parties in the conduct of our activities" and to "ensure that our activities are sensitive to *cultural considerations* [italics added], employee and public health, and the needs of future generations."[9]

With these principles, Noranda has acknowledged that sustainable development requires companies to address issues of equity as well as the environment. And that is by no means the only company to be moving in this direction. As discussed in Chapter 5, although it is still a relative rarity, more and more companies are discussing sustainable development in their annual environmental reports. For example, in NatWest's 1995 environmental report, CEO Derek Wanless declared, "[W]e are convinced that the [triangular values] of society, economy, and the environment are the determinants of the future and we will continue to take account of that fact in the way we run our businesses."[10]

Meanwhile that *rara avis* of corporate reports, the social audit — reports which assess corporate performance with regard to non-technical, social issues — is also getting more respect from mainstream companies. Not that they're exactly queuing up to publish them: still, they're not being dismissed quite as offhandedly as in the past. And as noted in the previous chapter, the occasional company — telecommunications giant British Telecom, for instance — has gone so far as to announce its commitment to stage a social audit.

Frank Frantisak, Noranda's chief environmental officer, sums up the emerging view when he says: "There's a growing understanding that eco-efficiency is a transitional strategy. We need to be focusing on sustainable development."[11]

— ○ —

And not just on the technical dimension of sustainable development, but also on its "depth dimension." Recall from Chapter 1 that sustainable development has a subjective as well as an objective aspect, and that both dimensions need to be honored. But in what ways? The philosopher and psychologist Ken Wilber points us in the right direction by observing that the subjective dimension has two aspects: one social (or collective), and the other individual (or personal). You might call the two dimensions "we" and "I", or alternatively "community" and "soul".

The business community has made inroads on both these fronts. Let's begin with the social (or "community") dimension. We have already seen that the chemical industry's Community Action Panels (CAPs) represent a step, albeit a modest one, into the social domain. It has been said that there are two consultative models: the "royal" and the "democratic." Under the "royal" model, input is solicited, but mostly as a courtesy — final decision-making power is retained. Under the "democratic" model, input is solicited and the decision-making is collaborative as well. The CAPs follow the royal model. Which is better than no consultation at all, but more watered-down than it might be.

An example of *democratic* consultation comes from Weyerhaeuser, the forest products company. The company regularly conducts "watershed analyses," comprehensive studies that examine the cumulative effects of lumber harvesting, road construction, and other forest activities on water quality, fish habitat, and public works. In its early-1990s analysis of the Tolt watershed in Washington State, the company worked with representatives of the Tulalip Tribes, the Seattle Water Department, the Washington Environmental Council, and the state departments of Natural Resources, Ecology, Wildlife and Fisheries to develop a collectively acceptable forest-management strategy. The final outcome was widely reported as having thrilled no one and being acceptable to all —

a strong sign that the negotiation was successful. Weyerhaeuser wound up setting aside two to three times more forest area as free from logging than it had planned but had the comfort of knowing it wouldn't have to fight a running battle against community resistance. The *Seattle Times* quoted Dave Somers, a fisheries biologist with the Tulalip Tribes, as saying, "I'm pretty pleased with the outcome and the working relationships we had with Weyerhaeuser. The protections we got for fish are quite a bit better than we had in the past."[12] The democratic-consultation model has been followed in some 30 analyses since the groundbreaking (and fish-saving) Tolt watershed initiative. When a company actually shares decision-making power with the local community, as Weyerhaeuser has done here, that represents a significant change in standard corporate operating procedures.

The entire socially responsible business movement, which was discussed in Chapter 3, is predicated on a commitment to the twin interior values of social engagement and personal development. Ben & Jerry's mission statement speaks to the need to initiate "innovative ways to improve the quality of life of a broad community: local, national, and international." Other socially responsible companies accord what by mainstream standards would be an inordinate amount of resources to the inner growth of individual employees. Rhino Foods, a specialty dessert manufacturer based in Burlington, Vermont, has "wants coordinators" who counsel employees on how best to meet their life goals. Levi Strauss & Co. has a 145-page binder, *Individual Readiness for a Changing Environment*, that offers a wealth of self-assessment and self-improvement resources, including a section called "Knowing Myself" that lets people measure their personal values, interests, attitudes, and values.

There's more. Consider, for instance, organizational learning, the management philosophy that has made major inroads into the mainstream corporate community. Organizational learning has five core disciplines, four of which address subjective "I" and "we" issues: 1) *building shared vision* (combination I/we: the "shared" is we, the "vision" I); 2) *team learning* (we); 3) *refining mental models* (I — mental models, our structures for understanding the world, are personal and subjective); and 4) *personal mastery*, which Peter Senge, the MIT professor and consultant with whom organizational learning is most often associated, defines as "approaching one's life as a creative work, living life from a creative as opposed to a reactive viewpoint" (emphatically an I).[13]

Another blossoming business movement can be called, generically, "soul in business." More and more companies — and mainstream ones at that — have decided it is in their interest to help their employees find meaning in their professional and personal lives. In a 1995 article entitled "Companies Hit the Road Less Traveled," *Business Week* magazine described the following scene:

> It's Spiritual Unfoldment time at the World Bank. Every Wednesday at 1 p.m., a group of bank employees sits in a semicircle in a conference room at the Washington-based agency and connects. Today, it's standing-room only. There's no stereotyping this crowd of about 60, which includes senior managers and young assistants. Group founder Richard Barrett, an engineer at the bank, leads the meeting, which begins with a moment of silence. Today's topic: "Ten Strategies for Attaining Soul Consciousness." After an hour of talk about such things as realigning soul and ego, even staffers who arrived looking wilted leave smiling.[14]

The World Bank is not alone. In a move to make hidebound materialists wince, major transnationals like Boeing, AT&T, and Dana Corp. have brought in poet David Whyte to speak to their employees about, um, soul. Reading his and others' poems, Whyte invites his audiences to discover a deeper, richer sense of themselves and to bring their whole selves to the job, i.e., to exercise organizational learning's "personal mastery." Whyte's book, *The Heart Aroused: Poetry and the Preservation of Soul in Corporate America*, has made the business best-seller charts.

More of this sort of thing is to be expected as baby-boomers steeped in counter-culture values graduate to positions of leadership. "Get used to it," warned *Business Week*. "Spirituality is creeping into the office."[15]

— O —

Over the past two decades, the corporate view of its responsibilities *vis-à-vis* the environment and sustainable development has matured steadily, graduating from barebones regulatory compliance (first era) to increased disclosure (second era) to "beyond compliance" (third era). Although the adoption of third-era strategies and values remains far from universal, much of the groundwork for the fourth era of corporate environmentalism has been laid.

But it is one thing to lay the foundation and another to build the building. There is no guarantee that the fourth-era strategies currently taking root here and there on the corporate landscape will blossom into a dominant *modus operandi*. Whether that happens will depend in large part on the outcome of a clash between two imperatives — the traditional corporate perception of self-interest, and our actual ecological circumstances.

It is a commonplace of environmental-science courses that human beings currently consume roughly 40% of the planet's net primary production (NPP), defined as the sum of all photosynthetic production minus the energy required to maintain and support the plants that are doing the "manufacturing." If estimates that the world population will double by the middle of the next century are on target, and if consumption habits do not decline, then our consumption will rise to a manifestly unsustainable 80% of the planet's NPP. Numbers like that suggest that we are hurtling toward chaos and collapse. Clearly we need to reduce consumption (and population growth too) quickly and substantially. But that runs squarely counter to corporations' perceived interest, which is premised on a very simple formula: More Consumption — More Revenue — More Profits.

Is it reasonable to expect corporations to torpedo their most fundamental value? Unlikely as it may seem, the answer just may be — yes. In the past few years, a new term has entered the sustainable-business lexicon: "sustainable production and consumption." Essentially, it calls for business to work both sides of the fence, reducing material inputs while simultaneously working to help reduce consumption. In a sense, the evolution is similar in structure to the one that moves companies from pollution prevention (end-of-pipe outputs) to eco-efficiency (front-of-pipe inputs); here, the horizon has expanded from "sell side" (production) to "buy side" (consumption). The emergence of sustainable consumption as a topic at business/sustainability conferences is not yet a cause for wild celebration — it's only talk at this point — but the fact that the subject is on the table at all is noteworthy. Dialogue creates familiarity, a comfort level, and with a comfort level comes, eventually, maybe, the willingness to change.

The corporate community is participating actively in the debate. The World Business Council for Sustainable Development has declared that "[s]ustainable production practices need to be matched by changes in the consumption and usage patterns of millions of individuals and businesses" and has issued a call for companies to "provide consumers with the clear, accurate and reliable information they need to make sound purchasing decisions" — a nice sentiment, but one that falls notably short of straightforwardly asking consumers to buy less stuff.[16]

Dow Europe has engaged the issue much more radically, helping to fund a provocative 1995 work by the U.K.-based consultancy

SustainAbility that projected — and applauded — drastically reduced consumption in the years ahead.

In the introduction to the report, Claude Fussler, at the time Dow Europe's vice president for environment, health, and safety, tried to explain why his company had chosen to "conjure the spirits of frugality and the devils of production restraints":

> The fact is, it takes 15 to 25 years to conceive a radically new solution and develop into a mature commercial success. Our market and product development teams must be aware of the fundamental forces at play. These forces will bring revolutionary changes in the way we will manage our material flows and create value over the next decades.[17]

— ◯ —

In the final analysis, the challenge is educational — a matter of changing what organizational learning specialists would call corporate executives' "mental model" about the gravity of the threat. Although talk about sustainable development can sometimes seem abstract and abstruse, the reality is anything but. There is an environmental imperative, and it is headed in our direction. If we do not voluntarily and promptly change our ways, it will do our changing for us.

Unfortunately, many executives — including many dedicated and sincere third-era corporate environmentalists — are so distracted by the present that they cannot see the juggernaut that is building up a head of steam just beyond their field of vision. Dow Europe's Fussler represents a more farsighted breed of executive. He understands the importance of looking into the future. And he understands another fact as well: that when the handwriting is on the wall, successful companies don't look the other way — they read it.

PART 3

THE CHALLENGE OF CHANGE

Progress is not an illusion, it does happen,
but it is slow and invariably disappointing.
— George Orwell

Mixed Messages

The human face is really like one of those Oriental gods:
a whole group of faces juxtaposed on different planes;
it is impossible to see them all simultaneously.
— Marcel Proust

IN THE 1951 FILM CLASSIC *RASHOMON*, a merchant and his wife are attacked by a bandit. The merchant is killed and the woman is raped. The movie retells the story four times, through the eyes of the three protagonists and a woodcutter who witnessed the event, and each time a sharply different story emerges. Director Akira Kurosawa seems to be saying that all we have is our perceptions, that there is no single, objective reality. Certainly the Rashomon principle holds true in the world of sustainable business. Companies aren't "good" or "bad" so much as complex, multi-faceted entities — much like humans, actually — whose "true identity," such as it is, is in the eyes of the beholder.

Consider, for instance, Asea Brown Boveri (ABB) which, with annual orders in excess of $35 billion, is one of the world's largest engineering and energy technology businesses. The company has been called "one of the founding fathers of corporate environmentalism," and with good reason.[1] Former CEO Percy Barnevik was an early and ardent supporter of the World Business Council on Sustainable Development. Billionaire Stephan Schmidheiny, author of *Changing Course* and (with Federico J.L. Zorraquin) the subsequent *Financing Change*, sits on ABB's Board of Directors and is one of the company's leading stockholders. ABB was one of the first companies to publish a freestanding environmental report and continues to position itself as a strong advocate of sustainable development. In a 1994 document, the company asserted: "ABB is committed to sustainable development. Protection of the environment is among our top corporate priorities. We address environmental issues

97

in all our operations and public policy."[2]

For many members of the sustainability community, however, one word puts the lie to ABB's environmental commitment — Bakun, a giant Malaysian hydro-electric venture intended to transport power from the Eastern Malaysian state of Sarawak across the South China Sea to Peninsula Malaysia via an 800 mile-long (1,300 km) 500 kilowatt cable.[3] The list of question marks about the project runs almost as long as the cable. Start with the fact that Malaysia doesn't even need the additional capacity. In 1995, the country generated an energy surplus of almost 64%, and by the time Bakun comes on line — slated for around 2003 — renewable energy alternatives such as solar are expected to be cost-competitive with conventional energy sources. Not only that, but the projected increase in capacity discourages energy-efficiency and demand-side management initiatives, locking Malaysian officials into precisely the "consume-more" mentality that contributes so heavily to our current crisis of unsustainability. When Ani Arope, the outgoing chairman of the Malaysian power authority, publicly complained about excess power supplies following a 1996 blackout, he was publicly rebuked by Prime Minister Mohammed Mahathir: "When you have a product, you have to go out and sell. If you sit down and say you have too much, you won't be able to."[4] So much for energy conservation...

Credible experts have attacked the economic and financial assumptions underlying Bakun as far too optimistic. According to Mark Mansley, author of *Bakun: High Dam — High Risk?* and a specialist in Asian energy issues with the firm Delphi International, "there's a huge amount of capital going into a project which is economically dubious and where the financial returns are at best uncertain."[5] The project has also been criticized as being environmentally destructive — over 400 square miles (1,000 sq. km) of rainforest will be flooded, and there is also the possibility of increased greenhouse gas emissions from rotting vegetation in the reservoir — and socially insensitive too: around 10,000 people, many of them indigenous tribespeople, will be forcibly relocated. Small wonder, then, that Gabungan, a 40-member coalition of Malaysian NGOs, has condemned Bakun as "socially destructive, environmentally disastrous, and economically misconceived," or that the project has been targeted by virtually every major transnational campaign group, including Friends of the Earth, Greenpeace, and the World Wide Fund for Nature.[6]

What does all this have to do with ABB? Simply this: until it was abruptly and unexpectedly relieved of its assignment by the Malaysian authorities — for reasons reportedly having nothing to do with the environment — the Swiss-Swedish conglomerate was to have been the leading outside contractor on the project, responsible for overall project management and the supply of electrical equipment. Bakun had been expected to contribute about $3 billion to ABB's coffers.

How did the company's intended participation in this dubious project square with its commitment, as stated in its formal environmental policy, to "involve itself in international activities devoted to solving global environmental problems and promoting sustainable development" and to "play its part in the transfer of environmentally sound technologies and methods to developing countries"? And how did its commitment to "foster openness and dialogue with employees and the public on environmental matters" square with the forcible relocation of 10,000 Malaysians?

The answers to those questions depends on who you ask. ABB's president and CEO Göran Lindahl has argued that his company has no duty to second-guess a decision made by the sovereign state of Malaysia:

> I put a clear borderline between what is the responsibility of the Sarawak and Malaysian authorities, and what is ABB's responsibility. Malaysia is like a sovereign state: we can't go in there like a colonial power, and try to take over. I must emphasize this point: it's the Malaysian government which has taken the decision to build the dam. Our job is to carry out the project.[7]

Critics of ABB dismiss this as the corporate equivalent of the infamous World War II "I was only obeying orders" defense, and argue that for projects like Bakun, which so directly and powerfully affect the global *problématique*, this argument no longer (so to speak) holds water. Tom Gladwin, director of the Global Environment Program at New York University's Stern School of Business, bluntly calls arguments like Lindahl's "… just a convenient smoke screen. Multinational corporations like ABB are among the most powerful institutions on the planet, and up to their eyeballs in the political and legal affairs of sovereign states when it suits their corporate interest."[8]

Lindahl has also argued that, given that the Bakun dam will in fact be built, it's best to have an environmentally sensitive company as project manager. ABB had intended to require all suppliers to get ISO 14001 certification, for instance — a not insignificant commitment. But even if you buy into Lindahl's arguments, there's no getting around the fact that ABB's willing — no, eager — participation in Bakun at a minimum raises questions about the depth of its commitment to sustainable development.

So will the "real" ABB please stand up? That's easier said than done. Environmentalist sorts who like to keep things simple dismiss the pro-sustainability behavior of companies like ABB as so much greenwashing, but that's a bit disingenuous. Corporate identity is more aptly viewed as one of those figure-ground images that allow a person to see one of two images — a vase, say, or a crone — but never both simultaneously. Only in ABB's case, the two images are a white hat and a black one.

The company is not at all atypical in this regard. The Roman god Janus had two faces, each looking in an opposite direction. So do most corporations.

General Motors, the world's largest industrial corporation, provides another example of how this is so. In 1994, the company became the third Fortune 500 company (and first Fortune 500 manufacturing company) to endorse the CERES Principles, a step that earned the company much favorable press coverage, and with good reason. For the company to sign a set of environmental principles that had been formulated by environmentalists and that required it to commit to regular, extensive public disclosure represented a courageous break from corporate business-as-usual.

Ask GM spokespeople, and the company's commitment to the CERES Principles is one more star in what has long been an illustrious environmental firmament. "GM has had a strong environmental program since the early 1970s," declares Dennis Minano, the company's senior environmental officer.[9] Glossy promotional materials sing the same song.

And indeed there is much that is positive in GM's environmental track record. TRI emissions have been reduced by over 40% since 1988. Packing used by suppliers to ship materials for GM cars and trucks has been reduced by over 500%, and nearly 60% of all packing waste is now recycled. Statistics like these, plus its commitment to driving eco-efficiency down the supplier chain, led to the company's receiving *Business Ethics* magazine's 1996 Award for Environmental Excellence.

GM has also been a leader in electric vehicle research and development. *Popular Mechanics* magazine called its Impact "the first real-world, practical electric-powered passenger car for the 21st Century."[10] *Popular Science* also heaped encomiums on it, calling it the "world's best electric car."[11] GM was also the first U.S. auto manufacturer to acknowledge the need to address global climate change.

But there is another side to the story. Even while the company was forging ahead with Impact R&D, it was working overtime to quash electric vehicle incentives in the northeast U.S.. A 1992 report by the New York City-based Council on Economic Priorities painted an unflattering portrait of GM. While acknowledging that the company was "in some ways an innovator," the study noted that "in other respects, GM's environmental policy is a troubling one." Among the problems identified: extensive criticism for making exaggerated claims about its environmental record, potential involvement at upwards of 200 Superfund toxic waste disposal sites, and extensive Political Action Committee (PAC) contributions to members of Congress with below-average environmental voting records.

For Paul Billings, Director of State/Government Relations at the American Lung Association, the environment has no bigger enemy than GM: "For years, the company has led the industry's opposition to good environmental controls in automobiles. They've been quick to take credit for every compromise they've been dragged into, but they've fought us kicking and screaming every step of the way. When you consider them environmentally, you have to take into account their products on the road and their campaigns in the public-policy arena against environmental improvements."[12]

With the rest of the auto industry, General Motors has announced its support for a higher gasoline tax as an alternative to higher fuel economy standards. According to Chris Calwell, a consultant to the Natural Resources Defense Council, there are two schools of thought on the reasons for the auto industry's stance — because they genuinely believe it would be better for the environment and business, or because they know it will never happen. Either way, he goes on to note, "Talk is cheap, and the industry has yet to back up its talk with any real action — no lobbying, no money spent to get a gas tax passed."[13]

GM has good reason to be ambivalent. By more actively supporting higher gasoline taxes, the company risks breaching its fiduciary duty to shareholders — basic economics tells us that if it costs more to drive, people will drive less, and less driving means fewer sales of GM cars and trucks. In addition, the company's customers don't want higher fuel economy standards, and if GM has taken anything to heart in recent years, it's the TQM maxim about listening to your customers. For years the company didn't do that, a non-starter of a strategy that brought it perilously close to bankruptcy in 1992.

The running battle over fuel efficiency incentives has been waged primarily in California. In 1991, the legislature passed a bill that would fund rebates on fuel-efficient cars with fees on inefficient ones. It was designed to solve the exact problem the industry complains about — the lack of economic incentives for people to buy more fuel-efficient cars. Nevertheless, Governor Wilson refused to sign the bill, and since then auto industry lobbying has kept it from clearing the legislature.

Again, the industry position is that regulators have no business getting between them and their customers. In addition, they argue that by giving energy efficiency such a high profile, the government is actually helping Japanese auto manufacturers, who have a better reputation in this area.

Another black mark against GM came to light in late 1995, when the EPA and the Department of Justice announced that the company would spend approximately $45 million to settle charges that it had illegally defeated pollution control devices inside nearly 500,000 Cadillacs since 1991, resulting in carbon monoxide emissions of up to three times the legal limit. That's hardly the behavior one would associate with an endorser of the CERES Principles.

Another sensitive issue revolves around so-called "light trucks" — sport utility vehicles, vans, minivans, and pick-up trucks. These vehicles are much less fuel-efficient than passenger cars, but that hasn't kept General Motors and other auto manufacturers from marketing them with such gusto that in November 1997 their light truck sales exceeded those of cars for the first time.[14] This shift in momentum has been fueled by the booming demand for sports utility vehicles: in the decade from 1986-1996, U.S. retail sales of those yuppie paeans to rugged individualism climbed from 5.0% to 13.8% of all U.S. sales.[15] On an annual basis, light trucks now account for over 40% of new-vehicle sales.[16]

This trend is a gross negative for the environment. Light trucks mean significantly lower fuel-efficiency, and that much more carbon spewing skyward. "The biggest single step we can take against global warming," says Dan Becker, director of the Sierra Club's energy and global warming program, "is to make more fuel-efficient vehicles."[17] Whereas the federal corporate average fuel economy (CAFE) standard for cars is 27.5 miles per gallon, for light trucks it is a much more paltry 20.7 mpg — and sports utility vehicles as a rule are much less fuel-efficient than that. The differential was created to give a break to workhorse trucks, but it also offered the industry a loophole, which it was quick to spot and exploit. And so, enter the sports utility vehicle, that playtoy for people with money to burn and an oxymoronic fantasy about getting back to nature in their automobile. "The industry exploited the law," says Becker. "The development of the light truck was a way to escape CAFE."[18]

Thus a core — and hugely successful — marketing strategy by General Motors and other auto manufacturers has directly and substantially increased greenhouse gas emissions.[19] Nor is this the only way in which company policies have been counter-productive. In 1997, the chief executives of General Motors, Ford, and Chrysler met with President Clinton, where they delivered, according to the *New York Times*, "an earful of complaints about the administration's interest in limited emissions of greenhouse gases that may contribute to global warming" — not a stance consistent with a commitment to environmental protection.[20]

Monsanto provides yet another example of the Janus face of business. The company has two spectacular sustainability feathers in its cap, having been not only the first U.S. company to formally commit to going "beyond compliance," but also the first one to formally commit to sustainable development as a core business strategy. The company has conducted two "Million Dollar Challenges" to spur development of innovative wastewater treatment technologies and has received Presidential Awards for Green Chemistry and for Sustainable Development.

Over the past few years, a steady stream of the nation's *greenerati* — the leading visionaries and spokespeople for a sustainable industrial system — has paraded through the company's executive suites, taking senior management through the paces of what's wrong with the world and how to fix it. Author and entrepreneur Paul Hawken; green designer and architect William McDonough; botanist Peter Raven; even David Korten, author of *When Corporations Rule the World* and a staunch foe of transnationals like Monsanto — the list of progressive sustainability thinkers who have provided input to Monsanto goes on and on. CEO Robert Shapiro now ranks as one the world's foremost industry advocates of fourth-era corporate environmentalism, having delivered his message in various forums, such as the *Harvard Business Review* which in 1997 published a wave-making interview with him.[21]

Monsanto warrants kudos for more quiet initiatives as well, such as its support of micro-credit, a breakthrough strategy pioneered by Muhammad Yunus of the Grameen Bank in Bangladesh that provides modest loans to people who normally would not qualify for bank financing. Monsanto recently helped sponsor a major international conference on micro-credit that was held in Washington, D.C. The company also hosted a follow-up conference in St. Louis in June 1997 to bring corporations and non-governmental organizations together to explore the possibility of creating partnerships for micro-credit in regions around the world. Monsanto's CEO, Robert Shapiro, is the co-chair of the Council of Corporations, the goal of which is to reach 100 million of the world's poorest families through credit by the year 2005.

Seen through another lens, however, the company is nothing but trouble. Part of the problem lies with the company's embrace of biotechnology, a stance that horrifies some observers. "The rush into biotech rivals the rush into nuclear power 50 years ago," says Ronnie Cummins, national director of the Pure Food Campaign. "It is creating the conditions for an environmental Auschwitz or Chernobyl."[22]

Monsanto has also taken hits for a variety of research and regulatory shenanigans. In the 1980s, the company was accused of manipulating research into the health effects of dioxin and, more recently, of muscling its genetically-engineered bovine growth hormone through regulatory channels despite unresolved concerns about its impact on human health. It has opposed labeling bills that would allow companies to notify consumers that the milk in their products came from cows that hadn't been treated with bovine growth hormone. It has also been implicated in the notorious "circle of poison" whereby chemicals banned in the U.S. are sold overseas and then make their way back into the country on the backs, so to speak, of treated products.

The bottom line is that Monsanto ranks high on standard lists of corporate environmental heroes, and of corporate villains, too. Which actually isn't all that unusual. Several years ago, I asked several experts to informally rate the environmental performance of 20 major corporations. The scores varied widely. In one instance, expert #1 gave Du Pont the highest possible rating, while expert #2 gave it the lowest. Du Pont had recently conducted an environmental image campaign, with one particularly memorable ad showing a sequence of applauding animals. The expert who gave Du Pont low marks confessed that he viewed these ads as a tacit admission of wrongdoing.[23]

— ○ —

The mixed messages that corporations deliver are of two basic types. The first can be characterized as black-hatted business-as-usual, i.e., good old corporate duplicity. It's a shopworn tale — companies doing their utmost to water down environmental regulations, often under cover of night, while loudly proclaiming their environmental commitment to all who will listen. One is put in mind of the professional wrestling villain who does something godawful to his opponent and then, wide-eyed, protests his innocence to the scowling referee. In these cases, charges of greenwashing are well-founded.

Our first example of corporate duplicity comes from the pharmaceutical industry. The issue involves ozone-depleting substances (ODSs), which for the most part were banned by the Montreal Protocol. The agreement did, however, allow for certain exceptions, specifically for "essential uses" where an ODS is deemed "necessary for the health, safety or is critical for the functioning of society," and "there are no available technically and economically feasible alternatives or substitutes that are acceptable from the standpoint of environment and health." Such an exemption was carved out for the use of CFC-11, -12, and -114 as propellants in so-called "metered dose inhalers" (MDIs), which are used in the treatment of asthma and other respiratory ailments.

The market for MDIs is quite substantial — about $4 billion — and growing rapidly, in large measure because of the rise in pollution-related lung disease. About 440 million MDIs were in use as of 1996, with the number expected to climb to 800 million by the turn of the century. With the stakes this high, it is not surprising — if discouraging — that major players in the pharmaceutical industry have done their best to slow down the phase-out of ODS-based MDIs.[24]

The effort was triggered by the introduction by 3M in 1995 of a non-CFC MDI, the first of its kind to reach the market. While less than ideal environmentally — it used the propellant HFC-134a, a rather potent greenhouse gas — the new product represented a significant improvement over the CFC-based products on the market. For rival vendors, moreover, it posed a significant competitive threat: it was priced at or below the level of CFC-propelled MDIs, and estimates gave it the potential to replace over half of the existing MDI market.

Unlike rival suppliers, the administrators of the Montreal Protocol were delighted to learn of the new product. A report by the organization's Technology and Economic Assessment Panel (TEAP) suggested that, given the 3M introduction and other promising developments, the phaseout of CFC-propelled MDIs could be sharply accelerated. Kate Victory, editor of *Business and the Environment*, a trade newsletter, reports what happened next:

TEAP's proposal was presented for discussion at the ... Montreal

Protocol's Open Ended Working Group, held from 26-29 August [1996] in Geneva, Switzerland. To the surprise of many observers, however, the proposal was vehemently opposed by a handful of developing countries — namely, India, South Africa, and Kenya. The countries cited concerns over the implications for health in developing countries as well as the potential cost of alternatives. As a result, no decision was reached at the meeting ....

Several observers felt that the objections expressed by Kenya and other countries were actually a result of lobbying by pharmaceutical companies opposed to the phaseout of CFC-propelled MDIs ....[25]

Pharmaceutical companies took other steps as well. Glaxo Wellcome hired a public relations firm, GPC Connect, which was quoted in a trade publication as saying it had been "appointed by Glaxo Wellcome to run an international lobbying drive to delay the ban on [CFC-containing] MDIs as used by asthma sufferers. Glaxo Wellcome is hoping to delay an eventual ban on [CFC-containing] MDIs to allow it time to develop alternatives."[26] A Glaxo Wellcome executive subsequently attempted to explain away this unfortunate foray into candor by writing that the company had "asked GPC Connect to advise on internal communications procedures to help facilitate the complex transition from CFC to non-CFC MDIs internationally" — an exercise in corporate gibberish that only lent credence to the original GPC Connect assertion.[27]

Pharmaceutical companies also took action inside the nation's capitol. Writes Victory:

Sources told BATE [*Business and the Environment*] that pharmaceutical companies wishing to delay the transition successfully lobbied in the U.S. Congress to attach a CFC tax repeal rider to unrelated legislation. Buried deep in the "Small Business Job Protection Act of 1996" (H.R. 3448) is Section 1803, which repeals the $5.80 per pound tax on CFCs used as propellants in MDIs. The bill became law on 20 August [1996]. The cost of producing a pound of CFCs ranges from $0.50 to $2.00, so the tax was clearly an incentive to cut back on CFC production and use. Changing the rules makes it harder for manufacturers of new alternatives to realize a timely return on investment.[28]

Our second example of corporate anti-environmentalism isn't industry-specific. It's about how the corporate community as a whole responded to the Republican takeover of the U.S. Congress in 1994. Readers will recall that the conservative uprising set into motion a no-holds-barred assault on business-as-usual in the federal government.

Among the targets: substantial portions of the system of environmental protection that had been painstakingly built up over the previous 20 years. For the most part, the corporate community responded with silence — or applause.

The Republican campaign had two faces: one relatively centrist, the other extremist. The more moderate one focused, legitimately, on regulatory reform. You don't have to be a Republican to believe that the country's regulatory system needs fixing: the question is how to do so without dismantling its safeguards. The so-called Dole bill proposed to achieve this by requiring cost-benefit analyses for regulation. The very thought produced howls from environmentalists, who argued that regulatory oversight would drown under a sea of red tape and endless litigation. But defenders argued, with some justification, that the bill would only impose the same logic on regulatory processes that businesses already apply to their own operations. "It would help federal agencies prioritize more effectively," argued John Cohen, executive director of the Alliance for Reasonable Regulation (ARR), an industry group that supported the Dole bill.[29]

A substantial majority of the business community favored the Dole bill. ARR members included companies with excellent environmental reputations such as AT&T and CERES Principles endorsers General Motors and Sun Company. Industry lobbyists worked closely with legislators to help make the Dole bill a reality. Indeed, rarely if ever has the collaborative process been so overt. In one memorable instance, three lobbyists with the law firm of Hunton & Williams sat beside the staff director of the Senate Judiciary Committee and answered questions as if they were themselves staff members. In another, a lobbyist represented herself to a federal agency as speaking for an aide of one of the senators who was drafting the bill. This boundary-blurring behavior invited the perception that, as one critic put it to the *New York Times*, the Dole bill was "by big business, for big business, and of big business."[30]

For Republican extremists, "regulatory reform" was essentially a pretext for rolling back environmental regulation. Tom Delay, who as the majority whip in the House of Representatives is one of Newt Gingrich's chief deputies, is not one to control his rhetoric: he has called the Environmental Protection Agency (EPA) the "Gestapo of government" and labeled the Nobel Prize, which was awarded in 1995 to two researchers for their work on CFCs, the "Nobel appeasement prize." Many Republican proposals reflected this unrepentant anti-environmentalism.

Did the corporate community resist this backlash? Hell no. Many businesses and trade associations were only too eager to leap aboard the anti-environmental bandwagon. Big business had a big hand in writing the House revision of the Clean Water Act, which if passed would have substantially reduced protection for wetlands and controls on polluted runoff from farms and city streets. The paper industry successfully inserted a provision calling for the EPA to give greater weight to cost-benefit analysis and risk assessment in determining what technologies should be used to meet water quality goals. The Chemical Manufacturers Association (CMA) won a clause softening pollution discharge requirements. These and other pro-business provisions came to legislative aides via a lengthy memorandum from an industry group that was headed up by a so-called "environmental manager" with the U.S. Chamber of Commerce.

In fairness, it must be added that there was the occasional corporate objection to Congressional extremism. Not many, but a few. Du Pont spoke out against attempts to repeal or postpone the country's phaseout of CFCs, and the Chemical Manufacturers Association objected to early proposals to cut the EPA's budget by a whopping 34%. Mort Mullins, vice president of regulatory affairs for CMA, told *Fortune Magazine*, "That much of a cut in one year would be disruptive and counter-productive. We must protect the EPA's core programs that are essential to the credibility of the agency."[31]

Skeptics would argue that positions like these come from enlightened self-interest, not genuine environmental commitment, and they have a point. Du Pont has invested heavily in CFC alternatives, while the CMA may have been concerned that attempts to roll back too much too soon might backfire. As indeed they did: the Republicans managed to pass remarkably few of their environmental rewrites, largely because the extremist rhetoric and proposals produced a powerful backlash. Overall, however, the impression one got from corporate America during these for conservatives heady times was unabashed delight at the goings-on in the nation's capital.

How is one to make sense of the apparent inconsistency between corporate claims of environmental commitment and their behavior inside the Beltway? In a phrase, by applying the concept of "cognitive dissonance." Corporations are made up of, and also operate within, a host of different cultures and value systems. In the words of Nigel Roome, a professor specializing in business and the environment formerly at York University's Schulich School of Business, they function in "interdependent systems which operate at different scales in time and place."[32] Far from being integrated entities, corporations contain what amount to multiple, parallel, and often unaligned universes, with each responding to different — and often contradictory — rules of engagement. As a result, it is the rule, not the exception, for environmental management and lobbying to occupy entirely separate tracks within a corporation — for the two to have nothing whatsoever to do with each other. And that seems to be what happened, as EH&S departments went one way, and regulatory affairs departments another, during the conservative Republican uprising of 1994/1995.

A glaring case in point comes from a Fortune 500 company with a strong environmental profile whose chief environmental officer was genuinely shocked when I told him that his company belonged to the Alliance for Reasonable Regulation. A few days later he called to tell me that the company's name was being removed from the list of ARR supporters.

And so, when Bob Banks, the chief environmental officer at Sun Company, points out that "the regulatory initiatives in Washington D.C. are having no effect on our overall commitment," and when Paul Tebo, vice president of safety, health and environment at Du Pont, says that "you need to look at the whole spectrum of what companies are doing," they're probably not engaging in greenwashing so much as communicating their sincere assessment of this complex state of affairs.[33] All of which is to suggest that companies can be green inside their factories and in their environmental-management policies, and brown inside the Beltway.

The bottom line is that businesses are complex organisms with often conflicting agendas: it's unreasonable to expect consistency from them. The fact that the corporate community didn't rally *en masse* against the Republican initiatives in Washington doesn't quite put the lie to its environmental commitment. But it doesn't sing hosannas to it either.

A more recent example of reactionary corporate thinking comes from the broadbased industry opposition to the movement for a strong United Nations treaty imposing meaningful limits on greenhouse gas emissions. In the United States, much of the campaigning has been conducted via the neutral-sounding Global Climate Information Project (GCIP), which includes among its members such powerful trade organizations as the American Automobile Manufacturers Association, the American Petroleum Institute, the U.S. Chamber of Commerce, the National Association of Manufacturers, Edison Electric Institute, as well as a host of others. The organization objected to President Clinton's cautious acknowledgment of the need for binding emission limits because it "isn't fair to consumers, workers, farmers, seniors and small businesses," and it opposed the proposed treaty that was ultimately agreed upon in Kyoto in December 1997 on the grounds that it would "have little or no environmental benefit."[34] The GCIP spent an estimated $13 million on an advertising campaign designed to pressure the Clinton Administration into watering down its position on the climate-change issue.[35] And the Global Climate Coalition, another industry organization, has for years been funding efforts to undermine the global scientific and public dialogue about global climate change.[36]

There have been some breaks in the ranks — Robert Campbell, CEO of Sun Oil Company, came out in favor of binding emissions, and executives at British Petroleum and Royal Dutch/Shell have expressed a similar readiness to take climate change seriously — but positions like these are very much the exception. Overall, business has done its level best to scuttle the United Nations' climate-change treaty.

— ◯ —

The second type of mixed message is more subtle. Sometimes an organization's conduct comes across as environmentally favorable from one perspective, and as obstructionist from another. Duplicity isn't the issue here — perspective is. These framing issues are tricky and don't readily lend themselves to clear judgments of right or wrong. They do, however, lend notes of ambiguity and complexity to the dialogue, and they also remind us to be skeptical in the face of corporate claims that a given position demonstrates environmental commitment. It is always useful to ask *What position and actions could have been taken but weren't?* and *How might the issue be re-framed to create a less favorable interpretation of the corporate position?* Not to put the corporation in the wrong, but because framing country is spin country, and questions like these serve as ritual incantations whose effect is to keep one's head clear and to ward off the magic of … *the spin.*

One example of a framing issue comes out of the forest products industry. No one questions the hugely important role that forests play in our global ecosystem. International forestry practices touch on all the key environmental issues: rainforest devastation, soil depletion, water pollution, fishery preservation, global warming, and loss of biodiversity, to name just a few.

Ask environmentalists and representatives of the forest-products industry how to address these issues, and both sides offer the same solution: sustainable forestry. However, they disagree on what the term means. Environmentalists argue for a broad definition that takes into account the long-term nurturing of the forest resource ("focusing on what's left, not on what's taken" is how one expert puts it), and that, more expansively still, addresses social issues such as the treatment of local communities and indigenous peoples. Historically, industry representatives have tended to favor a more limited definition, preferring to focus on what's quantifiable, i.e., on having a positive growth-to-harvest ratio and no net loss of forest land. In other words: cut one, plant one. They have used a similar rationale to argue against including biodiversity in the sustainable-forestry calculus — again, because it is not quantifiable.

The future of sustainable forestry hinges in large part on the outcome of this debate. There's no doubt that the future lies with sustainable forestry — but will this include monoculture or mean a quantum shift in forest management practices?

The American Forest & Paper Association (AFPA), the leading wood products trade association in the U.S., stepped into the fray in 1994 when it announced that beginning in 1996 compliance with a set of sustainable forestry principles would be a condition of membership. Whether the move was progressive or reactionary is largely a matter of interpretation. On the one hand, the AFPA's Sustainable Forestry Principles are a public commitment to environmental responsibility, and there is much that is specifically positive in them. For instance, they require clearcuts to be blended into the landscape, and they also limit the size of a company's clearcuts to an average of 150 acres (60 ha), a requirement that will put constraints on companies operating in flat pinewood forests where much larger clearcuts are possible.

Most importantly of all, the Principles go beyond the industry's "cut-one-plant-one" definition of sustainable forestry. Objective Four of the AFPA's Implementation Guidelines requires companies to "enhance the quality of wildlife habitat by developing and implementing measures that promote habitat diversity and the conservation of plant and animal populations found in forest communities."[37] In other words: *sayonara,* monoculture.

Does this mean that the AFPA has sided with the progressives? Not necessarily. The Principles contain more than a few gray areas. For instance, the "special sites" principle calls for companies to "manage [their] forests and lands of special significance (for example, biologically, geologically, or historically significant) in a manner that takes into account their unique qualities."[37] Precisely what this means is unclear. Does it preclude selective cutting of an old-growth forest? Not necessarily. Nowhere do the Principles require member companies to keep old-growth forests off limits.

Furthermore, the AFPA's initiative can be viewed as an ill-disguised effort to stunt the growth of the sustainable forestry certification movement, which is rapidly building up a considerable head of steam in North America. The American Society for Testing Materials (ASTM), a leading U.S. standards organization, is developing what it calls a "Standard Guide for the Assessment of Sustainably Harvested Wood," while on a less theoretical front the Rainforest Alliance's SmartWood initiative, the world's oldest timber certification program with over 50 certified enterprises, is expanding its expertise into North America through its SmartWood Network, which links regional non-profit certification organizations in the United States, Canada, and worldwide. The National Wildlife Federation, the largest U.S. environmental group, has agreed to provide certification services for the SmartWood Network in the northeastern United States — potentially a significant move, given the organization's excellent name recognition and its direct access to a 1.6 million-person membership base. SmartWood program certifiers will be accredited by the Forest Stewardship Council, a Oaxaca, Mexico-based organization that in the brief few years of its existence has managed to impose the beginnings of order on the burgeoning forest-products certification industry.

All these certifiers apply a much more holistic definition of "sustainable" than the AFPA. To the extent that the association succeeds through its Principles in creating the perception that its members practice sustainable forestry, it obviates the need for certification, blunts the movement's momentum, and ensures that the power to determine how they manage their resources remains in the hands of the forest-product companies themselves.

So are the AFPA's Sustainable Forestry Principles "green?" Yes. No. Maybe. You decide.

Another interesting framing issue is presented by Wal-Mart, the enormously successful mass-market retailer with close to $105 billion in annual revenue. Over the years, Wal-Mart Stores has developed an excellent reputation for environmental commitment, and its Lawrence, Kansas, eco-store is widely viewed as the jewel in its green crown. In many ways it is an impressive achievement, with features that include a

1,200 square foot (110 sq. m) permanent environmental education center and a one-stop recycling center for tin, glass, paper, and sorted plastics. More striking still is the extent to which environmental considerations have been incorporated into the building's design. Although steel is the usual roofing material for Wal-Mart stores, sustainably harvested wood was utilized for the Lawrence store's roof and ceiling structure. Altogether, 750,000 board feet of sustainably harvested wood were used, making it the largest amount of wood ever certified as sustainably harvested for a single project. The Lawrence skylight system operates in tandem with the building's fluorescent lighting system to minimize energy consumption. Photo sensors mounted at the base of the skylight walls continuously monitor the amount of light entering the building and automatically adjust the level of the dimmable light fixtures accordingly. In this way, only the exact amount of electrical light needed is provided beneath the skylight area. The parking lot contains recycled asphalt. Bumper blocks and directional signs are made of recycled plastic. Cart corrals are either made from recycled plastic or "recycled" from other stores. Even Wal-Mart's road sign is solar-powered.

Does all this make Wal-Mart, or Wal-Mart's eco-store, an environmental winner? Not if you ask David Morris of the non-profit Institute for Local Self-Reliance:

> Wal-Mart's Kansas eco-store has received enormous publicity but the context for the store is egregious. Wal-Mart has done the same thing everywhere. It moves into an area, drives out small businesses, drives out diversity — in short, undermines community. The fact that the Wal-Mart operation in Lawrence is an eco-store doesn't undo any of that.[38]

In Morris's opinion, even if you leave out the social component, the Wal-Mart eco-store fails on strictly environmental grounds:

> If you compare a Lawrence, Kansas, with a Wal-Mart store against a Lawrence without one, having no Wal-Mart wins hands down. The environmental costs of building a Wal-Mart store and parking lot are immense, even if you build environmentally. So is the mileage logged by people traveling to shop there. There is only one benefit in having a Wal-Mart in your town: you pay less. That doesn't make up for the social and environmental costs.[39]

Morris's critique serves as a valuable reminder that whether we hold something as good or bad, as favorable or unfavorable, in large measure depends on our frame of reference. It is also consistent with one of the core principles of fourth-era corporate environmentalism — the need, as articulated in the previous chapter, to "remember sustainable development." For Morris, sustainability requires us to look beyond relative environmental impacts and to consider other issues such as the quality of life and the impact on the community. Not only that, but he believes scale itself is intrinsically problematic. As green as it is, even the Lawrence, Kansas, Wal-Mart is still a superstore, and Wal-Mart is still a megacompany. For Morris, big is unsustainable, period.

— O —

Yet another set of framing issues might collectively be called the "curious incident of the dog in the nighttime." The phrase comes from a passage in a Sherlock Holmes story called *Silver Blaze:*

"Is there any other point to which you wish to draw my attention?"
[asked Watson].
   "To the curious incident of the dog in the nighttime."
   "The dog did nothing in the nighttime."
   "That was the curious incident," remarked Sherlock Holmes.[40]

The business/sustainability community is replete with similar "curious incidents." Behind the veil of corporate actions there lies another story — the things companies choose not to do; products and initiatives they do not follow up on; the white spaces in the text.

The "Greening-Up" Line in the Sand. Mainstream consumer-goods companies have devoted much time and expense to improving the environmental performance of their established product lines. Most detergent companies have introduced "Ultras," which substantially reduce packaging. The major soda companies have introduced two-liter soda bottles containing post-consumer recycled plastic. Packaging has been eliminated entirely for some deodorants, toothpaste, and other products. Many established products have been re-launched as refills.

The consumer-goods majors tend to position steps like these as proof of their environmental commitment, and from one perspective this claim is warranted. These exercises in product "greening-up" do indeed reduce materials consumption and waste. But their actions have a shadow side. In choosing to green up their products, the consumer-product majors have elected to steer clear of "deep-green" products, radically reformulated offerings whose core identities are built around their environmental assets. Moreover, their position entirely fails to address the even more fundamental issue of sustainable consumption.

One effect of the corporate embrace of product "greening-up" has been to diffuse and in the process to defuse consumer concerns about the environment. This in turn has reduced the marketplace appeal of deep-green alternatives, which for all intents and purposes have been foreclosed from mainstream distribution channels.

The consumer-goods majors have ample reason to want to keep the consumer marketplace from becoming very green. They have made substantial investments in capital equipment for their established non-green (or greened-up) product lines. In addition, by introducing "deep-green" products, they would be inviting a more critical appraisal of the environmental performance of their established brands. Moreover, by shifting the consumer-goods center of gravity to a point where the environment was a much more important buying considera-tion, the majors would run the risk of letting fresh air into a market structure that is pretty well sealed right now — and tilted very much in their favor. By going "deep-green," in other words, they would open the door to a new buying culture, with potentially grievous consequences for their established franchises.

These business reasons mitigate against the consumer-goods majors making the leap into deep-green products. But the fact remains that they *could* have chosen to do so.

Plastics Is As Plastics Does. Currently, two types of plastic — polyeth-ylene terephthalate (PET) soda bottles and high-density polyethylene (HDPE) milk jugs — are being recycled at rather high rates in the U.S., while all the other frequently used resins are hardly recycled at all. For Richard Denison, a senior scientist with the Environmental Defense Fund (EDF), the consumer-products industry is a prime culprit for the failure to expand plastics recycling beyond PET and HDPE — again, not for what it has done so much as for what it hasn't. He writes:

> Consider two reasons why recycling of soft drink bottles and milk jugs *is* working:
>
> **Single vs. multiple types of plastic:** Soft drink bottles are all made from the same type of plastic — easily identified by people and easily reprocessed. The same goes for milk jugs. In contrast, many other con-sumer products come in different types of plastic that look alike but can't be recycled together (except for low-grade uses such as making plastic lumber). This hodgepodge results not from any functional requirement but from short-term economics: these packagers buy the cheapest plas-

tic available at a given time.

EDF supermarket surveys found at least four different plastics used to make shampoo bottles and five or more for all-purpose cleansers. Colgate-Palmolive dishwashing liquid and Lysol disinfectant each come in three different plastics.

Clear vs. colored. Soft drink bottles and milk jugs are clear, in contrast to the broad palette of pigments used in most plastic bottles for purely cosmetic reasons. Companies like Procter & Gamble and Lever Brothers have won praise for using recycled plastic in their bottles. Ironically, they have done so by cornering the market on clear milk jugs, to which they add their trademarked pigments. The next time around, the bottles are lucky to be used even as plastic lumber — and far more likely to end up as trash.[41]

In Denison's view, the consumer-goods companies are perpetuating the plastics recycling *status quo* (or rather the plastics *non*-recycling *status quo*) by not giving environmental considerations enough weight in their plastics buying and processing decisions:

> Procter & Gamble has a color called Tide Red. It is its own color — no other company can use it. The company buys clear plastic and dyes it Tide Red. Theoretically it could use clear HDPE and a large Tide Red sticker but it doesn't. Instead it has chosen to link its brand image to a specific plastics processing technology.[42]

Does Procter & Gamble have good reason to stick with its "Tide-and-True" Tide Red marketing strategy? Absolutely. But it's also true that P&G could have elected to lead a shift in the packaging paradigm to clear plastic and big labels. It hasn't, opting instead for the lesser course of increasing its use of recycled plastic. And so we have another instance of a greener road not taken.

Twilight of the Champions. There are basically two types of corporate environmentalism. The first, which we might think of as Corporate Environmentalism #1, is largely operations and compliance-oriented — EH&S business-as-usual, essentially, with a handful of eco-efficiency electrons circling around a nucleus of regulatory compliance. The second, Corporate Environmentalism #2, is more aggressive, more creative, more unorthodox. It is the sort of corporate environmentalism that can lead to substantial breakthroughs, if given a home where it can endure and flourish.

Unfortunately, Corporate Environmentalism #1 — corporate environmentalism in its safe form — has proven to be the default option for virtually every company, while Corporate Environmentalism #2 — and its champions — are at risk.

At the Canadian utility Ontario Hydro, Brian Kelly and his team tried to make sustainable development a part of the core business strategy. At retailer Home Depot, Mark Eisen concentrated on motivating suppliers to deliver environmentally superior products. At consumer products company Church & Dwight, Bryan Thomlison's focus was on driving change through complex multi-stakeholder partnerships.

Unfortunately, all three champions of Corporate Environmentalism #2 were let go. In Kelly's case, it was because his champion, CEO Maurice Strong, left the company. Home Depot's Eisen fell victim to an organizational shuffle and a subsequent decision to focus on more strictly operational issues. At Church & Dwight, Thomlison got axed as part of a broader corporate downsizing. All these companies had the opportunity to do something dramatic, and opted instead to go back to their EH&S knitting. That's hardly a surprise, but it is disappointing. Corporate Environmentalism #1 is the rule. The bolder, potentially more significant Corporate Environmentalism #2 is vulnerable, and the rare exception. Still more testimony to how much could be done, and isn't.[43]

Who's Up First? The "After You, Alphonse" Syndrome. It is the rare company that goes against the business grain. It does happen occasionally, though. For instance, in 1990 Esprit International ran a "Plea for Responsible Consumption" in *Utne Reader* magazine:

> Today, more than ever, the direction of an environmentally conscious style is not to have luxury or conspicuous consumption written all over your attire. This is still our message. We believe this could best be achieved by simply asking yourself before you buy something (from us or any other company) whether this is really something you need. It could be you'll buy more or less from us, *but only what you need.* We'll be happy to adjust our business up or down accordingly, because we'll feel we are then contributing to a healthier attitude about consumption....[44]

More recently, the recreational clothing manufacturer Patagonia announced its intention to limit its growth in defiance of the hallowed capitalist tenet, "Expand or perish." To that end it has reduced its product lines, accompanying its move with printed materials asking consumers pointed questions about how many sets of outdoor clothes they really need.

But examples like these, which invariably come from privately-held companies with progressive political agendas, are very much the exception. If a publicly held company tried something similar, a rash of stockholder lawsuits would surely follow.

In some cases, however, the reluctance to lead by example cannot be fobbed off on fear of litigation. Consider, for instance, the case of Dow Chemical's Corporate Environmental Advisory Council (CEAC). As discussed in Chapter 5, the CEAC is an environmental management innovation of the first order. It brings together a group of highly respected and indisputably independent environmental specialists for regular meetings to advise Dow on environmental-management and related governance issues.

When Dow's CEAC was formed in 1991, it was met with some resistance by company managers, who were dubious about the wisdom of opening the corporate doors to outsiders. But those doubts dissolved over time as the CEAC proved to be a valuable management tool.

When companies make decisions without soliciting outside opinion, they run two risks. The first involves institutional parochialism — every corporate culture has its own biases and blinders. Second, the understandable desire of employees to stay on the right side of the boss can stifle dialogue. The CEAC kills both these birds with a single green stone. Indeed, about the only argument that can be mustered against the CEAC is the chestnut that you shouldn't give outsiders strolling rights within the corporate compound.[45]

In Dow's CEAC we have a proven idea, and an idea, moreover, whose time has come — one can scarcely imagine an initiative more in tune with the emerging values of collaboration and disclosure. Yet in the seven years since Dow founded the CEAC, not a single mainstream company has followed suit.

The CERES Principles provide another example of excessive corporate caution. In 1993 Sun Company became the first company to endorse the Principles. Since then only nine more Fortune 500 companies have come aboard. That's a mighty slow rate of acceptance, especially for a document that isn't even legally binding. Here, as in other environmental areas, companies want to be first to be second, or first to be third — or better yet, first to be 30th.

Over time, the recurring exposure to these mixed messages can get discouraging. We are clearly getting something less from the corporate community than the wholehearted engagement that the global *problématique* requires. No matter how we explain this unfortunate situation — as a function of unresolved internal conflicts, i.e., of having to operate within Nigel Roome's "interdependent systems which operate at different scales in time and place," or as the inevitable consequence of the imperatives of global corporate capitalism, as per critics like David Korten — we keep returning to the same picture: of a corporate sector that is playing both sides against the middle and continues to be largely in denial about the severity of the crisis.

One veteran of the corporate environmental wars, a person who spent years working diligently and ultimately unsuccessfully to get a public company to adopt an aggressive pro-environmental strategy, recently confided: "I have concluded that any corporation that is publicly traded is the enemy. We have to rebuild from the ground up, at the local level with neighborhood-driven "Mom-and-Pop" capitalism."[46]

My friend's despair is understandable. And widespread too, as evidenced by the emergence of a still-small but growing — and socially significant — global movement that favors such things as local self-reliance (keeping businesses small and ownership local) and voluntary simplicity (redefining happiness outside the context of western-style consumption). But while it is easy to sympathize with the impulse to put all one's eggs into the basket of local self-reliance, such a step would be misguided. Clearly there is a place for substantially more local self-reliance, and such initiatives need to be encouraged, but we just as clearly need to devote substantial amounts of time and energy to seeking points of leverage within the current industrial system. Whether the prospect pleases or pains you, the fact is that transnational companies are going to be with us for some time. And what this calls for from sustainability activists is, among other things, a sort of corporate strategic *aikido*, i.e., an approach that uses the language and values of mainstream corporate culture to create a business case so compelling that companies are left with little choice but to adopt more sustainable policies and practices.

True, corporations are working within significant constraints, but within those limitations individuals often have substantial freedom of choice, and can and do make a difference. Not always, but sometimes. In making sustainability a core business strategy, Monsanto's Robert Shapiro is making a considerable difference — that's true even if you take issue with the company's pro-biotechnology interpretation of sustainable development.[47] Ditto for executives like Claude Fussler at Dow Chemical, who was discussed in Chapter 6, and a whole host of other hard-working — and often under-appreciated (indeed, to the public eye largely invisible) — corporate sustainability champions. Is the road often rocky for them? Absolutely. But change does happen.

Not only can the sustainability initiatives of individuals like this have a positive impact inside their own organizations, but their efforts — if successful by the measure of business culture — can have a domino effect, inspiring other companies to follow suit and at a deeper level driving a shift in the dominant business culture toward ever greater levels of sustainability.

Let's say a progressive foundation were to underwrite the development of a sustainability master plan. Such a document, in my opinion, would have three distinct components. One would be relatively radical: work to build a strong foundation for alternative economic strategies and structures. A second would focus on reversing the considerable structural constraints that the global financial and economic system currently imposes on individual corporations and executives.[48] And the third would support the aforementioned corporate strategic *aikido*. Such an approach, it seems to me, would be sound practically and at the same time the best possible prescription against despair. And in fact this strategy already *is* being pursued by sustainability activists around the world, albeit in a random, chaotic, self-generating sort of way. While the precise outcome of their efforts remains to be seen, one thing *is* certain: everyone has their own path, their own "best strategy," and it is all these paths together that create change.

Across the Great Divide

As one digs deeper into the national character of the Americans, one sees that they have sought the value of everything in this world only in the answer to this single question: how much money will it bring in?
— Alexis de Tocqueville

IN THE PREVIOUS CHAPTER, we saw that one problem with corporate environmental conduct lies in the mixed messages companies deliver. There is another problem, too — the "mental model" most corporate executives have of the environment. Advocates of organizational learning believe that consciousness creates culture, not the other way around, and for the most part I agree. Which suggests that if we want to efficiently create changes in behavior, it is on the level of consciousness — of mental models — that we must focus.

In the corporate world, the term "environmentalism" over the years has had a special meaning — not positive "concern about the environment," but the same sort of negative connotation we find in "isms" like "racism" and "sexism." For the most part, environmental issues have had second-class citizen status in corporations — a place at the back of the bus.

The explanation for this can be found in the historical origins of corporate environmental concerns, which track back to regulatory compliance and its even more onerous aftermath, remediation. For the private citizen, environmentalism is an expression of compassion, a motion of the heart. In the corporate context, however, it has historically been a vexation, nothing more.

What turns people on in business? The prospect of making money, that's what — the thrill of seeing the product of one's creative efforts come back to one in the form of wealth and expanded opportunity.

Creativity translated into ever greater freedom — therein lies the lure of enterprise. Unfortunately the environment, as delivered gift-wrapped by a generation of command-and-control regulators, has come for the great majority of business executives to embody the very antithesis of that impulse. Bureaucracy, red tape, "cost centers" — these may be necessary aspects of doing business in these times, but they are certainly not fun. They are not really what business is all about — yet it is precisely these spirit-dampening associations with which the environment has historically been saddled. So long as this continues to be the case, i.e., so long as the environment is perceived as an obligation, not an opportunity — as a blight, not a delight — environmental considerations will inevitably receive only reluctant attention. Not for reasons of business (although it can be couched in those terms), but for reasons of the heart.

The importance of moving beyond this negative mental model can hardly be overstated. So long as the attitude of business executives toward the environment is defensive, so long as it lacks entrepreneurial gusto, corporations will not make significant progress in tackling the challenge of sustainable development.

In an earlier chapter we saw how far the small- and midsized enterprises (SMEs) are from operating sustainably. At larger corporations, the transition is beginning to happen, but only beginning. What progress has been made is due to the efforts of a group I think of as the "corporate mechanics," so named because they labor behind the scenes, with little public acknowledgement or acclaim. Around the country, these forward-thinking consultants and in-house proselytizers are laboring under the hoods of corporations in an effort to drag environmental management across the divide that separates liability containment and regulatory compliance — historically, the two main branches of environmental management — from the vastly more bracing world where MBAs gather to gambol: the world of the profit center.

The business philosophy they are advancing has come generically to be known as *strategic environmental management*, or SEM. The fundamental difference between traditional environmental management and SEM is one of attitude. Old-fashioned environmental management is essentially defensive: "How can we stay out of trouble?" SEM practitioners, by contrast, have a much more proactive orientation: "How can we use our environmental expertise to create competitive advantage?"

In the limited sense that its goal is to give environmental management a seat at the front of the corporate bus, SEM is the corporate-environmental equivalent of the civil rights movement. Although it lacks the flash of other sustainability concepts, it is a crucially important strategy. When environmental management crosses the great divide and begins to participate in the central business of business, which is to make money, it gains new momentum, indeed a whole new purpose. It leaves the mop-up crew and joins the ranks of "core competencies." This is a significant step, indeed a *sine qua non* of a more sustainable business paradigm.

— ◯ —

More specifically, the goal of SEM is to integrate environmental awareness into two levels of corporate practice: day-to-day business processes and line operations, and overarching strategy. Doing so offers several distinct benefits. For one thing, when EH&S operates as its own discrete fiefdom, it becomes all too easy for line managers to view the environment as somebody else's problem. This, of course, is a problem in its own right, and the one that enterprise integration — the merging of environmental awareness with line operations — is intended to solve. When environmental awareness is inculcated in the managers whose actions produce the environmental impacts in the first place, the EH&S function changes abruptly. No longer is it in the unhappy position of being the *de facto* corporate environmental scapegoat: the moral loop is closed and responsibility for environmental consequences returns to the people whose decisions created them in the first place. Enterprise integration reconnects responsibility for the *outcome* to responsibility for the *decision*.

A second benefit of enterprise integration is *improved feedback*. Donella Meadows, a writer, sustainability theorist, and charter member of the *greenerati*, tells of a housing development in the Netherlands where by happenstance half the utility meters were installed in the basements and half in the front halls, where the residents could see them. The result: 30% less energy consumption in the houses where the meters could be seen.[1] Enterprise integration has a similar effect: it puts the environmental "meter" squarely on the manager's desk.

Strategies for achieving enterprise integration differ. Dow Chemical conducts systematic EH&S Improvement Reviews in which products' strengths and weaknesses are assessed. According to David Buzzelli, who was Dow's chief environmental officer when the assessments were introduced, "They aren't conducted by environmental experts, but by the same people who run the businesses. It's a way for them to exhibit ownership and leadership."[2] This changes the role of the environmental staff, which becomes more of an educational and technical resource for line management — in Buzzelli's words, "a repository of specialized knowledge."[3]

BASF Corp. takes a somewhat different approach. It has a corporate "environmental opportunities" manager who functions as an internal consultant to help line managers climb the environmental learning curve, perform technology assessments, and identify environmental business opportunities. BASF has taken David Buzzelli's notion that EH&S managers should serve as "a repository of specialized knowledge" one step further. It has separated the compliance function from the money-making one and assigned an EH&S specialist solely to the money-making side of the business — a new and creative twist on the role of the environmental manager.

Research data, although somewhat outdated, support the notion that many companies are integrating environmental management with other management functions. A 1992 Abt Associates study of mostly Fortune 200 non-service firms found that 63% of the companies assigned environmental responsibility to manufacturing management, while product development and R&D departments had eco-responsibilities in more than half of the firms surveyed. Marketing, purchasing, and quality assurance occupied a second tier at 25-30% of responding companies, with finance coming in last at under 20%.

Similarly, a 1991 survey of international corporate environmental practices by the United Nations Centre on Transnational Corporations found that many different functional areas had a hand in initiating environmental programs. Strategic planners were involved in environmental initiatives at roughly 50% of responding companies, with R&D participation at above the 40% level.

But there is integration, and then there is integration. Formal corporate policy and the underlying reality are often at odds. And indeed a late-1995 survey by the management consultancy Arthur D. Little indicates that what the company dubs a "green wall" continues to stand between the environmental and business staffs of many companies. ADL's poll of 185 EH&S managers at U.S. and Canadian companies found that despite their belief that good environmental management can be an important contributor to a company's overall business performance, the EH&S function is still commonly viewed as an outside operation whose sole mission is to keep the company out of trouble.

Nor is enterprise integration necessarily synonymous with SEM: it is one thing to make line managers responsible for environmental impacts, and another to embrace SEM as an overarching management philosophy. As a theoretical construct, SEM is still very much at the leading edge. As recounted in Chapter 4, a 1994 survey by Environmental Research Associates found that only 18% of executives said their companies treat environmental management as a profit center — and even this number, modest as it is, was probably inflated by the so-called "halo effect," a market-research phenomenon whereby respondents give what they believe to be the "right answer" even though that answer does not accord with the facts.

How does one explain the disparity between the relatively high level of enterprise integration on the one hand and the relatively low level of SEM buy-in on the other? One reason is that all too often companies fire environmental managers, assign their responsibilities to line managers, and call it "integration." It is, in other words, a way to put a nice shine on something nasty — the wolf of downsizing dressed up in eco-clothing.

Even when enterprise integration *is* legitimate, for the most part it involves the integration of SEM on an *à la carte* basis through the adoption of specific tools such as life-cycle analysis, design for environment, and strategic environmental auditing. In other words, to the extent that SEM is establishing itself, it is doing so not from the top down, but largely by accretion.

There are many reasons why business executives have been slow to accept SEM. They include the usual ones of inertia, distraction, and denial, as well as others: a generalized distrust of abstract concepts, plus the suspicion that SEM is merely the latest in a long line of management flavors-of-the-month conjured up by the Society of Starving Consultants.

How do you get executives to view SEM more positively? You start by sending SEM to school, i.e., by inculcating an appreciation of SEM in the next generation of business executives. This is the explicit mission of the Washington-based Management Institute for Environment and Business, which is supporting the development of environmental-management curricula in business schools around the U.S.[4] Thanks in large part to this group's efforts, over 100 business schools currently have courses on environmental management, up from less than five in the late 1980s. Other organizations have targeted this niche as well. The mission of the Massachusetts-based non-profit Second Nature is to help universities adopt sustainability principles and curricula, while Bridges, a Houston-based start-up (and also a non-profit), will provide international, inter-disciplinary teams of interns to businesses around the world, advising them on environmental-management and sustainability issues.

The next step is to build a persuasive business case for SEM. Michael Porter of the Harvard Business School has led the way here, arguing persuasively, albeit in the face of much entrenched resistance, that analyzing business problems through an eco-lens encourages innovation and resource productivity. By way of example, Porter points to the Dutch flower industry, where "[i]ntense cultivation of flowers in small areas was contaminating the soil and groundwater with pesticides, herbicides and fertilizers." The Dutch, Porter reports, responded by developing a closed-loop system where flowers "now grow in water and rock wool, not in soil" — a step that produced many environmental benefits, including reduced fertilizer and pesticide use and lower water consumption, as well as competitive advantages: "The tightly monitored closed-loop system also reduces variation in growing conditions, thus improving product quality. Handling costs have gone down because the flowers are cultivated on specially designed platforms." Porter's conclusion:

> [T]he Dutch have innovated in ways that have raised the productivity with which they use many of the resources involved in growing flowers. The net result is not only dramatically lower environmental impact but also lower costs, better product quality, and enhanced global competitiveness.[5]

Other examples come from the U.S., where SEM has been shown to reduce costs and to encourage new-product innovation. For much of the decade, Bristol-Myers Squibb has analyzed the environmental performance of many existing and new products under its *Environment 2000* program. The initiative has improved the company's competitive positioning in more than one instance. For instance, a product life-cycle assessment of the company's *Ban* roll-on deodorant pinpointed changes in chemicals usage that enabled the company to reduce its manufacturing cycle time by 12.5%, a move that improved its cash flow management. Responding to pressure from California calling for reduced volatile organic compounds in consumer products, the company's Clairol subsidiary went beyond compliance and developed the first alcohol-free hairspray for permed or color-treated hair. The competitive advantage: being the first to market with a new, environmentally superior product. And when another consumer products company, S.C.

Johnson Wax, reformulated its RAID Ant 'n Roach pesticide from a solvent-based to a low-VOC (volatile organic compound), water-based format, it avoided costly regulatory demands and reduced storage costs for an estimated annual savings of $2 million per year.

In the long run, it is examples like this — and not just one example, but multitudes of them — that will persuade business executives to take SEM seriously. Nor will it suffice for these examples to appear solely in the form of sermons delivered by wandering consultants and sustainability advocates. One kind of evidence alone will be truly persuasive — the between-the-eyes jolt that comes when executives find themselves losing market share to companies that have embraced SEM.

Specialized SEM tools include *strategic environmental auditing, design for environment* (DFE) and its various subsets (design for disassembly, design for recyclability, etc.), *full-cost accounting, environmentally conscious manufacturing,* and *life-cycle assessment.* I have chosen in this overview chapter to limit our discussion to the first three:

- *Strategic Environmental Auditing* — because auditing for compliance is extremely widespread and because it requires only a relatively modest shift in focus to audit strategically;

- *Design for Environment (DFE)* — because it is arguably the splashiest SEM tool (and also because it is making considerable headway);

- *Full-Cost Accounting (FCA)* — because it is probably the most important SEM tool of all.

Strategic Environmental Auditing. As we saw in Chapter 4, most environmental audits — 86%, according to an Ernst & Young survey of Canadian companies — are conducted primarily for compliance, i.e., to assure conformance with existing regulations. But that is not the only role for audits, which can and indeed should be more ambitious. Within an SEM context, they can be used to create competitive advantage through the identification of opportunities for resource productivity. More aggressively still, audits can be conducted against *sustainability* — a standard that, as we have seen, goes well beyond eco-efficiency. (In Chapter 11, we will explore structures for auditing against sustainability; here, we focus on the more modest but nonetheless important *audit for competitive advantage.*)

An eco-audit by Green Audit, a New York City-based consultancy, for Motherwear Inc., a Massachusetts-based manufacturer of women's clothes for breastfeeding mothers, demonstrates the benefits of the strategic environmental audit. Green Audit's review uncovered several opportunities for reducing environmental impacts while improving the company's financial performance. For instance, the audit revealed that about 25% of the fabric purchased for manufacture was wasted. Commented Green Audit: "With this knowledge the Company can act by 1) making an effort at minimizing the waste in manufacturing, 2) reusing the fabric wastes and/or recycling the waste fabric."[6]

The audit also found that Motherwear's back-order software didn't consolidate multiple back-orders to the same customer. This created another eco-opportunity: by shipping back-orders at the same time, the company could reduce the amount of packaging used, save on packaging and shipping costs, and use its personnel more efficiently.

Design for Environment (DFE). The aim of design for environment is to build environmental considerations into the entire product-design process.

IBM's *PS/2 E* personal computer (the "e" stands for "environment"), which was introduced in 1993, used the DFE process to create competitive advantage. The computer had a host of eco-features, including design for disassembly and reusability, and the use of recycled content. The machine also consumed relatively little energy, exceeding the requirements of the Environmental Protection Agency's *Energy Star* program by a generous amount — a fully loaded *PS/2 E* operated at a maximum of 24 watts, whereas *Energy Star's* 30 watt requirement applies to units in their bare-bones configuration.

Another energy advantage came from the fact that the *PS/2 E* was one of the first desktop computers to use PCMCIA technology. This allowed full-scale add-on applications such as fax/modems to be placed on credit card-sized cards that plug into external bays, thereby eliminating the need for space- and energy-consuming internal components. Because PCMCIA cards were initially designed for portable and laptop computers, where energy considerations are paramount, they are extremely energy-efficient.

The combination of PCMCIA technology and other energy-efficient features produced several performance breakthroughs. For instance, the low power consumption and use of PCMCIA technology reduced the size of the *PS/2 E's* "footprint." The system unit measured a mere 12" by 12" by 2.5" (30 cm x 30 cm x 6.4 cm) and could actually be wall-mounted. Silent operation was another advantage, achieved because the energy-efficient design eliminated the need for a fan.

These are the sort of benefits that customers prize — benefits that spell competitive advantage. And they evolved out of IBM's application of SEM to the product development process.

Although it too is very much a leading-edge concept, DFE has made deeper inroads into the mainstream than SEM. There are six reasons why this is so.

First: Design is the big bang of the product development process. Because design decisions reverberate throughout the entire life-cycle of the product, this is the most efficient stage at which to shape environmental performance.

Second: DFE is more hands-on than strategic environmental management. Whereas DFE is more about *praxis*, SEM is more about theory.

Third: DFE is relatively straightforward and can be implemented without much ado. It is also quite flexible. Like the environmental audit, it can be used by companies for different reasons — by Alpha Corporation to tweak existing products, by Beta Corporation as a tool for more substantial change.

Fourth: DFE works. A project currently underway at the Microelectronics and Computer Technology Corp. (MCC), Austin, TX, demonstrates the power of DFE to move environmental improvements directly to the bottom line. The electronics industry R&D consortium is reinventing how printed wiring-boards are fabricated. Early indications are that the new approach will reduce hazardous waste by 30-100%, water use by 50-90%, energy use by 50-75% — and costs by 20-70%.[7]

Another example comes from Xerox Corporation, through its ambitious Environmental Leadership eco-efficiency program. Preliminary analysis conducted when the program was first proposed indicated that the program would save the company $10-$20 million annually when implemented on a limited scale and up to $250 million in its full-blown form. Today the company is on track to meet the $250 million target, in large measure through the application of what the company calls "asset management," a DFE process characterized by a Harvard Business School case study as "...the process of reusing an asset (machine, subassembly, part, or packing material) either by re-manufacturing to its original state, converting to a different state, or dismantling to retrieve the original components ... a complex process which required the integration of design, engineering, and re-manufacturing activities."[8]

Fifth: The electronics industry is driving the acceptance of DFE, especially at the transnational level. Not only are electronic product life-cycles extremely short, which makes the industry very receptive to change, but electronic product takeback laws, which require companies to take responsibility for the ultimate disposal of their products, are looming in Germany, the Netherlands, and other jurisdictions. All this is leaving the industry with little alternative but to design their products for disassembly and reuse.

Sixth (and last): DFE fits neatly into the pod of fashionable management practices alongside concepts such as:

— *Total Quality Management.* DFE reflects a basic TQM tenet: Get It Right the First Time.

— *Concurrent design.* Increasingly, design, manufacturing, and marketing decisions are being made in parallel. Writes Gregory Eyring of the now-defunct U.S. Office of Technology Assessment:

> Companies are discovering that they cannot afford to have designers develop a concept in isolation and then toss it "over the wall" to production engineers. Instead …[t]he product evolves continuously through a spiral of design, manufacturing, and marketing decisions. As a product progresses along the "design helix" toward commercialization, multidisciplinary product development teams take part in every major design iteration. This multifunctional approach safeguards product integrity and expedites product development from stage to stage.[9]

Integrating this sort of systems orientation into the product-development process is the trickiest aspect of DFE. Once a company has de-linearized the product-development process by switching to concurrent design, adding environmental considerations to the mix is a relatively minor step.

— *Integrated logistics.* Companies are discovering that there are distinct advantages in working more closely and collaboratively with their suppliers. Eyring tells how General Motors, in what amounted to an exercise in "virtual DFE," shifted to a single supplier to meet and manage the chemical requirements for a plant and geared the supplier's compensation to the productive output of the factory, rather than to its consumption of chemicals. The result: a roughly 25% reduction in chemical usage.[10]

Two obstacles stand in the way of more widespread acceptance of DFE. First, there is the by now familiar problem of the small- and mid-sized enterprises, who have been slow to adopt DFE, even in the eco-friendly electronics industry. In this era of integrated logistics, this is particularly problematic. The entire supplier chain needs to be on the same environmental wavelength.

The second problem, a dearth of DFE software tools, is more readily resolved, and indeed a number of projects are underway that aim to meet this critical need. MCC is supporting the development of DFE advisor software for printed wiring boards, while IBM has developed a prototype internal on-line system linked to a computer-aided design package that flags environmentally troublesome products. Meanwhile, the sustainable-development task force of the American Association of Engineering Societies is working to create a more qualitatively-oriented template that will give designers throughout the engineering profession basic good/bad/neutral information about the eco-performance of their product options.

DFE appears destined for more widespread acceptance. Not only is it a first-rate eco-efficiency tool, but international regulatory and quasi-regulatory trends make it the only logical course to take. As noted earlier, takeback legislation is pending for electronics products, and there are also initiatives in respect to batteries, automobiles, appliances, tires, and packaging. In addition, there are close to 20 national eco-labeling programs worldwide, and these create a substantial market incentive to improve products' eco-performance.

Full-Cost Accounting (FCA). This brings us to full-cost accounting which, relative to the broader goal of sustainability, may be the most critical SEM technique of all.

Let's begin with some background. For our purposes, we can say that there are three general types of accounting:

- *National income accounting* tracks macro-economic data. While important changes are occurring in this area — in 1994, for instance, the U.S. Commerce Department published its first "green" tabulation of domestic GNP — that is not our focus here.

- *Financial accounting* has to do with how companies structure their books in order to report their performance to interested outside parties such as stockholders, creditors, banks, and the government. Financial accounting must conform to what are called generally accepted accounting procedures (GAAP). Here, too, there is much "green" activity. The U.S. Securities and Exchange Commission, for instance, recently increased the disclosure requirements for publicly-held companies about potential environmental liabilities.

- *Managerial accounting*, which is our focus in these pages, is the method by which companies keep track of their internal affairs. A strictly intracompany activity, it helps businesses operate as efficiently as possible.

Increasingly, business executives are coming to view current managerial accounting practices as inadequate because they fail to provide sufficiently detailed information about business operations. "Corporate overhead," to take just one example, is a very blunt instrument with which to perform cost surgery: it would be much more useful to have that overhead attributed to specific activities. Similarly, environmental costs are usually carried as a separate line item or not at all. More specificity, closer linkages, are required. Not for environmental reasons, but for business ones.

The need for more useful managerial accounting systems is behind the rising popularity of "activity-based costing" (ABC), whose aim, as the name suggests, is to pin costs to a specific activity. But here the issue starts to gets tricky. What costs? For businesses have both visible and hidden costs, and to make matters more complicated, some of these hidden costs are internal — the inefficient use of resources, for instance — while others are external: the cost to society of disposing of a product at the end of its useful life, say, or the cost in terms of habitat loss of having a tree farm instead of a natural forest.

It is here that full-cost accounting (FCA) comes into play. Although the exact meaning of the term is still in some dispute, FCA is viewed by many as essentially an expansive form of ABC — expansive in the sense that it accounts for both visible and hidden costs. *The function of FCA is to allocate all direct and indirect costs, including environmental ones, to a specific product, product line, process, service, or activity (or whatever).*

These indirect environmental costs can be substantial. Several years ago the non-profit World Resources Institute (WRI) developed a series of case studies examining how companies account for environmental costs. Its conclusion: "[E]ven where environmental costs are sizable, they are often systematically underappreciated."[11]

The corporate and professional communities are starting to put cautious toes into the environmental-accounting waters. The ubiquitous Monsanto has a task force on the subject. The Society of Management Accountants of Canada has developed a set of guidelines for dealing with environmental cost issues, and the United Kingdom-based Chartered Association of Certified Accountants, the world's largest trade association for accountants, has published a document called *Business Conceptions of Sustainability and the Implications for Accountancy.* All of which makes for a beginning.

But it is still very, very early. One critically important issue that is still largely being danced around concerns whether managerial FCA should account for "social" (also known as "external") costs. Those who believe the answer is yes argue that our corporate/economic and environmental systems are linked, not separate, and that as long as we continue to draw down our natural capital without accounting for its use, we are headed for ecological and financial bankruptcy. The value of these resources is staggering: a 1997 paper published in the prestigious journal *Nature* by 13 ecologists, geographers, and economists placed the annual value of these ecosystems at *between $16 trillion and $54 trillion* — that's compared to the current U.S. gross domestic product of about $27 trillion.[12] Until these external costs are included in our financial accounting practices, this argument goes, "corporate environmentalism" will be an oxymoron.

There is an indisputable logic here — and managerial quicksand too. For one thing, many external environmental costs defy valuation. How, for instance, does one value loss of biodiversity? Who is to decide and on what basis? Moreover, including external environmental costs grossly limits the usefulness of full-cost accounting as a management tool. Remember the purpose of FCA — to help companies compete effectively in the so-called "real world." This is done by identifying "real" costs, "real" in the sense of *actual expenditures*. Advocates of this more conservative version of FCA argue that adding external environmental costs to the mix when other companies are not doing so places companies at a competitive disadvantage and ultimately discourages them from using FCA at all.

Can the apparently incompatible social and competitive agendas be merged? Is "win-win" possible here? Maybe — but only transitionally. Remember that managerial accounting is a decision-making tool, nothing more. To borrow a phrase from the National Rifle Association: Accounting systems don't make decisions, people make decisions. FCA, in other words, provides information that is only one variable in a decision-making process that must, or should, consider citizenship as well as profits, values as well as economics. AT&T's Brad Allenby puts it this way: "External costs should be included in the business planning process, not in the internal accounting system."[13]

Allenby's solution makes sense, but only on an interim basis. Sooner or later our ecological and corporate accounts will have to be reconciled.

Whitecaps, Green Consumers, and the Infrastructure-Building Blues

The world's greatest events are not produced, they happen.
— G.C. Lichtenberg

PEOPLE HAVE MULTIPLE AND OFTEN CONFLICTING AGENDAS, just like corporations. It is the rare individual whose shopping and other life choices are consistently informed by environmental concerns. For the great majority of citizens, the environment is one of many signals flickering across their radar screen. In this world of constant distractions, how do you get companies to commit to offering environmentally superior products at prices customers can afford? There are essentially two strategies — increase supply, and stimulate demand. That, in a nutshell, defines the challenge of infrastructure-building. It has not come easily. Neither business nor government nor the consuming public has been able to muster the sort of energy and resources that would create a truly thriving market for environmentally superior products.

There has been activity, but it has been largely inadequate to the challenge. On the corporate front, a number of green business networks have been established that directly target infrastructure development. The Buy Recycled Business Alliance, a project of the National Recycling Coalition, has over 1,600 members. Recycling at Work, a program of the National Office Paper Recycling Project, has over 600 companies participating with the EPA as well as state and local governments in a campaign to significantly increase the collection of office and waste paper and the purchase of products containing recycled material. The

Recycled Paper Coalition has over 220 corporate members nationwide who commit to making their best efforts to buy recycled paper. In 1996, member companies collectively purchased nearly 260,000 tons of recycled paper and recycled 53,000 tons of office paper.

Efforts by individual companies to green their supply chains are bearing fruit, too. Over the years, McDonald's has purchased over $2 billion in recycled goods from suppliers, Du Pont spends over $200 million on recycled products annually, and there are many similar examples.[1] But efforts like these, praiseworthy though they are, fall far short of what is required to create a truly level playing field for recycled products.

As for the public sector, it is hampered by limited resources, plus a conservative political climate that discourages the implementation of an aggressively proactive environmental agenda. However, the Clinton Administration has taken some modest steps to build an infrastructure for green products.[2] In October 1993, President Clinton signed an Executive Order requiring federal agencies to purchase paper with a minimum of 20% post-consumer recycled content starting at the end of 1994, with the percentage of post-consumer content climbing to 30% by the end of 1998. This was widely viewed as a victory for environmentalists; industry had lobbied for lower levels.

The rationale for requiring government agencies to purchase green products is twofold: to stimulate demand directly, and to inspire state/local governments and the private sector to follow suit. With the federal government's purchases of goods and services totaling over $200 billion annually, its purchasing power can send clear market signals about the preferability of green products to manufacturers, other levels of government, and the public.

The 1993 Executive Order also requires EPA to develop a general guidance document for environmentally preferable products and services. EPA hopes to expand the procurement focus beyond a single characteristic of a product, such as recycled content, to a broader array of life-cycle considerations, ranging from the gathering of raw materials through to final disposal. EPA's position is that a comprehensive approach that goes beyond recovered materials, although much more difficult to implement, is likely to result in more sustained environmental gains, especially in view of the fact that a huge range of items — everything from cleaning products to satellite systems — is on the federal government's shopping list.

Although the Executive Order does not authorize federal agencies to pay a premium for green products, it does call for them to consider products' "life-cycle cost," which it defines as "the amortized annual cost of a product, including capital costs, installation costs, operating costs, maintenance costs and *disposal costs* [italics added] discounted over the lifetime of the product."[3] This can work to a green product's advantage. If it costs more up front than a non-green product, as is often the case, it can make up the difference at the back end with lower disposal costs. Thus life-cycle costing that more fully costs out products, as called for in the Executive Order, has the potential to help level the procurement playing field for green products.

There has also been a fair amount of activity at the state and local government levels, although here too scarce resources have been a considerable constraint. Market development initiatives at this level have three goals: 1) to assist companies with environmentally beneficial products get off the ground; 2) to help create a stable equilibrium between supply and demand; and 3) to create jobs. Strategies for meeting these objectives include grants, loans, tax incentives, and technical assistance. The great majority of states are active in most or all of the four major areas, and market-development activity is also heating up at the local level, where urban efforts are at different stages of development. Some cities are initially focusing on designing for sustainability, i.e., on creating a quality of life attractive to ecologically-oriented businesses. Other cities have built support of environmental businesses into their policy statements but have not yet developed specific initiatives, while some cities are further along. Scattered about the country, concrete programs are emerging. Philadelphia has formed a Recycling Economic Development Consortium to encourage the growth of recycling businesses in the city. San Jose has a formal Green Industries Initiative that includes an $800,000 Green Industry Loan Fund and two Green Industry Districts. Chattanooga has a multi-pronged market development strategy that includes an annual environmental conference, greening up its own act — the city built its own electric trolleys for downtown — and doing whatever else it takes to attract environmental businesses. And plans are underway to turn the East Bay of San Francisco into what amounts to a Silicon Valley for environmental technologies. Local military bases and national research laboratories scheduled for de-militarization are part of the master plan.

All in all, the momentum at the state and local levels is considerable. Still, the challenge for government at all levels these days is to do more with less. Their creativity and good intentions notwithstanding, federal, state, and local governments are spread too thin. Market-building efforts need more public dollars than they're getting.

— ◯ —

Consumers, i.e., people in their role as shoppers, represent another critically important piece of the equation. Basic economics tell us that to the extent that consumers vote with their wallets for green products, suppliers will provide them. Buy them and they will come. It seems so simple. Or did, once upon a time.

Our story begins close to a decade ago, in the flush of excitement surrounding Earth Day 1990, when market researchers grandly announced that a new creature had been discovered prowling the supermarkets of North America: the so-called "green consumer." This individual, they proclaimed, would transform the consumer products marketplace, ushering in a new generation of eco-sensitive products. The green revolution had arrived, and this time it wasn't about agriculture.

However, things haven't worked out that way, not by a long shot. Green consumerism hasn't been a complete bust, but it hasn't boomed either. In the years since 1990, the movement has followed a bell curve, showing a mild rise followed by a decline that brought many of the indicators back to 1990 levels or below. For instance, 9.7% of new product introductions in 1995 made some sort of green claim, compared to 11.4% in 1990 (and a peak of 13.0% in 1993).[4] And according to the annual "Green Gauge" survey by market researchers Roper Starch Worldwide — probably the most extensively cited green-consumer poll in North America — in 1995 12% of consumers "avoid[ed] buying products from companies not [considered] environmentally responsible" compared to 17% in 1991, and 20% of consumers "read products to see if their contents are environmentally safe" in 1995, compared to 29% in 1991.[5]

Overall this track record has been quite a letdown, especially in view of the initial — and in hindsight inflated — expectations. With the exception of a few countries, most notably Germany, green consumerism — demand-side pressure — has made hardly a dent in global industrial practices.

The blame for this goes all around. The major consumer-product companies responded to the new market-research gospel by gussying up their products with green pitches — "good for the environment," "biodegradable," and so on. Most of these claims were innocuous but there were enough forays into dubiousness and deception to attract regulatory scrutiny. The resulting publicity soured many consumers on green claims.

Even when mainstream companies didn't overstep the bounds of labeling propriety, their strategies had a dampening effect on green consumerism. As discussed in Chapter 7, the consumer-product majors started introducing "greened-up" products while turning their backs on "deep-green" offerings whose identities were based on their claimed environmental assets. This took the edge off what might otherwise have become a much more significant social movement.

Not even "deep-green" product vendors were entirely free of responsibility. Their hearts were in the right place but their products were often second-rate, especially in their earliest incarnations. Many consumers tried deep-green products once or twice and then returned to their standard brand because of its clearly superior performance.

As for supermarket retailers, they were doing just fine with what they had, thank you very much, and were disinclined to cut the deep-green product vendors any slack, for instance by foregoing slotting allowances — steep up-front fees that many retailers demand to stock product on their shelves. Most deep-green product suppliers were small start-ups without much capital, and slotting fees priced the supermarket channel beyond their reach.

Retailer gullibility was another factor. In the early 1990s, market study after market study indicated that consumers would pay a premium, often a substantial one, for green products. This turned out not to be the case. When market researchers probed into people's willingness to pay more for a green product, the so-called "halo effect" — the impulse, mentioned in the previous chapter, to seek the interviewer's approval — biased them toward answering in the affirmative. Retailers accepted at face value the market-research fairytale about consumers being willing to pay a significant premium for deep-green products, priced them accordingly — and then, when the products failed to move, dropped them like hot potatoes.

What the decade has taught us is that consumers are a fickle bunch when it comes to voluntarily taking action on behalf of the environment. Require them to do so — for instance, to recycle — and they will: the percentage of the public that claims to engage in recycling has not shown the same S-curve decline as other types of behavior. Ask them if they are concerned about the environment, and once again a high proportion of respondents will answer in the affirmative — the figure typically comes in at over 60%.[6] But ask them to make a voluntary sacrifice on behalf of the environment — for instance, by paying a premium for green products — and the universe of participants shrinks abruptly.

Roper Starch Worldwide's 1996 "Green Gauge" survey placed the total number of green consumers at 15% of the population. The "True-Blue Greens," defined as "true environmental activists and leaders," comprised 10% of consumers, and the second-greenest group, the "Greenback Greens" (who "express their commitment by a willingness to pay significantly higher prices for green products"), comprised an additional 5%.[7] And even these numbers may be high. In a 1996 survey, the Hartman Group identified the "True Naturals," comprising 7% of the population, as the "core group ... of consumers that have integrated environmentalism into their lives and are strong proponents of organic foods."[8] To my mind, these are the real green consumers — or, more precisely put, people who have made a serious attempt to cast off the "consumer" label entirely and to engage a non- (or post-) consumerist set of values.

Another 23% of the populace (the "New Green Mainstream") were characterized by the Hartman Report as "curious about environmentalism and ... receptive to overtures."[9] The study went on to state: "The primary barrier to current purchase [of Earth-sustainable products by the New Green Mainstream] is lack of availability (out of sight, out of mind), inconvenience (having to go to stores other than where they usually shop), and price."[10] In other words, make it easy and they'll do it. Maybe. These are *potential* green consumers, not the real thing. Green-consumer wanna-bes, so long as it all gets simpler and cheaper.

The bottom line is that the proportion of actual green consumers is probably fairly steady at 10% or less of the population.

— ◯ —

How are we to explain the sharp differential between the high expressed levels of concern about the environment (concern that is "vague, diffuse, and unfocused," in the words of the Hartman Report[11]) and actual behavior? In a phrase, by the difference between *issue* and *ideology*. M. Jimmie Killingworth and Jacqueline S. Palmer write:

> [T]he discrepancy ... hints that the great majority of the American people continue to see environmental protection as an issue, not as the foundation of a "total ideology" as defined by Daniel Bell, "an all-inclusive system of comprehensive reality ... a set of beliefs infused with passion" that "seeks to transform the whole of a way of life."[12]

Issues are transitory concerns: they do not inspire commitment. The vitality of an issue depends on the mood of a moment, on the stimulus of a question, on a report one tunes into on CNN. An issue in the newspaper stops being an issue after morning coffee and is entirely forgotten in the supermarket.

Ideologies, by contrast, are forever — pervasive in the sense that they drive all of a person's behavior, not just some of it. The Hartman Report's "True Naturals" are green ideologues: the members of its "New Green Mainstream," by contrast, are just flirting. By most estimates, up to 40% of Americans are indifferent to the environment. Among the great majority of the remaining 60%-plus who profess to care, it is an issue, not an ideology, and issues are sometime things.[13]

As Killingworth and Palmer point out, green consumerism is important precisely because it bridges the gap between issue and ideology:

> While the various environmentalisms set their sights on distant futures ("Utopias," as [Dennis] Pirages says), green consumerism looks to the transition, offering ways of acting that reinforce the mentality of the convert and, to use the language of pragmatism, "fix belief" by making it habitual, bringing consciousness into contact with daily practice and with the body .... Green consumerism ... offer[s] a means of fixing belief on a mass scale, so that the ordinary householder and not just the environmental activist and outdoor enthusiast has a habitual way of reinforcing awareness and commitment. It takes the old habitual "stopping places" of shopping and housecleaning and treats them as "starting places" for new associations and flash points of emerging identity.[14]

Unfortunately, green products all too often tumble into the chasm that separates issues from ideology. A case in point comes from Whirlpool Corporation, which in 1993 won $30 million in a utility-sponsored competition to design a CFC-free, super-efficient refrigerator. The following year the company began to market the refrigerator to the general public in all 50 states and Puerto Rico (the design competition required the winner to market the product in the territory covered by the 24 sponsoring utilities). The refrigerator was priced at about $1,500 — about $100 over competing offerings — but Whirlpool, which had received numerous inquiries about the product, was optimistic. Two years later, the company was singing a different song. It abandoned its national marketing campaign due to disappointing sales. "[L]ike any company that has to make a living, when [a product] doesn't sell, we have to let it go," Whirlpool's Carolyn Verweyst told the trade newsletter *Business and the Environment*.[15] Although consumers are somewhat likelier to pay a green premium for high-ticket items such as cars or refrigerators, the same basic principle applies across the spectrum of product offerings: their bucks don't match their bark.

— ◯ —

But this by no means tells the whole story about green consumerism. The additional news is both good and bad. The bad news is contextual and cultural, and lurks in the very terms "green consumer" and, more generally, "consumer." This is how market researchers typically describe what once were called "members of the public" — or, better yet, "citizens." The term "consumer" neatly redefines the individual as … *a person who buys stuff.* This linguistic insult is troubling in its own right, and doubly so when we consider the extent to which it has gone unnoticed by the press and public. Culturally, we seem to take for granted that this is an accurate and appropriate self-identity.

This variation on the Cartesian theme — "I buy, therefore I am" — has troubling repercussions. It limits our relatedness to products, and in so doing strips away our moral and civic dimensions — the dimensions that bring us into relationship with other people and the world, with all the attendant responsibilities. It neuters us in a quite fundamental way, and then lulls us into forgetfulness by showering us with … *things.* Not even the most environmentally conscientious person among us is a "green consumer." We are, or need to be, "green citizens."

Let me give a concrete and personal example of what I mean. For the last three or four years I have met socially and informally every other week with a group of men. A year ago I moved, so that I now must drive an hour and a half to participate. Clearly there are benefits in these regular meetings — friendship, community-building (of a sort), and so on. If I were to gauge my participation through the lens of green consumerism, I would not be able to find anything objectionable in it — I'm not buying anything, after all. As a *green citizen*, however, I am compelled to consider the possibility of abandoning this biweekly pilgrimage, agreeable as it is. As I drive from my home in the Hudson River valley to Connecticut, I use up gasoline and spew carbon into the air. And so I find myself asking questions like: Do the benefits outweigh the costs? If I thought of my responsibilities solely in the context of what I buy, the fact that I drive an energy-efficient Honda Civic would have "cleared me" for the trip.

As a consumer, my moral responsibility is limited to the products I buy. As a citizen, it extends to every choice I make — such as the choice to drive an hour and a half to hang out with my friends. By re-defining us solely as what we buy, our culture encourages us to lead commercially excessive and morally simplistic lives. Most of the talk of green consumerism, well-intentioned though it is, misses this critically important point.

As for the good news, if we take as our point of departure the actual state of consumer environmentalism in North America in the late 1980s, rather than the (inflated) hopes for green consumerism that attended the movement's emergence a year or two later, we find that in addition to the disappointments recounted above there has also been significant progress. For one thing, the environment is now a buying consideration for many shoppers. In the euphoric early days of the green-consumer movement, it was widely believed that shoppers would pay extra for green products, i.e., that the environment would be a first-tier buying consideration alongside price, performance, and ease-of-use. Although things didn't work out that way, the environment *has* settled in as a second-tier buying consideration for most of the everyday consumerist public. The first-tier concerns of price, performance, and ease-of-use being equal, consumers will opt for the environmentally superior product. Recalling the labeling for "dolphin-safe tuna," some environmental-marketing wags put it this way: "The tie goes to the dolphin." That's modest but real headway.[16]

Another hidden positive lies in the fact that at this point virtually every school has some kind of environmental education program, and this is creating a generation that is much more environmentally aware than its parents. Standard market-research surveys don't register this fact because they poll adults.[17] In one poll by Environmental Research Associates, 23% of parents reported avoiding a product because their children said it was bad for the environment. As today's kids move into adulthood — and assuming their environmental ardor doesn't fade — statistical levels of environmental commitment can be expected to rise, possibly dramatically.

Finally, although the size of official green consumer segments has declined of late, green *values* are steadily penetrating mainstream culture. Readers may recall a much-publicized 1993 article in the prestigious *New England Journal of Medicine* which reported that holistic and other alternative therapies had been tried by over one-third of the public.[18] More recently, research underwritten by the Merck Family Fund found that over 25% of respondents had "in the past five years …

voluntarily made changes in their life which resulted in making less money" in order to have "a more balanced life." Not only that, but over 80% of respondents agreed that "we buy and consume more than we need."[19]

Other tantalizing data items come out of the natural products sector, where sales grew 22% in 1995 and 26% in 1996, according to the trade publication *Natural Food Merchandiser*.[20] Not only that, but these sales are by no means confined to natural product stores. *Private Label*, another trade magazine, reported in its March/April 1996 issue that sales of natural foods in supermarkets grew almost 20% from 1994 to 1995. The study, based on Infoscan supermarket scanning data, determined that natural foods were the sixth fastest-growing category of the 243 tracked. (Water filters were the fastest growing, with a 55% growth rate.[21]) Sales of organic foods in the mass market have also been growing sharply, increasing by over 22% in both 1994 and 1995 to a total of $210 million.[22]

Another hint of change comes from the success of natural product supermarket chains like Whole Foods and Fresh Fields, which are spreading rapidly through the country. Supermarket-sized but with a strong natural-product orientation, they offer a bridge to consumers who are drawn to green products but prefer the convenience of supermarket shopping.

— ◯ —

What we have, then, are surveys indicating that levels of green consumerism are flat or receding, and other evidence that people are increasingly seeking alternative therapies and buying "natural" products. What are we to make of this apparently contradictory information? Part of the explanation is to be found in how we define "green consumer." If we define green consumers as people whose personal ideology is based on their environmental beliefs, that helps make sense of the contradiction — lots of "dating," not much "serious commitment."

There is a more substantive explanation as well. Something is happening here, Mister Jones, and it has relatively little to do with shopping or even, for that matter, the environment. Largely unnoticed by the media, a fundamental cultural transformation is taking place. In intellectual circles it is a commonplace to observe that we have come to the end of the modernist era — hence the term "post-modern." But for some reason that awareness seems not to have trickled across to the worlds of social and market research. Yet the intellectuals are correct. The modernist institutions that throughout this century formed the bulwark of our society are widely perceived as lacking authority and credibility, hence the widespread cynicism about such things as corporations and government and allopathic medicine. Gun-toting militia members and mantra-chanting devotees of acupuncture may seem to have little in common, but they share something quite fundamental: an avid distrust of modernist institutions. The increasing numbers of these and other similarly disposed cohorts point to a phenomenon about which the *New York Times* (the modernist publication of record) and the inside-the-Beltway crowd (the modernist power brokers) seem remarkably oblivious — the spectacle, all around us, of modernist institutions wavering and toppling over.

Why is modernism dying? For a very simple reason: the world has changed, and once effective modernist strategies now no longer work.

The modern nation-state no longer works.

The modern United Nations — basically a federation of nation-states — no longer works.

Modern management principles such as the "organization man" and highly-controlled, top-down information flows no longer work.

Modern command-and-control regulation only sort of works.

Our modernist, resource-intensive industrial system no longer works, not if "working" is understood to include thriving natural and human environments. In fact our current crisis of unsustainability is the smoking gun, the ultimate proof positive that the modernist way of doing things no longer works. Or rather, that the world is governed by modernism, and no longer works.

People may not be able to articulate it in so many words, but around the world the awareness is building that modernism is largely bankrupt as a principle of sociocultural organization. I suspect that the intuition is more pervasive among those who don't hold positions of power, largely because political and corporate movers and shakers tend to be blinkered by their investment in the *status quo*. Hence the curiously schizophrenic discourse about what's wrong with this country, as the spokespeople for modernism — the walking dead, only they don't know it — try to explain the malaise through a lens that's flawed (only they don't know it), while in parallel a sort of *vox populi* dialogue takes place — on local access TV, not on CNN — that treats being fed up with modernist structures as a given.

Moralists like the neo-conservative William Bennett propose that things will get better if we can only muster up some of that good ol' time virtue, but arguments like this, while not without merit, miss the point. Which is: change happens. Not because people are short on moral fiber, but because, as the Bible itself reminds us, everything has its season. And the modernist season is over.

It is a badly-kept secret that we are in an interregnum between the death of the old and the birth of the new. While no one quite knows what the phoenix that is rising from the ashes of modernism will look like, one thing is certain: it will differ in important ways from what we have known. The implications of this can make for a shattering insecurity, if we allow ourselves to head in that direction. Our so-called "leaders" — the people upon whom we have traditionally relied to deliver us into a safe future — are riding something much bigger than they can control or even understand. Arrogant or naïve leaders may continue to operate in the belief that they're in control of the ship, but sharper ones know better.

Sarah Van Gelder is the editor of *Yes!* magazine, a publication that tracks the emergence of a post-modern — and positive — future. In 1996 she interviewed Mark Luyckx, a member of the Forward Studies Unit of the European Commission, a think-tank within the administration of the European Union in Brussels. Luyckx offered a compelling metaphor:

> The change we're seeing is a drastic, profound, and very important change. The political leaders are not the organizers of change; we are caught up by the depth and the rapidity of the change. We had not foreseen that.
>
> Nobody has mastery over the change. No one. The image that comes to my mind is that we are in a big truck, and the steering is not responding, the accelerator is pushed to the floor and won't release, and the brakes are not functioning. And a lot of indicators are flashing red: ecological, social, industrial, also violence in the streets, problems in schools and universities.
>
> Now beside the steering wheel that's not working is another steering mechanism, a post-industrial one, that's still in its package. No one has dared unwrap and use it. Our challenge is to learn quickly and use it, otherwise the truck could go off the road.
>
> Living partly in an industrial society and partly in a post-industrial society is not comfortable. You have to master your own anguish as a politician to be able to tell people the truth about that, and it's not easy. It's also difficult to talk about these issues and still get votes.[23]

In this transitional period, it is only the dense or defended who do not experience a profound malaise about the current state of the world, only the dense or defended who do not cast about for new solutions. Militia members find one in radical libertarianism ("No more modernist Big Government!"). Devotees of acupuncture find one in "meridians" and "*ki* energy" ("No more modernist medicine!"). Advocates of local self-reliance discover one in small-scale businesses ("No more modernist corporations!"). Whatever the focus, whatever the solution, the basic impulse is the same — to embrace a set of beliefs that will put an end to the hegemony of modernism.

It is in this broad and dramatic context that phenomena like green consumerism and consumer environmentalism are best understood. Most of the market research misses the forest for the trees. The issue isn't so much whether people "shop environmentally" as the extent to which they are what social researcher Paul Ray calls "Cultural Creatives" — people who are leading the transition into post-modernism, who in Ray's words are "coming up with most [of the] new ideas in U.S. culture, operating on the leading edge of cultural change."[24] Green consumers are whitecaps, superficial symptoms of a powerful sea change.

As important as top-down efforts to build infrastructure are, they can seem quite trivial when set against the backdrop of the grand cultural shift that is occurring. The transformation that is taking place can be supported but not fabricated. Its scope is too massive for that; it emerges from too-great depths. It is happening, and will continue to happen, without much regard for conscious human intervention one way or the other. Infrastructure-building strategies are extremely valuable, but they are like fertilizing a garden — there to support a natural process but incapable of creating it *ab novo*. And in this case the organic process that is taking place is the transition into the uncharted and hopefully sustainable waters of a post-modern, post-industrial culture.

10

The Data Game

Oh, how much is today hidden by science!
Oh, how much it is expected to hide!
— Friedrich Nietzsche

S ELF-PRESERVATION," wrote American founding father Alexander Hamilton, "is the first principle of our nature."[1] We humans seek out security as naturally as flowers turn toward the sun. However, it is not only our physical selves that need to feel secure. We create myths, share dreams, devise theories, and traffic in narrative, and we hunger for security in this "noetic" realm, too. Life is all flux and flow — surprises both pleasant and unpleasant await us around every corner. The mind tries to protect itself from the insecurity of the future by, so to speak, not going around the bend, by creating a world whose inhabitants — concepts all — are immutable and therefore, in a sense, fixed in time. *Et voilà:* the sanctuary of eternity! Inside the mind not even "change" changes: change is a construct, not a motion, and its meaning remains constant. The philosopher Henri Bergson put it this way: "The human intellect feels at home among inanimate objects, more especially among solids, where our action finds its fulcrum and our industry its tools; ... our concepts have been formed on the model of solids; ... our logic is, preeminently, a logic of solids."[2] In the life of the mind, security takes the form of what is fixed and unchangeable.

And that, in a word, is knowledge as it is conventionally understood — as verities that are fixed and unchangeable.

Our sources of knowledge, however, have changed dramatically over the centuries. In the Middle Ages, it was religious faith that provided people with their moorings. Life might be nasty, short, and brutish, but at least there was order in the heavens, a purpose to it all. In the 16th century along came a new form of knowledge — science — and with it a new sort of faith. Since then, science has established itself as one of our main sources of security. This is no wonder, given the increasingly secular nature of our age and the extraordinary and largely positive transformation scientific inquiry has wrought in the human condition. But the emergence of science as a source of knowledge has not been solely a blessing. "When we say 'science'," writes Wyndham Lewis, "we can either mean any manipulation of the inventive and organizing power of the human intellect: or we can mean such a thing as the religion of science, the vulgarized derivative from this pure activity manipulated by a sort of priestcraft into a great religious and political weapon."[3]

In its cheapened form, science becomes an ideology, and ideologies are always suspect. Why? Because they are driven by a need for emotional certainty that will brook no obstacles. It rolls over everything in its path — including, where necessary, the search for truth.

So powerful is this need that it can make science itself unscientific. In their headlong rush to suckle at the breast of Mother Science, people abandon the orderly, analytic thought processes upon which the scientific method itself is premised. And this, in a nutshell, describes the fatal flaw of scientism, which is, essentially, science recast as ideology.

Those who fall victim to the scientistic fallacy commit two logical lapses in particular. The first confusion involves the boundary between the objective and the subjective, i.e., between the worlds of "quantity" and "quality." While the scientific method is extraordinarily effective at elucidating principles about the nature of objective reality, it is basically useless at doing the same for subjective reality. Scientific ideologues tend to deal with this limitation in one of two ways. Either they ride roughshod over the boundary between objective and subjective in the irrational belief that scientific methods will work perfectly well in that domain — a sort of scientific imperialism — or they simply deny the existence of subjective reality entirely, thereby committing the sort of ontological reductionism that creates what Ken Wilber calls a "flatland" worldspace.

Whereas this first confusion involves what might be described as the horizontal "reach" of science, the second involves its "vertical leap" — how high it can go, how many empirically accurate answers it can actually provide. Scientific ideologues tend to assume that science is up to just about any challenge — that it can deliver a sort of secular equivalent of papal infallibility. Unfortunately, this is not the case, not by a long shot — certainly not, as we shall see, in matters environmental.

Measurement has a hugely important role to play in the

business/sustainability domain. Corporate executives need to measure their progress relative to established baselines and future goals. Corporate watchdogs, investors, and others need to be able to benchmark the environmental performance of one company to that of other companies as well as to industry norms. Public officials and other concerned citizens need to be able to effectively assess risk — for instance, with regard to hazardous waste sites. All this is done by measurement. Unfortunately, the measurement state-of-the-art is sadly lacking. Many eco-measurements give only approximate directions, while other measurements are not available at all. As a result, we cannot be positive that our choices, which are based on the science of measurement, are actually taking us in the right direction. To some extent we are flying blind, and there is nothing we can do about it.

Scientific ideologues are terrified at this thought and resist it with a passion, thereby setting into play a critically important conflict that pits those who think scientistically (and who may or may not be scientists) against those who think scientifically (and who may or may not be scientists). This conflict as well as strategies for nurturing alternative valuation systems that reduce our reliance on strictly empirical measurement are the subject of this chapter.

There are three basic reasons why measurement is as problematic as it is: 1) gaps in the state-of-the-science; 2) too much subjectivity; and 3) problems of normalization. Let's examine each in turn.

Gaps in the State-of-the-Science. Measurement has two components — collecting data, and assessing them. Sometimes the required data are not available because we lack the tools to collect them or because we don't know what data we need to collect. In other cases, the data are available but our knowledge base isn't up to telling us what to make of them. In each instance, the basic problem is the same: the state-of-the-science isn't sufficiently advanced.

Problems like these tend to be exacerbated when the situation calls for the projection of consequences over time. Consider, for instance, global climate change, where models projecting the consequences vary immensely — the current state-of-the-science is simply not up to saying where global climate change will take us 50 or a 100 years from now.

Even if we sharply limit our spatial and temporal focus — to a hazardous waste site, say — the best that risk assessment, which is the relevant science, can do is provide very general statements about what may happen.

Too much Subjectivity. We humans are intrinsically unreliable —
biased, emotional, unpredictable. Our eyes and ears deceive us constantly. We make mistakes, then we go out and make them again. The
good news is that we know these facts about ourselves all too well. That
is why we seek out methods for safeguarding ourselves against our frailties. Science is one such method. It is a system for discovering objective
truth, a mechanism for protecting us against ourselves.

In the limited sense that it is primarily a technique for insulating us
against the consequences of our fallibility, measurement — rigorous
measurement — is also a science. But it is by no means as objective as
we would like to believe. The barrier between objective measurement
and our subjective biases is constantly being breached.

One reason for this is our need for *boundaries*. We never measure
everything. Something is always off the map — A and B get measured, X
and Y do not. Determining boundaries is a subjective human decision,
and it strongly affects the measurement process.

Let's say, for example, that we want to measure a corporation's environmental performance. Immediately this raises a host of boundary
issues. Should we limit our analysis to the company's waste and emission outputs? Shall we also include input data such as materials
consumption? What about corporate policies such as the existence of a
written environmental policy statement? If so, how deeply into policies
should we go? Should we include an environmental education program?
How about environmental philanthropy? The outcome of our analysis
will depend on where we set our frame.

Or let's say we want to assess the risks associated with a hazardous
waste site. In large measure, our conclusions will depend on which
chemicals we choose to analyze.

Framing the measurement is not the only layer of subjectivity that
we impose on the process. Numbers, measurements, are only that —
numbers. We have to figure out what they mean, and this too is a subjective process.

At one level, *data interpretation* can be very straightforward. If emissions of a certain toxic chemical are 10,000 units in Year 1 and 1,000
units in Year 2, we can safely say that this represents a decrease of 9,000
units. This is strictly mathematical: in no way are we contaminating the
process with subjective judgments.

However, many measures of corporate environmental performance
don't lend themselves to this sort of value-free calculation.
Environmental performance evaluations cover two categories of corpo-

rate activity: 1) *results* — wastes, emissions and the like; and 2) *process-es* — a company's policies and practices. Many "results" are directly quantifiable — returning to our earlier example, we can say with confidence that the value of our reduction in emissions from 10,000 units to 1,000 units is 9,000 units. With environmental processes, however, measurement is not so easy. What is the value of a corporate environmental policy? Or an environmental educational curriculum? Or a Design for Environment program? The only way to establish the worth of processes like these is by arbitrarily assigning a value to them. There are no external referents — our valuations travel directly from brain to paper. Our judgments are inescapably subjective.

Not only that, but dig beneath the surface of results measurements and things start getting murky there as well. Let's take our example of a reduction in emissions of chemical A from 10,000 to 1,000 units. We know this "means" a reduction of 9,000 units, but what in turn does this reduction "mean?" To find this out, we must probe further by asking questions like: What is the value of any resulting reductions in danger to human and ecosystem health? What is the value of the peace of mind experienced by people living near the plants as a result of the reduced emissions? Again, any answers will necessarily be subjective.

Furthermore, some results don't naturally lend themselves to objective measurement. Let's say a telecommunications company runs cable through a rainforest. How does one measure any resulting reductions in biodiversity? Or let's say a clearcutting operation indirectly causes a nearby river to silt up, thereby reducing the salmon spawn. Impacts like these are very difficult to quantify. And even if we *do* manage to do so, that quantification remains a fabrication of the mind.

Yet another source of contamination is *data aggregation*. Let's say a results analysis produces 25 measurements. We could list them all separately, but that would annoy the many stakeholders who simply want to know what the numbers "mean" — the environmental bottom line.

How are the needs of these people — senior management, investors, green consumers, environmental activists — to be met? By the straightforward but by no means simple expedient of aggregating those 25 data items into a readily digestible number or cluster of numbers.

In his presentations, Frank Consoli, formerly an environmental executive with Scott Paper, likes to show a slide depicting a sign that reads "Entering the town of Hillsdale." Immediately below are several rows of figures. "Population — 15,000." "Elevation — 2,000 feet." "Established — 1800." And then: "Total — 18,800."

That this is a nonsensical outcome is, of course, precisely Consoli's point. Simply aggregating dissimilar data items makes no sense at all. A different and more sophisticated series of operations is required. Grades must be given each of those raw data items relative to a goal or standard, and then those grades must be weighted against each other based on a subjective assessment of the relative importance of the categories.

As we climb up the performance-measurement chain, this weighting process must be repeated over and over again. Wastes must be weighted against other wastes, emissions against other emissions, total results against total processes, and so on. The more we try to compress our data into a single all-inclusive number, the more our analysis becomes saturated with subjective evaluations.

As if all this contamination were already not more than enough, there is another set of problems as well. This one involves *personal values,* as distinguished from the less emotionally-charged "valuations" discussed above.

Let's say a risk assessment has produced two possible strategies for dealing with a hazardous waste site. Strategy A poses a 1 in 1,000 risk to humans and a 1 in 2 risk to wildlife. Strategy B poses a 1 in 100 risk of damage to both humans and wildlife. Which strategy do we adopt? Our choice will depend on the relative value we ascribe to humans and wildlife.

Or let's say a town composts its sewage sludge and proposes to make it available as fertilizer to local farmers. At the same time, the farmers are considering selling out to a golf course developer. Some members of the community may lobby for the golf course, based on various unconscious assumptions they make — golf courses symbolize wealth and are therefore desirable, golf courses are green and therefore environmentally superior, compost comes from sewage and is therefore unhealthy, and so on. Other neighbors may argue for a different outcome based on a different set of assumptions (compost is "natural" and therefore good, golf courses are status symbols and therefore objectionable, and so on). Although the debate may ostensibly be about environmental risk, at this level it is about something else — about symbols, about self-image, about values.

Problems of Normalization. It is rarely enough simply to measure something on a stand-alone basis. More often, we need to compare equivalent items — one product's performance against another, say, or one company's performance in the current year versus its performance in a prior year, or one company's performance against another's.

In all these cases, we need to be certain that we are measuring apples against apples and oranges against oranges, and this is not easily done.

Consider, for instance, Scientific Certification System's *Environmental Report Card* (ERC), which is discussed at greater length later in this chapter. At one point in its evolution, this label displayed the environmental burdens of a given product in the form of a bar chart on the product's packaging. To help consumers evaluate the information, Scientific Certification Systems considered displaying the ERC of the product in question alongside that of a "typical" product. But what precisely is a "typical" product? There is only one way to answer that question: subjectively. Not only that, but — how are we to define the product category? Are water-based paints to be compared against other water-based paints or against solvent-based paints as well? How we define the category — again, the boundary we set — affects the location of our midpoint; and, by extension, the impression created by documents like the ERC.

Similar problems arise in attempting to compare corporate performances. Even subtle differences between companies can make a comparison inapposite. Imagine two companies, identical in all ways but one — Company A has a vertically integrated supply chain, while Company B uses outside suppliers. Company A will show higher levels of environmental burden because its environmental supplies are part of the calculus. But this variation will reflect a difference in strategy, not in environmental performance. To get a truly accurate measure of how the companies stack up against each other, one would have to factor in the performance of Company B's suppliers, and this in turn would open another can of worms — how much of the suppliers' environmental performance? Only that portion directly attributable to the materials and services produced for Company B? What about environmental "overhead?" And so on.

Even the seemingly mundane operation of comparing companies within specific industry categories is problematic. Again, let us imagine two companies, identical in every way but one: Companies C and D are both mining companies, but Company C has a software subsidiary. Company D will probably score worse on an environmental rating, but again that rating is misleading. Company C is not only a mining company, it is also a software company, and software companies have lower environmental burdens. And of course there is no industry category for "mining companies with 4% of revenue derived from software sales."

— ○ —

The measurement conundrum extends to risk assessment, an important emerging science with extremely broad applicability: pesticide usage, site selection and remediation, the evaluation of existing and new technologies, corporate risk reduction and management programs, and the identification of emerging ecosystem hazards, to name a few. Yet for all its utility — and despite its indisputable methodological rigor — risk assessment is a problematic discipline. Why? Because the measurements it produces are fraught with uncertainty. Like a gun loaded with buckshot, risk assessment produces a broad pattern, not a single hole — a range of possibilities, not a definitive conclusion.

A typical risk assessment proceeds through a four-step sequence. Each phase is riddled by uncertainty, and in combination that uncertainty is compounded.

The first stage, *data evaluation and hazard identification*, determines what materials should be included in the assessment. Sources of uncertainty at this stage include the accuracy of the sampling program that determines which chemicals to include in the risk assessment, and the health impacts, either individually or cumulatively, of excluded chemicals.

The second stage, *toxicity (or dose-response) assessment*, examines the health impacts of the included materials. Among the sources of uncertainty in this phase are the availability of data on the chemicals in question — extensive toxicity data are currently available for only about 600 out of over 70,000 chemicals used in commerce; and the reliability of available toxicity data (for instance, the extent to which research findings based on experiments on mice can be mapped onto humans is not yet clear).

Exposure assessment, the third stage of risk assessment, attempts to determine who is at risk. Uncertainties arising at this stage include the accuracy of models calculating how the chemicals will migrate from the site or how populations might otherwise be exposed.

The last stage is *risk characterization*, which aims to assess the likelihood of adverse consequences. Risk is typically defined in terms of an equation: Risk = (Severity of Consequence) x (Probability). The conclusions reached in stages 2 (toxicity assessment) and 3 (exposure assessment) are combined into a single characterization of risk that typically takes the form of "Site X represents a 1×10^{-x} excess lifetime risk." This process compounds any errors built into the earlier stages and also fails to account for any additional risk caused by chemical interactions.

As if this catalog of uncertainties were not enough, there are two more problems: — *variability*, and *pure uncertainty*.

Variability refers to the substantial differences that exist within any population. If we have five people, one may weigh 100 pounds, another 200 pounds, and so on. These differences, this "variability," will affect the risk exposure of each individual. The 200-pound person is less likely to be at risk when exposed to a chemical than the 100-pounder. Risk assessments do not account for these individual variations.

As for *pure uncertainty*, let's say we have two people whose basic physical attributes are identical — same weight, same gender, same complexion, same age, and so on. External appearance does not tell us anything about the idiosyncrasies of individual reactivity — these two people may respond very differently to the same exposure. Just as there's no accounting for taste, there's no accounting for individuality. People are truly unique.

Put all these uncertainties together, and they add up to a tentativeness of conclusion that defies belief. Uncertainty in risk assessments typically runs to *two to three orders of magnitude,* i.e., they are *only accurate to within a factor of 100 to 1,000.* "The odds of your getting cancer from that hazardous waste site around the corner are somewhere between one in one thousand and one in one million" — that is about the best risk assessment can do. Small wonder, then, that risk-management expert Rao Kolluru says, "We make environmental decisions based on what we don't know more than on what we know."[4]

The extraordinary levels of uncertainty inherent in risk assessment were made dramatically clear during the brouhaha surrounding Intel's defective Pentium computer chip. As recounted by *Rachel's Environment and Health Weekly*, the way the company chose to address the crisis was not to "[b]ite the bullet and offer to replace all those chips ..." but "to maintain silence and do a risk assessment."[5]

According to Intel's analysis, *Rachel's* went on to report, "'average' computer users would only get wrong answers once every 27,000 years of normal computer use. A 'heavy user,' such as an accountant or financial analyst, might see an error once every 270 years."[6] Based on this risk assessment, Intel announced that "the flaw is not meaningful for the vast majority of commercial PC applications."[7]

IBM saw the matter differently. Two weeks after Intel's attempt to soft-pedal the problem, IBM announced that it had conducted a risk assessment of its own and would be halting all sales of computers containing Intel's Pentium chip. According to IBM, *Rachel's* reported,

... a large company running 500 Pentium-based computers might get 20 errors every day. Thus IBM's risk assessment concluded that the Pentium problem was roughly 400,000 times worse than Intel said it was .... A scientist might say that the risk assessments by the two companies differed by more than 5 orders of magnitude — a large difference indeed ....[8]

Rachel's went on to inquire:

Who are we to believe? If two of America's most resourceful corporations, analyzing a well-defined arithmetic problem in a computer chip about one inch square, get answers that differ by a factor of 400,000, what hope is there for reaching agreement on the hazards posed by a huge, complex machine like a solid waste incinerator, a nuclear power station, or a petrochemical processing plant? Clearly, risk assessment is not a tool for reaching true and reliable conclusions ....[9]

Rachel's then discussed a major study of risk assessment that was conducted by 11 European governments at the end of the 1980s and published by the Commission of the European Communities as the *Benchmark Exercise in Major Hazard Analysis* in 1991. The participating countries, *Rachel's* wrote,

... established teams of their best scientists and engineers and set them to work on a single problem: analyzing the accident hazards of a small ammonia storage plant. Private companies like Rohm & Haas, Solvay, Battelle, and Fiat contributed experts as well. The results were stunning: the 11 teams varied in their assessments of the hazards by a factor of 25,000 — a difference of more than 4 orders of magnitude. Analyzing the hazards of a single small plant handling only one chemical, these world-class experts reached wildly different conclusions. For example, the individual risk at the "refrigerated storage site" was calculated by one group of experts to be one-in-400, but by another group of experts to be one-in-10-million.[10]

These accounts make it eminently clear how extraordinarily uncertain a science risk assessment is.

— ○ —

The term "good science" has been much abused of late. In its pure form, if such a thing can be said to exist, the "good science" movement proposes to ground the environmental policy-making process in "sound" or "good" science. Taken at face value this makes good sense: one would have to be overtly, irrationally anti-science to take a different position. But "good science" has come to have a more dubious meaning as well. In the mouths of representatives of conservative business interests, it has become a code word justifying green-bashing and the dismantling of federal environmental protections.[11]

Advocates of this vulgarized version of "good science" make the by now familiar error of assuming that science — "good science" — can produce certainty. They position Science (capital-S science) as a sort of techno-truth serum — Inject and Thou Shalt Know. But science isn't a magic bullet; and it is also the wrong tool for the job. The scientistic bias would "rationalize" the political decision-making process, and while there is much to be said for encouraging people to think in a clear and orderly manner, we must not let science — and certainly not scientism — imperialize the political domain. Ours is a democracy, more or less, and this requires us to operate by consensus. In order to bring everyone into the consultative process (or at least to give the impression of doing so), we cut a corner here, a little slack there — we diverge where necessary from the straight and narrow path of "rationalization." Moreover, even if we could rule by fiat (scientific or otherwise), we could still not have a fully-rationalized policy-making process for the simple reason that the current state-of-the-science does not come even close to providing definitive guidance. Like it or not, in the final analysis it is up to us — uncertain, subjective us — to determine our directions.

This is an age of rapid change, of overwhelming uncertainty. To the extent that science holds out the promise of "truth," it also holds out the promise of certainty. There is solace in that — but the flight into certainty is also a flight into irrationality, for it takes only a moment's objective reflection to realize that science does not have all the answers.

Nowhere is this irrationality more evident than in the "good-science" movement's embrace of risk assessment, which is regularly trotted out as one of the prize exhibits in the "good science" armamentarium. (For instance, making risk assessments and cost-benefit analyses mandatory for all new regulation has been a lynchpin of the so-called "regulatory reform" movement.) The new role contemplated for risk assessment is, to put it mildly, misguided. Not only does it badly overestimate the state-of-the-science — we have seen how little guidance risk assessment actually provides — but it also thrusts science into a role for which it is not suited. Policy-making is not intrinsically a scientific activity, i.e., it is not about the pursuit of an objectively discoverable truth, but about helping to keep our democracy afloat by integrating multiple perspectives into final policies. It is an exercise in negotiation, in diplomacy, in consensus-building, none of which is the stuff of scientific inquiry.

In what can only be interpreted as a grand exercise in wish fulfillment, the good citizens of "good science" have positioned risk assessment as a great gleaming sword that cuts through emotionality and uncertainty and delivers clear answers and directions. The more apt analogy is the Peter Principle, as the proponents of the new scientism confer upon risk assessment an authority far beyond its qualifications.

— ◯ —

There are four valid alternatives to the over-reliance on science and quantitative measurement, and they are all being actively pursued. The first of these might be called: *an emphasis on consensus.* Earlier in this chapter we saw that our capacity to measure and compare environmental outcomes leaves much to be desired. But this does not mean we have no choice but to throw up our hands and walk away. There is much that we can do within the boundaries set by our uncertainty. We can make the best possible policy — not the *right* policy, for that is unknowable, but the best possible policy under the circumstances. To do so, however, requires us to abandon the notion that the science of measurement — or any science at all, for that matter — can provide a detailed road map that frees us of the burdens of uncertainty. Science must be positioned as a servant rather than as a dictator of public policy.

What is called for, in the final analysis, is a human-oriented, not science-oriented policy. In the absence of certainty, *consensus* becomes the compass for environmental policy-makers, if only by default. Collaboration and cooperation within a community-oriented context become paramount. If we cannot be sure of our directions, at least we can agree on where we *want* to go — and work as a team to get there.

In the business/sustainability arena, the contrasting philosophies of two small U.S.-based environmental labeling organizations, Washington-based Green Seal and Oakland-based Scientific Certification Systems (SCS), as they evolved in the earlier years of the decade provide a clear case study in the consensus- and science-oriented approaches. Our focus is on the 1993-1995 time period, when SCS was showing its Environmental Report Card (ERC), since somewhat amended and renamed the Certified Eco-Profile.

The public-policy benefits of labeling environmentally superior products are straightforward — such labels make it easier for consumers to "shop green." In theory, this gives businesses with green products a competitive advantage, which in turn inspires companies to compete on the basis of their products' environmental performance. Germany (then West Germany) introduced the first eco-labeling program, the Blue Angel, in 1977, and there are now about 20 programs worldwide. These programs are federally funded in every country but the U.S., where it was left to Green Seal and SCS to do the heavy work of developing acceptable methodologies and building marketplace support. It has been a struggle for both organizations: for all practical purposes, eco-labeling in the U.S. has not gotten off the ground.

Temperamentally and philosophically, the two organizations were and remain as different as night and day. Green Seal was founded by environmentalists; SCS was launched and is run by Dr. Stanley Rhodes, a toxicologist. Green Seal is a straightforward non-profit; SCS is for-profit. And whereas Green Seal has publicly embraced consensus, SCS has leaned heavily on hard science.

Because much of the debate between SCS and Green Seal involves the field of life-cycle analysis (LCA), let's begin with a brief overview of that area. The aim of LCA is to measure the environmental burdens that are generated by a product and its related processes on a "cradle-to-grave" (or "cradle-to-cradle," if the materials are reused) basis. For every stage in the product life-cycle (material acquisition, manufacturing/processing, distribution and transportation, and disposal or reuse), LCA measures environmental "inputs" (energy and raw materials) and "outputs" (water effluent, air emissions, solid waste, and so on). Despite its technical-sounding name, LCA is a very rough science, a useful but highly subjective tool for measuring eco-impacts.

At this point we come to a confusing but inescapable terminological subtlety, namely the difference between life-cycle *analysis* and life-cycle *assessment*, which is the subset of life-cycle analysis that aspires to scientific rigor. The latter term ("life-cycle assessment") has been coined by the Society of Environmental Toxicology and Chemistry (SETAC) to describe a formal process for quantifying environmental burdens, determining their impacts on human and ecological health, and minimizing their impacts. SETAC divides life-cycle assessment into three stages:

- *Life-Cycle Inventory* — environmental inputs and outputs are quantified.

- *Life-Cycle Impact Analysis* — the effects of these environmental burdens are characterized and assessed.

• *Life-Cycle Improvement Analysis* — a systematic evaluation of the strategies available for reducing the environmental impacts identified by the impact analysis is carried out.

Although fairly rapid progress has been made in recent years, formal SETAC-style life-cycle assessment is still in a relatively early theoretical stage. While the state of the art for formal life-cycle inventory is fairly well along, useful impact and improvement analyses are not yet feasible.

Even at the relatively advanced inventory stage, formal life-cycle assessment is problematic. For one thing, it is constrained by a severe boundary problem. Let's say a company manufactures a product that incorporates a certain mineral. Few people would disagree that the eco-impacts of extracting that mineral from the Earth's crust should be included in the life-cycle assessment. But what about the environmental impacts of manufacturing the machinery used to extract the mineral? How about the energy required to transport the miners to and from the mine? Or the environmental impacts associated with disposing of mine tailings? Thus we find ourselves back in familiar territory: our conclusions depend on where we set our boundary.

Another problem involves the variable relationship between environmental *loads* and environmental *impacts*. Let's say a factory discharges a given quantity of effluent into a river. The amount is fixed — so much discharge goes into the river daily. But the impact of that discharge may vary depending on the depth of the river, i.e., it may be much more harmful to aquatic life when the river is low than during flood season. Life-cycle inventory doesn't measure impacts at all, much less subtle variations of this sort.

A third problem with life-cycle assessment concerns the indeterminate nature of the relationship between different types of environmental loads. To continue with our example, let's suppose that management decides to reduce the amount of effluent being discharged into the river. As things turn out, however, this can only be done by increasing the amount of energy consumed, a move that increases air pollution and produces greater environmental loads at the materials-extraction end of the life-cycle. What to do? To answer that question with any certainty, management would have to be able to compare the relative impacts of Alternative A (lower effluent, higher energy consumption) against those of Alternative B (higher effluent, lower energy consumption). They would need a scoring system that produced a single rating. But no database for rating environmental loads exists.

Someday, hopefully in the not too distant future, sophisticated systems for performing truly scientific life-cycle assessments will become available. In the meantime, corporate managers — and eco-labelers as well — must make do with vastly more subjective life-cycle analyses.

With this brief overview of life-cycle analysis and life-cycle assessment for background, let's return to Green Seal and SCS. Green Seal embraced subjectivity as a fact of life and proceeded from there. The organization rejected formal life-cycle *assessment* as a public-policy instrument and elected to rely instead on the vastly more subjective life-cycle *analysis.*

In the words of eco-labeling analyst Roger Wynne, Green Seal's stance "...demonstrates an ambivalence toward, if not outright suspicion of, more quantitative decision-making tools."[12] Using publicly available data, Green Seal identifies selected areas of significant environmental burden for a given product category and then uses life-cycle analysis to address any outstanding questions regarding relative environmental impacts. These essentially technical activities take place within an unabashedly subjective context. Wynne writes:

> Green Seal staff, sometimes with the help of outside advisory panels and consultants, make tradeoffs and value judgments to draft standards that focus on those factors that provide significant opportunities to reduce pollution and other negative impacts on the Earth. Thus, Green Seal promises only to make decisions that are grounded in available technical information, somehow influenced by quantitative, life-cycle data, and ultimately based on qualitative assessments.[13]

Once draft standards have been established, they are subjected to notice-and-comment procedures that mimic the federal rule-making process.[14]

Whereas Green Seal made consensus, not the pursuit of a higher, empirically-derived "truth," its first priority, SCS clung to the belief that it could deliver scientific objectivity. Its vision was essentially one in which a mechanical "good science" spewed out unimpeachable data that SCS, in the role of information handmaiden, organized and passed on to the consumer. It was a model that relied heavily — indeed, excessively — on life-cycle assessment and, more specifically, on life-cycle inventory.

SCS's Environmental Report Card (ERC) presented detailed life-cycle inventory information about a product in the form of a bar chart listing 18 so-called "critical environmental burdens."

The ERC had its fair share of supporters, most conspicuously in the hardware industry, where Home Depot was a prominent defender. But it also drew much fire. The Environmental Defense Fund's Richard Denison was sharply and loudly critical.[15] So was Roger Wynne's 1994 analysis, which called the ERC "fundamentally flawed" in its use of life-cycle inventory and "extremely troubling" as an instrument of public policy.[16]

The ERC reflected a misguided faith in the power of quantitative data. Not only did SCS rely heavily on a database that was well over a decade old, but the company's strategy for filling in data gaps was overly ambitious. Roger Wynne put the matter gently:

> ... SCS betrays a sanguine view of conducting LCIs [life-cycle inventories]. This optimism seems particularly inappropriate in light of the awesome amount of data that its complete "cradle-to-grave" inventories will require. Although SCS will place some nominal bounds on the systems it defines for its studies, it still seeks to account for all inputs and outputs for each system. This presents an extremely formidable task to SCS, which proposes to collect current, high-quality, site-specific data for a wide array of systems, studying each system for an entire year and updating that information annually. Despite SCS's self-described "aggressive recovery approach," the challenge remains daunting.[17]

In addition, the need to compress detailed life-cycle inventory data into a limited series of ERC bars created severe data-aggregation problems. Commented Wynne:

> Even assuming that SCS could collect all relevant, high-quality data, subjective steps would still compromise the supposed objectivity of SCS's methodology because compressing data into an LCI that fits on a product label necessarily involves choices, and such choices necessarily involve subjective judgments....[18]

SCS's Environmental Report Card pretended to objectivity but did not achieve it. It was "scientistic," not scientific, and as such emblematic of our cultural enchantment with the Siren of Science.

— O —

A second way to avoid asking too much of the science of measurement is by focusing on *processes* rather than on *results*. That is, rather than measure (or attempt to measure) the environmental burdens themselves, measure the *management systems* whose efficacy goes a long way toward determining the level of those burdens.

This is what ISO 14001 does with its focus on management systems, and it is also the direction in which forest-product certification is headed. Whereas eco-labelers examine the impacts of the *product* in question, forest-product certifiers focus on the systems and practices of the *company* that produces the wood, thereby sidestepping many of the issues associated with life-cycle inventory. It is much easier to determine whether a management practice or system meets a predefined standard than it is to, say, quantify levels of erosion. This eyes-on-management approach helps sustainable-forestry certifiers dodge the quicksand of quantitative measurement.

What it fails to do, however, is let performance be compared on more than a superficial (i.e., certified or not-certified) basis. As noted earlier, from a public-policy perspective it is important to be able to benchmark companies against each other as well as against their own past performance. Simply certifying that a management system meets a certain standard does not allow this to be done.[19]

Another emerging approach attempts to split the difference between pass/fail certification and detailed quantitative measurements. Eco-Rating International, a Swiss company with U.S. headquarters in Pasadena, California, grades companies on a scale of -5 to +5, with grades of +4 or +5 signifying a level of performance that will compromise economic performance, at least for the near- or medium-term. Companies that hire Eco-Rating can make use of their grades as they wish — for internal use, to attract green investors, or for general marketing purposes.

More recently, White Plains, NY-based Benchmark Environmental Consulting has developed a system that rates the extent to which the behavior of transnational corporations conforms to the recommendations of Agenda 21, as measured by their codes of conduct and published environmental guidelines. To some 30 categories of behavior in four general areas (global environmental management, environmentally sound production and consumption, risk and hazard elimination, and full-cost accounting), Benchmark assigns one of four grades: 1) "distinguished contribution"(★); 2) "full commitment" (●); 3) "partial conformity" (▲); and 4) "not mentioned" (o). Both Eco-Rating International and Benchmark Environmental have the same goal: to build a successful consulting practice out of the sizable and to date completely unmet demand for useful, reliable measures of corporate environmental performance.

— ○ —

A third way to account for the subjective quality dimension is by measuring for it quantitatively. While philosophically conservative and intrinsically problematic — we have seen that quality resists translation into quantity — this approach does at least take the critically important first step of acknowledging that quality is a consideration that warrants measurement.

As we saw in Chapter 6, Noranda Inc. has developed a set of corporate sustainability principles. Well, when a corporation has principles, it needs to measure for them, and this has brought Noranda squarely up against the challenge of measuring for sustainability — and, more specifically, the hard-to-quantify subjective aspects of sustainability. For instance, Noranda's principles call for the company to "foster constructive dialogue with interested parties" — but how do you measure for that? As of this writing, the final decision hasn't been made but it looks as if Noranda's basic answer will be, by counting — 12 public meetings this year as compared to 10 last year, 18 communications with environmental groups as opposed to 15 last year, and so on.[20]

There are obvious shortcomings to this approach. Noranda's reliance on numeric quantification is badly reductionistic. The number of dialogues with stakeholders is a useful indicator of commitment, but it tells us absolutely nothing about the *quality* of those conversations. Still, Noranda *is* acknowledging the importance of the subjective dimension and making a serious effort to measure for it. That's progress.

Similar "translation" strategies are being implemented around North America by the many communities that are developing sustainability indexes. Toronto, Seattle, Jacksonville, and Minneapolis are among the major North American cities that have launched projects in this area. Nationwide, there are currently about 150 initiatives to develop sustainability indicators.[21] Community strategies for quantifying the social aspect of sustainability include such measures as divorces involving children, runaways per 1,000 children, the amount of gardening activity, public library book circulation per capita, and public participation in the arts. All of which suggests that in many cases the subjective dimension of experience *can* be captured quantitatively, at least to some degree.

— O —

T he fourth and most radical way to measure for quality is by straightforwardly assessing subjective performance without trying to force it onto the procrustean bed of hard numbers. This is the approach for which The Body Shop has opted. In its *Values Report*

1995, the company's first plunge into sustainability reporting, the company acknowledged the difficulty of measuring for sustainability: "One thing that stands out in this social audit process is the difficulty of measuring the intangibles," the document has CEO Anita Roddick and her husband Gordon saying. And elsewhere: "[W]e need to find a new qualitative instrument to measure human development...."[22]

In a companion document, The Body Shop calls for "new techniques" that go beyond technical devices such as life-cycle assessment and eco-efficiency:

> These techniques may borrow from existing management theory and practice, including techniques used in environmental, health and safety, or quality management and auditing. But business will need a broader and more holistic set of values, together with systems for implementing those values, if it is to make a genuine commitment to sustainable development. A paradigm shift is needed, complete with methodological underpinning.[23]

What The Body Shop calls "integrated ethical auditing," as embodied in its Values Report, is a first crack at this new approach. The document, which contains separate "statements" on the environment, social issues, and animal protection, basically steers clear of trying to pull off any "quality-into-quantity" alchemy. It quantifies what is straightforwardly quantifiable — e.g., the amount of paper recycled, the percentage of employees availing themselves of the company's policy of providing paid time for community service — and doesn't try to force the square peg of social impacts into the round hole of hard numbers. Instead, it relies on subjective stakeholder input to assess its performance in the field.

Philosophically, this is a hugely important step. It cuts the management decision-making process loose of the umbilical cord of statistics to which it has been attached for the greater part of this century. In relying on the mechanism of *social feedback* rather than the scientific (or pseudo-scientific) rigor of hard numbers, The Body Shop's Values Report represents a radical and crucial departure from the standard business approach to measurement.

It remains to be seen how many companies will follow The Body Shop's lead, and how soon. Corporate executives are very leery about subjective measurement generally, and they also tend to be horrified at the thought of turning over control of anything, including assessment, to a bunch of outsiders — all the more so when they're not even members

of a respectable guild! Given these antipathies, it is unrealistic to antici-
pate rapid movement in the direction of subjective outside assessment.

There is a countervailing pressure at work, however. The increasing
recognition of the need for effective alternatives to strictly empirical,
quantitative measurement is a cultural phenomenon and by no means
limited to The Body Shop alone. The field of education is representative.
"Grades" as we know them did not exist until 1792, when they were
instituted at Cambridge University at the suggestion of an otherwise
unremarkable tutor named William Farish. For Neil Postman, this was a
most significant event:

> [H]is idea that a quantitative value should be assigned to human
> thoughts was a major step toward constructing a mathematical concept
> of reality. If a number can be given to the quality of a thought, then a
> number can be given to the qualities of mercy, love, hate, beauty, cre-
> ativity, intelligence, even sanity itself. When Galileo said that the
> language of nature is written in mathematics, he did not mean to include
> human feeling or accomplishment of insight. But most of us are now
> inclined to make these inclusions. Our psychologists, sociologists, and
> educators find it quite impossible to do their work without numbers.
> They believe that without numbers they cannot acquire or express
> authentic knowledge.
>
> I shall not argue here that this is a stupid or dangerous idea, only that
> it is peculiar. What is even more peculiar is that so many of us do not find
> the idea peculiar....[24]

To Postman's observations about grades — that they are an artifact of
modernism, and an oddly reductionistic one at that — we might add
that they teach a wrong lesson, too. Grades train students to be outer-
directed rather than inner-directed in their learning, i.e., to derive their
satisfaction through awards proffered by others rather than through the
learning process itself.

The emerging educational philosophy known as "lifelong learning"
attempts to remedy this by making learning a value in and of itself, irrespective of external recognition. So does another emergent, the
so-called "Alternative Assessment" school, which focuses on the development of methodologies for evaluating performance that focus on the
actual learning that takes place, rather than on how well one does at traditional testing. By no means is this interest in subjective learning the
dominant thread in the educational community, but it is not off the map
either. For instance, the College Board, which is the most prominent

educational testing institution in the U.S., is exploring these alternatives quite seriously.

This trend also extends to the field of law, where, according to the *Wall Street Journal*, "[Stanley] Smith is the high-priest of 'hedonic damages' urging juries in death-related law suits to award huge sums to the estates of victims deprived of the pleasure of life. Usually, payment in death cases is based on what the victim might have earned in the future. But life is more than a paycheck, argues Mr. Smith: 'We are worth more than we earn.'"[25]

All of which is a quite predictable response to the demise of modernism. The image all this leaves us with is one of conflict, with the cultural momentum swinging toward subjective measurement and the corporate community virtually without exception digging in its heels against the trend. Lengthy habituation with quantitative measurement, terror at the loss of control implied by subjective assessment, the incapacity to relate emotionally or intellectually to the need to measure quality — all these factors help explain the resistance. But this sort of tension tends to get resolved, or at least reduced, and in this case this will probably happen in part as a result of a broad corporate bending-in-the-wind — bending always being better than breaking. For the foreseeable future, we can expect more and more companies to develop and implement quantitative measures for assessing performance in the subjective "quality" arena, much as Noranda has done. In so doing, they will be following the lead of the many communities that have developed tolerably effective, quantitatively-oriented sustainability indexes.

Down the road, as a new set of cultural values takes hold, perhaps we will see the widespread implementation of more radical strategies for assessing the subjective aspects of performance. And then again, maybe not. Remember Bergson's admonition about the human intellect feeling most at home among solids: subjective experience is intrinsically vaporous and insubstantial, and perhaps for that reason will always be resisted.

Meanwhile, pending the resolution of that question, we seem to be on the way to getting half a loaf. For that, we should probably be grateful.

11

From Here to Sustainability

Where there is no vision, the people perish.
— Proverbs 29:18

I N THIS BOOK, we have seen that both corporations and consumers deliver mixed signals in terms of their commitment to the environment and the larger cause of sustainable development, and that a host of structural, institutional, and cultural factors contributes to the lack of progress. Clearly it will not be easy to find a way past all these hurdles. But much that is positive is occurring, too. Models and tools are emerging that will enable individual corporations and our global industrial system to operate much more sustainably. In addition, entire industries are slowly but surely shifting toward sustainability, like super-tankers coming around in the open sea. This chapter surveys these more positive developments: the models, tools, and transitions that collectively give us reason to hope for the emergence of a sustainable future.

Y ou can't solve a problem at the level at which it was created, Albert Einstein is reputed to have said. Applied to sustainability, that means we can't retrofit our way out of our current dilemma, i.e., we can't use the same linear, non-holistic approaches that created the global *problématique* in the first place. What I called in Chapter 6 "Principle #2 of the Fourth Era of Corporate Environmentalism" — whole-system thinking — is required, and that is precisely the approach that the industrial design team of German chemist Michael Braungart and U.S. architect William McDonough has taken. What they propose, in essence, is that all products be designed so as to be waste-free.

If this sounds simple, it is. Still, to understand their concept fully, we must get a better understanding of their non-ordinary definition of "waste."

For Braungart and McDonough, waste isn't what remains after the useful life of a product (and its various components) is complete. It consists, rather, of all end-of-life outputs that are not *organic nutrients*, i.e., "food" for a natural system, or *technical nutrients*, i.e., "food" for an industrial system. Compost is an example of food for a natural system, while the materials in, say, a computer — precious metals, plastics, etc. — are food for an industrial system.

There are no neutral quantities here. If something is not an organic or a technical nutrient, if in other words it is waste, then it is also — by definition — a poison. Why? Because all waste eventually makes its way back into the natural system, and, as in the human body, any buildup of non-nutrients in an ecosystem is by definition toxic.

Another way to put this is that waste is bad because it reduces "quality," i.e., because it reduces the complexity, usefulness, and efficiency of the system or process in question. In this sense, *zero waste* is a variation on the Total Quality Management theme of "zero defects." When waste is designed out of a process, you have advanced well beyond the "end-of-pipe" (compliance) and even "front-of-pipe" (eco-efficiency) approaches to environmental management. You have instead what McDonough calls a "no-pipe approach." "You don't filter smokestacks or water," he says. "Instead, you put the filter in your head and *design the problem out of existence.*"[1]

McDonough is proposing something very important — an aggressive re-definition of Design for Environment, a lifting of its Do-it-Right-the-First-Time mentality beyond the relatively narrow confines of eco-efficiency and into the broader domain of sustainability.

Can zero waste work in the real world? An award-winning collection of textiles designed by McDonough suggests that the answer may be yes. To identify appropriate materials for the project, he and Braungart ran some 8,000 chemicals through a sustainability filter that screened for carcinogenicity, teratogenicity, and mutagenicity.[2] In the end, only 38 chemicals — less than one-half of one percent of the total — passed muster. Using this modest list of environmentally acceptable chemicals, McDonough designed the DesignTex line, and with great success despite these seemingly severe constraints: it received the 1995 NeoCon award as the best fabric of 1995 and found its way into the permanent collection of the Chicago Athenaeum. Strictly speaking, this wasn't a zero-waste product – the chemicals were petrochemically-derived dyes that could not healthily be re-introduced to the environment – but it did represent a huge advance over product-design-as-usual.

What if the list of permissible chemicals had been such that even the best designers couldn't work with it to create a beautiful and useful product? For McDonough, there is only one possible answer to this question. Don't loosen the sustainability filter. Instead, climb up the design hierarchy and come up with a new way to satisfy the need in question. Don't fudge the parameters. Redesign.

In McDonough's view, the benefits of a universal zero-waste industrial-design ethic will be more than ecological. They will be esthetic ("How can something be beautiful if it makes you sick?") and socio-structural as well: do away with waste, and the need for regulation goes. What an improbable "win-win" outcome: an end to all that big-government oversight, and a healthier environment too!

At this point, let us pause for a moment and imagine that McDonough's no-pipe dream has come true and we have arrived in a zero-waste world. In ways it is almost unrecognizable. Industrial processes are super-efficient; regulation is either non-existent or a rusty relic of historical inefficiencies. So boggling are these transformations that, returning to the present, we cannot help but wonder if it is realistic to conceive of such a radically transformed system coming into being at all, much less in the relatively near future. For McDonough, the answer is an unequivocal yes. "Revolutions happen fast," he says. "Only ten years ago, who could have predicted the end of the Cold War and of the Russian communist state and of apartheid in South Africa?"[3]

Furthermore, there is a compelling business rationale for shifting to a zero-waste industrial economy. The reason, in a TQM-word: *quality.* "We got access to those 8,000 chemicals because a major chemical company let us inside their door," says McDonough. "Why did they do that? Because they understood that our analysis would help them. It would help in their pursuit of quality."[4] How so? Because less waste means more quality — *environmental* quality — and quality is a key to competitive advantage in the global marketplace.

We are still at the very beginning, but the idea of zero waste is beginning to take hold. Günter Pauli's Zero Emissions Research Initiative, which was discussed in Chapter 6, is premised on the belief that "[a]fter the quest for zero defects and zero inventory, zero emissions will become a standard objective for industry over the next decade .... [I]n 20 years zero emissions will have become the standard."[5]

No-pipe design isn't an idea whose time has come. Not yet. Not quite. But it is on the way.

— ○ —

Imagine, if you will, a ship — a very large ship — on the ocean. Its destination: a port called Sustainability. Among the thousands upon thousands of passengers on board are a handful who have carefully calculated their position and determined that the ship is off course. If these passengers decide to head off in the right direction, they will not get very far. It will be a few steps and splash! — sharks and a watery grave. They are as much prisoners of the ship as they are passengers, and have little choice but to go where it takes them.

Similarly, corporations' freedom of action is constrained by the larger industrial system of which they are a part. There is only one way to help these companies, only one way to "set them straight": by re-orienting the ship on which they are traveling.

From this perspective, initiatives such as Design for Environment, which are usually internal to a company (or to a company and its relatively narrow matrix of suppliers), have a quite limited capacity to produce change. What is required is for the basic principle of DFE to be applied simultaneously to a great many corporations. In other words, it's not enough just to redesign a product (or products): you have to redesign the entire industrial system.

Ambitious? You bet. And once again, McDonough and Braungart are at the forefront of efforts to re-conceptualize the industrial rules of the game. Zero-waste products and processes, it turns out, are only one piece of a larger puzzle.

By way of explanation, consider the following thought-experiment. Granted that the goal is to eliminate the dispersion of waste, i.e., non-nutrients, into the environment, the following question arises: What economic structures will optimize the odds of success? An elegant answer comes from Michael Braungart, who has erected what amounts to a conceptual shelter around the shrine of zero waste by proposing, essentially, that products be divided into three types. First, *consumables* — products which, once we are done with them, become organic nutrients: an organic cleaning product in a biodegradable bottle, or a hamburger in a compostable wrapper. Second, *products of service* — products which, once their useful life is complete, are recycled as technical nutrients. For the most part, these are so-called "durables": appliances, electronics and the like. Finally, there is everything that remains — so-called *unsaleables,* such as dioxins, that are neither organic nor technical nutrients and that are therefore pure, unadulterated waste. Ideally, these unsaleables would be designed entirely out of the product/service system. However, pending the arrival of that zero-waste Promised Land, the best option, Braungart argues, is to make the producers of unsaleables responsible for safeguarding them until such time as it becomes possible to dispose of them safely by upgrading them into organic or technical nutrients.

Nor is this the only change Braungart envisages. Just as unsaleables would remain the property of the producer, products of service, i.e., technical nutrients, would remain the property of the manufacturer. That is, non-organic products would be *leased* instead of *sold*.

The shift to a lease-based economic structure makes sense for three reasons. First, it simplifies the challenge of product stewardship enormously. If the raw materials remain the property of the manufacturer, that puts an end to the many logistical problems associated with "returning to sender" when there are multiple owners. It also shifts the enterprise from a *product* (or *manufacturing*) focus to a higher-level *service* orientation. This means jobs, and jobs are critical components of sustainability in a world where one billion people are currently unemployed but are eager to work, and another two billion people will be entering the market over the next 20 years.[6] Finally, when the link between product sales and profits is broken, new and more environmentally favorable business missions often emerge. Earlier we saw how chemical consumption at a General Motors factory decreased when the supplier's compensation was geared to overall productive output rather than the amount of chemicals consumed. Similarly, when utilities switch from selling energy (a *product* orientation) to providing energy-management services (a *service* orientation), overall energy consumption declines. And when a pesticide company shifts from the (product-based) business of selling chemicals to the (service-based) business of helping maximize long-term yields, its focus switches from peddling pesticides to managing the fields sustainably, and pesticide usage declines.

There is a compelling business rationale for the service-based approach as well. Currently, businesses buy raw materials, convert them into products, and then give up ownership and control of those products and their embedded materials by selling them. By the current system of reckoning, the faster a company loses control of its products and materials, the more successful it is! Now let's suppose the same company does not relinquish ownership and instead retains control of those materials. As McDonough points out, this produces two benefits: the materials are transformed into an asset on the company's books, and also into a source of competitive advantage by virtue of their being stockpiled. From McDonough's vantage point, the current approach is wildly irrational. Instead of materials being exploited as an asset, "the money goes into a hole in the ground [in the form of waste], where it toxifies."[7]

To be sure, the lease concept is not new. AT&T leased its telephones for much of this century, when it was operating as a monopoly. And on a much more moderate (and more ecological) note, in the 1970s the Witkar electric car "utility" in Amsterdam took the novel approach of leasing cars by the minute. Convenient pick-up and drop-off locations were scattered throughout the city; subscribers used a car for as long as they needed but never took ownership. All the players benefited: customers paid only for actual use (and nothing for parking), the utility maintained control of the fleet, and downtown Amsterdam enjoyed less pollution and congestion.

Fast-forwarding to the present, in 1995 Interface Inc., a privately-held $1 billion manufacturer of industrial carpeting tiles, introduced its Evergreen Lease, under which it maintains control of its carpeting, replacing individual tiles as they wear out. Theoretically, this too is "win-win": the customer is freed of maintenance obligations and gets carpeting that consistently looks new, Interface maintains control of the product and embedded raw materials, and the sustainability cause gets the benefits of the service orientation — more jobs, drastically reduced consumption of raw materials, and so on.

In launching the Evergreen Lease, Ray Anderson, founder and chairman of Interface, led with his heart: the company still has to figure out how to recycle its carpeting cost-effectively. The concept is less than perfect for other reasons as well, not least of all because it poses a threat to other participants in the product-development and distribution cycle, ranging from designers to retailers. Nor does Interface's carpeting meet McDonough's "no-pipe" sustainability standard. But Anderson is moving forward on that front as well, having hired the designer to help the company reach its goal of becoming one of the world's first zero-emission companies.

Meanwhile from the world of business *praxis*, a separate set of forces is also beginning to build a powerful case for a service orientation. The prospect of product takeback legislation is forcing companies into a product stewardship mode wherein they manage their products on what has come to be known as a "cradle-to-cradle" basis. In addition, corporate customers are requiring manufacturers to assume end-of-life responsibility for the disposition of their products. For instance,

Interface's three main suppliers of nylon fibers — BASF, Du Pont, and Monsanto — have all established carpet-recycling initiatives due to pressure from institutional clients.

While the combination of institutional and regulatory pressure has not yet snapped companies out of their sales-oriented mindset, leasing is such a logical response that mass migration to a service framework seems a real possibility for the future.

— ○ —

The proposals of McDonough and Braungart address, at a system level, a *technical* sustainability issue — the ongoing consumption of natural capital. Only indirectly do they target the equity aspect of sustainable development. However, provocative work to directly target sustainable development's equity component is occurring as well. One particularly exciting strategy is *micro-credit*, the granting of modest — often tiny — loans to entrepreneurs living below the poverty level. The average micro-credit loan is $150, and they can run much smaller than that. Most banks won't touch loans at this level — administrative oversight is a fixed cost, and at that level it eats up any profit. Enter micro-credit to fill this financing gap.

In large measure the concept owes its existence to the pioneering work of two individuals: India's Ela Bhatt, who in 1975 launched the Self-Employed Women's Association with a loan of $1.50 to a woman to buy herbs for resale, and Muhammad Yunus of Bangladesh, who in 1976 founded the Grameen Bank by loaning tiny sums to 42 poor people. Today, the bank reaches two million borrowers, has lent over $1 billion, generated $18 million in savings, and helped inspire a worldwide movement that in the words of journalist Paula DiPerna "...is a global and heterogeneous industry consisting of hundreds of financial institutions and micro-credit banks reaching roughly eight million people in both developed and developing countries and handling billions of dollars a year."[8]

The data suggest that micro-credit really works. In El Salvador, 380 villagers who borrowed funds from the Foundation for International Community Assistance increased their weekly incomes by 145%. A study by the U.S.-based Aspen Institute found that 68% of participants in seven U.S. micro-credit programs increased their household incomes by 25% over a three-year period, with 42% registering an increase of about 75%. The programs are effective for the lenders as well: payback rates typically exceed 90%.

The first global Micro-credit Summit, which was held in Washington D.C. in February 1997, established the goal of reaching 100 million of the world's poorest families by the year 2000. While this will not be easy to achieve, major institutions are starting to take notice and even to come on board. The United Nations Development Programme has launched Microstart, a $41 million micro-financing program. In 1995, the World Bank allocated $32 million over three years to its Consultative Group to Assist the Poorest, a micro-credit initiative. The Inter-American Development Bank has committed $400 million to micro-credit over the next five years, and the U.S. Agency for International Development earmarked $120 million a year in 1996 and 1997.

Corporations are starting to show interest too, with the philanthropic arms of Citicorp, Monsanto, and MasterCard International each having provided $100,000 grants to help underwrite the summit.

For the summit's ambitious goal to be reached, or even approached, it will be necessary to secure considerably more support from mainstream financial institutions, and there will have to be massive progress in micro-credit infrastructure-building as well. In the meantime, micro-credit has already been shown to be a viable strategy for helping to address the social-justice side of the sustainability equation.

Strategies like "no-pipe design" and micro-credit are macro-level models intended to operate at the level of the overarching financial-industrial complex. But the pursuit of sustainability also calls for strategies at the individual institutional level, and these too are emerging. *The Natural Step* is one such tool. The movement was born in Sweden, where it has enjoyed an extraordinary measure of success. With the support of the king, a mass mailing consisting of a color booklet and an audiocassette explaining The Natural Step's framework for sustainability was sent to every school and household in Sweden, reaching close to nine million people. The Natural Step organization sponsors an annual Youth Parliament on the Environment in which as many as 150,000 Swedish students have participated in an interactive video teleconference. In 1994, 40,000 students participated simultaneously in a Natural Step board game, qualifying for the Guinness Book of World Records. The Natural Step's impact on business has been substantial as well: over two dozen leading Swedish companies, including internationally-known ones like IKEA and Electrolux, use the Natural Step to map their environmental and strategic directions.

How did The Natural Step become the toast of Sweden? Through a combination of three factors — the extraordinary will and commitment of Karl-Henrik Robèrt, a physician and cancer researcher by training, who is the charismatic force behind the movement; the good fortune of having been launched in one of the environmentally progressive countries in the world; and the power of a good idea.

At one level, The Natural Step is an uplifting personal story, testimony to the ability of a single determined individual to make a difference in the world. An environmentalist by disposition, Robèrt's training and work as a cancer researcher only strengthened his intuitions about the interdependence of natural systems. Again and again he observed how the human body could only tolerate certain levels of toxicity without expiring. From there it was a small step — a "natural step" — to draw the same conclusion about the larger organism that is the planet. From Robèrt's perspective it was really quite simple: keep degrading the *quality* of systems by loading them down with useless (or, worse still, harmful) stuff, and sooner or later — the exact date was unknown but the outcome inevitable — a "junk threshold" would be crossed, with disastrous results.

Central to this model is the notion of "quality" — but "quality" uniquely defined. The second law of thermodynamics tells us that the world is winding down, i.e., that structures of greater complexity are breaking down into structures of lesser complexity, and that these substructures are in turn breaking down in a regression that will eventually return the planet to the inorganic chemical soup whence it came. At the same time, however, matter is evolving into structures that are ever more complex and efficient and elegant. It is these attributes — the sophisticated (and interdependent) architecture of living systems — that Robèrt has in mind when he speaks of "quality." And it is precisely this quality which is at risk through the progressive junking of the planet.

It was speculations like these that in 1988 led Robèrt to write a paper attempting to define the basic conditions for sustainability. He distributed it to colleagues in the scientific community, and it came back heavily edited. Many of his assumptions, it seemed, were incorrect or in dispute. Robèrt revised his paper and sent it around again, and once more it came back heavily redlined. Yet another time he tried to winnow out what was not agreed upon, and once again his revised draft proved inadequate. Thus began an extended review process that did not end until it had gone through fully 21 iterations. What remained at the end was a paper whose contents the entire Swedish scientific community agreed upon. The impossible had been achieved: there was now consensus on the basic conditions for sustainability.

From this document there emerged what Robèrt variously calls a "pedagogy" and a "compass" — a tool, in short, that helps steer institutions and individuals toward sustainability. The strength of The Natural Step lies in its simplicity — or, more specifically, in what Robèrt calls "simplicity without reductionism." It distills sustainability into four basic principles, which it calls "system conditions."

System Condition #1: *Substances from the Earth's crust must not systematically increase in nature.* Essentially, this means that the by-products of fossil fuels, metals, and other minerals must not be spewed into the air and water. "In practical terms," Robèrt writes, "this means: radically decreased mining and use of fossil fuels."[9] From there he proceeds to a challenge: "Does your organization systematically decrease its economical dependence on underground metals, fuels, and other minerals?"[10]

System Condition #2: *Substances produced by society must not systematically increase in nature.* Non-degradable materials such as plastics and toxic chemicals such as dioxins "must not be produced at a faster pace than they can be broken down in nature or deposited into the Earth's crust .... In practical terms this means: decreased production of natural substances that are accumulating, and a phase-out of all persistent and unnatural substances."[11] And again Robèrt challenges companies: "Does your organization systematically decrease its economical dependence on persistent unnatural substances?"[12]

System Condition #3: *The physical basis for the productivity and diversity of nature must not be systematically deteriorated.* This principle focuses on the need to maintain high levels of fertility and biodiversity: "[T]he productive surfaces of nature must not be diminished in quantity or quality, and we must not harvest more from nature than can be recreated .... In practical terms this means: sweeping changes of our use of surfaces in, for instance, agriculture, forestry, fishing and planning of societies. Does your organization systematically decrease its economical dependence on activities which encroach on productive parts of nature, e.g., long road transports?"[13]

System Condition #4: *There must be just and efficient use of energy and other resources* (particularly tricky because of its values orientation). "Basic human needs," Robèrt writes, "must be met with the most resource-efficient methods possible, including a just resource distribution."[14] This requires two sets of changes: sharp increases in technical, organizational, and environmental efficiency as well as what Robèrt calls "a more resource-economical lifestyle" (reduced consumption, in other words) in wealthy countries. This brings Robèrt to his challenge: "Does your organization systematically decrease its economical dependence on using a large amount of resources in relation to added human value?"[15]

The four system conditions are *non-negotiable*: violate any of them and by definition you are behaving unsustainably. Despite this requirement (which Robèrt argues is derived from natural laws, not The Natural Step), the organization is quite pragmatic in its orientation. It does not call for companies to meet all four system conditions in the short term. It is enough to work systematically in their direction, to do what Robèrt calls "investing for the future."

Nor does The Natural Step claim to be a sort of eco-Napoleonic code providing companies with infallible guidance about what to do in every situation — it is a compass, not a code, and an excellent one at that. In his speeches and articles, Robèrt returns repeatedly to our collective preoccupation with issues of secondary importance, which he calls the "leaves on the tree." The Natural Step draws attention to the trunk, relentlessly reminding sustainability strategists to focus on the most basic level of inquiry.

Technically, what The Natural Step provides, in essence, is twofold: first, a clear (if in the final analysis incomplete) image of what the end goal — sustainability — consists of; and second, a filter for determining if one's decisions are taking one in that direction.

To see how The Natural Step works in practice, let's examine how ICA, a Swedish supermarket chain, used the process to decide what coolants to use in its refrigeration systems. Senior management knew that CFCs (which Robèrt calls "hard freons") should be avoided, but they were less clear about CFC alternatives such as HCFCs ("soft freons"). When placed under the lens of The Natural Step, however, it became apparent that soft freons also violated System Condition #2. Although probably less damaging than CFCs, they too were a "persistent and unnatural' substance and therefore had to be phased out. As a result, instead of switching all refrigeration systems to soft freons, ICA resolved to do so only where absolutely necessary, and then only on an interim basis. In all other cases the company would seek solutions that complied fully with System Condition #2.

But The Natural Step is not solely technical. It is also a powerful social tool, powerful in that it is a mechanism for bringing together disparate stakeholders to engage in dialogue about the broader set of sustainability issues. The Natural Step has scientific underpinnings but its premises are not at all scientist. It is a way to bring people together —

a way to create awareness and, beyond that, shared mental models. For this reason it finds application outside corporations in communities and other settings where the all-important first step is to create a dialogue. And indeed it is The Natural Step's dual personality – one part technical, one part social — that gives the organization its unusual strength.

In recent years, The Natural Step has been making the transition into an international movement. In the U.S., where the prime mover has been TNS-U.S. chairman Paul Hawken, it has embraced a de-centralized, partnership-oriented management model and is steadily becoming a more pervasive presence. A strong TNS organization has set up shop in the United Kingdom, led by Jonathan Porrit and Sarah Perkin. TNS also has an established presence in the Netherlands and Australia. Canada's program is fairly well advanced, France and South Africa are launching operations, and Japan and New Zealand are coming along as well.

The specific role of The Natural Step varies from country to country. In Sweden, where it was founded, there are very few non-governmental organizations (NGOs). The Natural Step filled this NGO gap, with the result that it quickly became quite powerful — and, predictably, drew some fire in the process. In the U.S., by contrast, NGOs number in the hundreds of thousands. The Natural Step couldn't be the proverbial 800-pound NGO if it wanted to be, and for that reason has forged alliances with a broad range of NGOs and other organizations.

In the final analysis, The Natural Step is embedded in and embodied by the people who understand and communicate its message. In my home town of Kingston, NY, for instance — hardly a hotbed of radical change — a community dialogue around the subject of sustainability is just beginning. At an early organizational meeting, a person familiar with The Natural Step made a presentation. Eventually, The Natural Step may end up providing the language and structure around which dialogue takes place. This is where the real value of the organization lies – as a potentially pervasive tool for facilitating dialogue and helping corporate and other communities assess their sustainability strategies.

— ◯ —

Yet another significant emergent is *Factor Four.* This term, along with a companion term, Factor Ten, first appeared on the business/sustainability scene in the mid-1990s, in parallel with the growing recognition that the northern industrialized companies needed to reduce their consumption by up to an order of magnitude in very short order. This led to the formation of an international group of sustainability experts, the Factor 10 Club, at the initiative of a German think tank, the Wuppertal Institute for Climate, Energy, and Environment. Since then the concept has been toned down to Factor Four, and a book of the same name has been authored by Ernst von Weizsäcker, president of the Wuppertal Institute, and Hunter and Amory Lovins, who together head the Rocky Mountain Institute (RMI), an influential U.S.-based research and educational foundation that develops innovative eco-efficiency solutions. (The American edition of *Factor Four*, this one co-authored by the Lovinses and Paul Hawken, is scheduled for publication in fall 1998 under the title *Natural Capitalism: The Next Industrial Revolution.*)

Essentially, Factor Four proposes that businesses can be four times more efficient in their use of resources than they are currently, and that they can do it *using currently available technologies*. In other words, it's not new *inventions* that are required — *fresh thinking* is. In this regard, Factor Four advocates are delivering much the same message as Braungart and McDonough — make the changes inside the head, not out there in the world.

The *hypercar*, a concept pioneered by RMI, provides an example of how Factor Four thinking can be applied to a real-world product like the automobile. Featuring ultralight, aerodynamic design and a hybrid-electric drivesystem ("hybrid-electric" because it is powered by an electric motor or motors, the energy for which is generated onboard by a small engine or other device such as a fuel cell, rather than by batteries), the hypercar is projected to get 90 miles per U.S. gallon in the near term, and eventually up to 200 mpg (That's right, Factor Four above the current 40-50 mpg maximum.) These gains in efficiency would not come with any downside: air emissions would be comparable to those of battery-electric vehicles, and there would be no fall-off from the current standard in performance, style, or safety.

Automobile manufacturers are taking hypercar design very seriously. RMI expects the vehicles to become commercially available by the turn of the century:

> Light battery-electric vehicles like GM's EV-1 production model (released in late 1996), Honda's four-seat EV (scheduled for release in 1997), and Solectria's all-composite four-seat Sunrise (1998) are two-thirds of the way there — they have ultralight, aerodynamic bodies and electric propulsion. Replace the heavy batteries with a small engine, generator, and buffer storage device and you've got a functional hypercar. Adapting an existing battery-electric vehicle would still involve many technical

hurdles — development and testing would take at least an extra year or two — but it would be easier than building a hypercar from scratch.

We wouldn't be surprised to see this sort of modified battery-electric vehicle officially come on the market by the year 2000. GM announced in November 1996 that the EV-1 will be the first of a series of battery- and hybrid-electric cars with halved weight and drag — early hypercars in all but name. Such first-generation hypercars would probably be manufactured in small volumes, and hence would be relatively expensive and not widely available; as such, they'd probably appeal more to "early adopters" than to the average motorist. However, hints from Toyota suggest that the automaker is contemplating starting production of 80-mpg Corolla-class hybrids at a rate of tens of thousands per year as early as the end of 1997, which would really fast-forward the hypercar future.

In any event, affordable, production-volume hypercars are likely to appear in the first few years of the next decade.[16]

Certainly the arithmetic of Factor Four is appealing. Currently, 20% of the world's people consume 80% of its resources. If this group were to be four times more efficient in its use of resources, then we would find ourselves with an equitable consumption ratio — 20% of the world's people consuming 20% of the world's resources. Factor Four thinking, applied across the board, makes this possible. What is required at this point is for the word — and the ingenuity — to get out.

In the previous pages, I have tried to show that innovative solutions to the global *problématique* do exist and in fact are part of the current business/sustainability discourse. And this is not where the good news ends. Entire industries are beginning to make the shift into sustainability — slowly, to be sure, but inexorably. One example comes from the all-important energy industry, which is undergoing a fundamental transformation, with boom times on the horizon for sustainable energy alternatives such as wind power, solar energy, and fuel cells.

There are four basic reasons for this market turnabout. The first is demographic. An estimated two billion people worldwide currently have no power whatsoever, and another one billion have access for only a few hours a day. In addition to testifying to the immense gap between rich and poor — in industrialized societies, we tend to yammer when a momentary power outage short-circuits our computer — these sobering figures also speak to the staggering size of the worldwide energy market. A 1995 study by the consultancy Arthur D. Little estimated that over the next 10 years developing countries would spend over $700 billion on electric supply and transmission infrastructures, and while energy forecasts are notoriously unreliable, ADL's number does give a rough sense of the market's extraordinary potential.

The second trend, or cluster of trends, is technological. Steady progress has been made in reducing the cost of sustainable energy alternatives, so much so that in some situations they are now directly competitive with conventional resources. In addition, energy technologies are undergoing the same process of miniaturization and modularization that information technologies have been going through for the past several decades. Just as computing power has migrated from the mainframe to the PC, so are energy technologies becoming smaller and better suited for local usage. Experts agree that the energy architecture of the future will be modular, with utilities managing a portfolio of technologies that includes sustainable energy alternatives and large numbers of consumers opting to stay entirely off the central grid.

The third transformative trend is the opening of the power industry to competition, both in the U.S. and around the world. Policy-makers in developing countries are increasingly coming to the rather obvious conclusion that a clunky, bureaucratic, underfunded monopoly is probably not the best way to bring electricity to the masses. In the U.S., a similar recognition — namely, that market forces cut costs and improve services — underlies the move toward market restructuring.

Finally, there is the environment itself. With scientific consensus building that global climate change represents a legitimate threat, it is becoming increasingly difficult for even harrumphing businessmen to dismiss talk of the greenhouse effect as so much, so to speak, hot air.

Wind power has been an immediate and dramatic beneficiary of the opportunities that these converging trends have opened up. In 1995, global installed wind capacity grew to more than 5,000 megawatts (MW), representing a 1,300 MW increase over 1994. For the first time, equipment sales soared above the $1 billion level. In 1996, the growth continued, with global wind capacity climbing by 1,200 MW, or another 24%. Driving this spectacular upturn have been sharp improvements in price and performance. In the U.S., the cost of wind power is down to 4.2 cents/kwh (kilowatt-hour), making it cost-competitive with traditional energy sources, while improvements in blade design, power conditioning equipment, and system electronics have made the technology vastly more efficient and reliable than it used to be.

The market for *solar power* is also thriving. Manufacturing capacity has expanded sharply in recent years, driven largely by developing-country interest in bypassing traditional non-renewable power sources. For instance, Thailand has invested $8 billion in a phone system that will be mostly cellular — and driven in large measure by photovoltaics. And in Kenya and Brazil, more homes in recent years have been electrified via photovoltaics than through the extension of the electrical power grid. In countries ranging from South Africa to Vietnam, national governments are actively supporting solar electrification. The non-U.S. market for solar technology has been growing at 30% annually for several years, and the pace is expected to continue through the end of the decade.

Interest in solar is not limited to developing countries. Over 1,000 buildings in Switzerland and Germany have been solarized under government-funded programs, while Japan, ever ready to take a good idea one step further, plans to install some 62,000 solar generators in buildings by the turn of the century. Even in the U.S., where utilities for the most part have been gun-shy about investing in sustainable energy alternatives, solar is starting to make headway as one of several renewable options within a portfolio of modular technologies.

Fuel cells are another sustainable energy alternative with exciting market potential. This remarkable technology, which was first used in the 1960s to provide electricity for orbiting U.S. spacecraft, generates power through an electrochemical process rather than through combustion. It is reliable, extremely flexible in terms of its fuel sources, and virtually pollution-free. So why doesn't everyone have one? The answer, in a word: price. The technology is in a relatively early stage of the commercialization process — the world's first commercial fuel cell factory opened for business in late 1995 — and still rather expensive.

Particularly striking about fuel cells is how improbably few the obstacles to market penetration are. Once prices decline, the sky appears to be the limit, with potential application areas including small-scale power plants, battery alternatives, and also the great white whale of the energy world — transportation. Imagine (as John Lennon might have said): the world's vehicles powered by zero-emission engines. It is by no means an impossible scenario. The spade work is already well underway, with British Columbia-based Ballard Power Systems among the companies that are developing fuel cell engines for mass transit.

This isn't to suggest that oil and gas will go off the map completely. The likelier outcome is the one projected by the improbably named Roger Rainbow, who develops long-term scenarios for Royal Dutch/Shell:

We don't see oil and gas declining for the next thirty years or so, but after that the situation may change. What will happen then? History shows that people tend to find solutions. And when we ask what those solutions will be, we find that there are at least ten potential alternative energy sources out there. Some are direct energy sources while others are energy transformation methods, ranging from batteries to flywheels to you-name-it.

Most of them are relatively new technologies, and their costs are coming down rapidly. As costs continue to decline, the niches for these products will expand and they will gradually fight their way into the market. While it's impossible to predict which technologies will prevail — that's part of the magic of the market — virtually all the winners will be what we call "new renewables" — "old renewables" being things like chopping down forests to make firewood.

We don't expect oil and gas to give up the fight easily. They have many advantages and demand will continue to grow for both of them. Thus, if you look ahead to 2040 or 2050, we expect to see an energy world that is even more complex than the one we have today, with many more competing fuels, many more niche markets and much more blurring of boundaries. It won't even be clear what the energy industry is anymore.[17]

If Shell's scenario is on target, the world won't be relying entirely on sustainable energy alternatives by the middle of the next century. But it will be doing so in considerable measure. And the shift is already beginning.

A nother industry in transition is agriculture. In a sense it's a case of "back to the future." In the time before petroleum, agricultural products — plants, in a word — provided the raw material for a host of non-food consumer products ranging from dyes to synthetic fibers to paints to plastics. Then along came "black gold," and with it inexpensive petrochemicals, and the next thing you knew, the industrial world had been turned upside-down. Among the losers: plants, whose share of the industrial materials market dipped from 30% to less than 16% between 1925 and 1989.

Now, however, without fanfare, the pendulum is swinging back to *industrial crops*. The shift has been gradual, but that doesn't make what's happening any less important or impressive. Petroleum-based economies spew carbon dioxide into the air and deposit soldiers in far-off lands. Plants, by contrast, are renewable, pollute less, and can be grown at home. In addition, industrial crops create jobs, both on the farm and in local "biorefineries" — facilities that convert plant matter into biofuels, biochemicals, and other industrial products. The range of industrial applications for agricultural products is staggering — paints, inks, and dyes; surfactants; solvents, plastics, and other chemicals; and fuel, to name just a few. Slowly but surely, policy-makers are coming to realize that a "carbohydrate economy" has distinct advantages over one that's soaked in oil.

Around the world, countries and businesses are making commitments to industrial crops, boosting demand and lowering prices. In Europe, countries are emerging as leaders in different niches. France and Austria are strong supporters of biodiesel, while more northerly countries are showing the way with regard to biopolymers. Scandinavian nations are the world leaders in terms of manufacturing capacity. Germany is an especially strong source of demand. In part this is due to regulatory policies, especially the country's strict packaging law, and in part to German consumers' demonstrated willingness to pay a premium for green products and packaging.

Nor is the interest in industrial crops by any means limited to Europe. Brazil is active in ethanol. Japan is putting substantial resources into agricultural products as specialty chemicals. And in the Philippines, the government has made a significant commitment to reducing the country's dependence on foreign oil by developing a domestic biobased infrastructure for fuels, chemicals, and materials.

As for the U.S., in a 1993 report entitled *The Industrial Uses of Agricultural Materials,* the U.S. Department of Agriculture hailed industrial crops as "one of the greatest potential market opportunities in history." That's extravagant language. But not off-the-wall, considering the timeliness of the idea. A mid-1980s USDA task force estimated that new uses for agricultural products could generate $30 billion in increased farm income in the U.S. along with 750,000 new jobs. The USDA document identified three main reasons for industrial crops' potential. First, increases in agricultural productivity, which are driving agribusinesses to search for new applications for their products. The second factor is technical: "Changes in the materials and biological sciences are reducing the costs of producing and processing renewable resources into industrial products." The third contributor is the environment: "More and more questions are being asked about the true costs of non-renewable resources. There is mounting evidence of the high environmental costs of recovering, transporting, and using nonrenewable resources...."[18]

Not that the success of the industrial crop industry was — or is — a foregone conclusion. In the products' 10 years of post-oil crisis commercialization, there have been only two clear winners in the U.S. — ethanol, with a 1.5 billion gallon/year (5.7 billion liters/year) production capacity, and soy-based inks, with a roughly 10% market share. However, if anything, the global prospects are even better than they were in 1993, when USDA issued its enthusiastic endorsement.

One reason for this is an upsurge in interest from Wall Street. "Investment companies look for technologies that aren't rocket science, and for products that can be sold directly into a currently existing market. Agricultural crops applied to industrial applications meet both requirements," says Irshad Ahmed, a bioproducts specialist with the consultancy Booz Allan & Hamilton. Wall Street's interest is paralleled by multilateral institutions such as the World Bank, which see industrial crops as a way to hasten rural economic development in lesser-developed countries.

A second factor, often indirect but no less important for that, is the globalized economy. In the U.S., one chemical company after another is looking to shed its commodity chemical business because competition from China and other countries is too stiff. Monsanto, Du Pont, Allied Signal — all are following the same trajectory. These transnational powerhouses are looking for alternative lines of business, preferably ones less environmentally burdensome than petroleum-based chemicals. Not surprisingly, they're fastening on biochemicals.

In the U.S., another important change is federal agricultural policy. The Federal Agriculture Improvement and Reform Act of 1996 essentially eliminates farm subsidies. Without the government to rely on, farmers will have to get creative — and this will mean aggressively pursuing new applications for their products.

Don't expect the worldwide biobased product market to show short-term explosive growth. Cost-effective technologies take time to commercialize, and wary customers must be weaned from familiar ways of doing business. Nor, as with energy, will non-renewable options leave the stage completely. However, with national interests in security, economic development, and environmental protection all aligned — and buttressed, moreover, by the technological imperative of biotechnology — the emergence of a substantially more extensive carbohydrate economy seems pretty well assured.

— ◯ —

The energy and bioproduct markets are examples of *evolutionary* change, i.e., of industries that are making a gradual but steady transition into sustainability as technologies evolve, costs come down, and the environmental noose tightens. But the future holds out more radical possibilities as well. Many sustainability advocates are leery of technological solutions to environmental problems out of concern that they treat the symptom while ignoring or (worse still) masking the problem. Thus the derogatory term "techno-fix"; but these anxieties notwithstanding, the fact remains that technology has a critically important role to play in the pursuit of sustainability.

Consider, for instance, the problem of zero waste. If all products could be designed and manufactured in a way that produced no waste, as per the design strategy of McDonough and Braungart, and furthermore if the great masses of accumulated waste could somehow be upgraded into organic or technical nutrients, what an extraordinary improvement in the quality of our natural systems that would mean!

If this sounds wildly fantastic, it isn't. A technology capable of both these feats may be headed our way. It is called *nanotechnology,* and if there is anything at all to the hype, it could transform the nature of manufacturing.

Historically, manufacturing has involved making things smaller — hewing out of wood, etching out of silicon. Instead of manufacturing "down," nanotechnology makes it possible to manufacture "up," atom by atom, molecule by molecule. Not only does this make it possible to manufacture a vast array of new products, but their fabrication can conform precisely to design specifications — literally down to the last atom. Whereas today's clunky bulk manufacturing technology makes compromises inevitable, with nanotech what you want is what you get, or will get.

Clearly, the arrival of a technology this powerful is a mixed blessing. Nanotechnology can theoretically be used, for instance, to build horrific weapons. But it can also do a world of good. In medicine, for instance, nanotechnology may make it possible to build devices that target cancer cells without harming their neighbors — a vast improvement over the mayhem wrought by today's shotgun chemo- and radiation therapies. In healthy people, nanotechnology-built cell repair machines may be able to identify abnormal cells and return them to their healthy state, thereby retarding ageing. As for the environment, here, too, nanotechnology could have an extraordinary impact. It may make it possible to fabricate lighter, stronger, longer-lasting materials, thereby reducing materials consumption. It may even make it possible to manufacture products without producing chemical or solid waste. Pollution is a function of inefficiency, and nanotechnology is a super-efficient manufacturing technology. The more control .over the production process you have, the less pollution you produce — and nanotechnology gives you absolute control. Nanotechnology may also make it possible to fabricate specialty products that tackle specific environmental problems head-on. One possibility: molecular cleaning devices that neutralize dangerous chemicals such as dioxins by rearranging their atoms.

As improbable as it may seem, scientists are already knocking at nanotechnology's door. Several years ago, for instance, IBM researchers constructed an image of the corporate logo using 35 xenon atoms. Even conservative technology forecasters expect commercially viable nanotech applications to be with us within 25 years, if not sooner.

Thus the "no-pipe" model of sustainability does not necessarily require the future to be no-tech, or even low-tech. "Appropriate technology," i.e., technology that is compatible with sustainability, can have a high-tech face. It may just be the wizards of nanotechnology who end up jump-starting the McDonough/Braungart vision of a zero-waste world.

Much headway, then, has been made in the development of tools and models that will accelerate the transition into sustainability. Furthermore, trends in market and technology development are favorable. But that leaves unresolved a critical issue — the matter of *collective will*. To what extent has the business community accepted the severity and immediacy of the sustainability crisis? To what extent has it resolved to take prompt and decisive action? With only the occasional exception, the business response historically has ranged from a cautious "wait-and-see" attitude to outright obstructionism. Through lobbying groups like the Global Climate Coalition, the fossil fuels industry has been doing its best to create the impression that the debate over global climate change is much ado about very little and that the scientific community is split down the middle on global climate change, neither of which is the case.

Recently, however, cracks in the industry's armor have begun to appear. In October 1996, British Petroleum (America) and the Arizona Public Service Company withdrew from the Global Climate Coalition, basically because they found the organization's positioning untenable. And in May 1997, John Browne, Group Chief Executive for BP America, gave a speech at Stanford University in which he made a quite extraordinary pronouncement:

> The prediction of the IPCC [Inter-Governmental Panel on Climate Change] is that over the next century temperatures might rise by a further 1 to 3.5 degrees centigrade, and that sea levels might rise by between 15 and 95 centimeters. Some of that impact is probably unavoidable, because it results from current emissions.
>
> Those are wide margins of error, and there remain large elements of uncertainty — about cause and effect — and even more importantly about the consequences.
>
> But it would be unwise and potentially dangerous to ignore the mounting concern.
>
> The time to consider the policy dimensions of climate change is not when the link between greenhouse gases and climate change is conclusively proven but when the possibility cannot be discounted and is taken seriously by the society of which we are part.
>
> *We in BP have reached that point.* [italics added]
>
> It is an important moment for us. A moment when analysis demonstrates the need for action and solutions.
>
> To be absolutely clear — we must now focus on what can and what should be done, not because we can be certain climate change is happening, but because the possibility can't be ignored.
>
> If we are all to take responsibility for the future of our planet, then it falls to us to begin to take precautionary action now.[19]

For several years, the insurance industry has been taking global climate change seriously, not out of general principle but because they are already being affected by it in a big way. In the 1980s, payouts for weather-related losses averaged less than $2 billion a year. From 1990-1995, they soared to over $10 billion a year — a sort of "bad news Factor Five." What makes BP's shift particularly noteworthy is the fact that unlike insurance companies the corporation isn't getting hammered financially by global climate change — the company has adopted its new stance to protect its long-term business interests and as a statement of social concern. While it remains to be seen how much the company will actually *do* in support of its position, the mere fact that the company has taken the first step of aligning itself with the precautionary principle represents a refreshing change of heart for a company with a deeply entrenched interest in fossil fuels. Shifts like this suggest that corporations have the capacity not to play ostrich, and that it is not entirely out

of bounds to hope for, in due course, the emergence of a collective —
and pro-sustainability — corporate will.

— O —

This brings us to the end of our narrative. During the course of our
journey, we have seen that the performance of business with
regard to sustainable development has been mixed. There has
been progress on many fronts, ranging from improvements in eco-efficiency to the emergence of more sophisticated communication
strategies to the still-dawning realization that sustainability, not the
environment, is the real issue, and that it is a system challenge with a
strong equity dimension. We have seen clear signs that a fourth era of
corporate environmentalism is emerging, and that many of the pieces
are in place for a rather dramatic transformation of our current corporate and industrial practices.

But the corporate community has fallen short in many ways as well.
Even as the leading edge pushes forward, most companies remain
blithely oblivious to the challenges presented by our current circumstances — and to the opportunities, too. For a complex set of historical,
structural, and psychological reasons, environmental and sustainability
issues still tend to rank low on the hierarchy of corporate priorities.

We have seen that the corporate understanding of the sustainability
challenge is lacking in another way too. Corporations tend to take an
altogether too technical and empirical view of sustainable development. They fail to account adequately for the fact that sustainability has
a subjective "quality" dimension and that this aspect of experience
needs to be honored equally alongside those characteristics that are
more readily susceptible to empirical measurement.

In adopting this attitude, the corporate community reflects the cantilevered perspective of the broader culture of which it is a part. In this
limited but important sense, sustainable development requires a deep-
level shift in cultural assumptions and values such that quality is
privileged equally with quantity, depth equally with surfaces, and the
subjective equally with the objective.

Is it merely wishful thinking to hope for such a transformation? One
is tempted to say yes, until one recalls that it was precisely such a shift,
roughly four centuries ago, that created our current cantilevered circumstances. What shifted once can shift again — and most likely will, as
we continue our transition out of modernism.

These are times that encourage us to focus on surfaces. However, when we go deeper, we find that the current hubbub of activity is taking place within the context of two parallel exercises in what the economist Joseph Schumpeter called "creative destruction."

The first of these is the aforementioned transition out of modernism, with its myriad implications for our institutions of governance and, on a more personal level, our values and self-sense.

The second is the passing of our petroleum-based industrial culture. In the colonial era of the 17th through 19th centuries, western nations amassed wealth by exploiting indigenous (and usually darker-skinned) people. In the 20th century, it was the land itself that was increasingly violated as technologies of extraction became more sophisticated and the chemical revolution took hold. The transition from people to nature was, so to speak, the next logical step in an enduring strategy of exploitation.

With each passing day, it is becoming increasingly clear that the strategy of environmental exploitation that characterized the 20th century is reaching the end of its natural life. We are in the early stages of a transition from an attitude that, in Herman Daly's felicitous phrase, "treats the Earth like a business in liquidation" to one that is committed to preserving the planet's "natural capital." The principle underlying this shift is really quite simple: if we want a high quality of life for ourselves and future generations — a high quality of life in all its senses — we cannot continue to degrade the quality of the natural systems of which we are a part.

Personally, I have little doubt that this broad historical transformation is occurring — not because *homo sapiens* is especially foresighted or clear-thinking, but because the harsh realities of the global *problématique* leave us with little choice. True, we cannot rule out the possibility that we will let ourselves fall blindly into the abyss of a post-industrial, eco-apocalyptic Dark Age. However, peril is a mighty powerful — and usually effective — wake-up call. If only for this reason, it seems to me that the really pertinent questions at this juncture focus more on *when* than *if.* Will we continue to limp and stagger toward sustainability, with the cultural and political mainstream largely oblivious to the urgency of the challenge? Or will we at some point, preferably sooner rather than later, display the collective wit and will to commit massive resources to accelerating the transition into a more sustainable industrial culture? In very broad terms, these are our two options.

Whichever path we take, I have little doubt that we will be living in a vastly more sustainable industrial society by the time the 22nd or 23rd century rolls around. But if we take the first route — the route ruled by distraction and denial and business-as-usual — the journey will be much more painful.

If one thing is certain as we stand on the verge of the next millennium, it is how little we actually know. It is beyond our capacity, for instance, to say definitively when a more sustainable culture will emerge, or how powerfully, or how much unnecessary suffering will have to be endured in the meantime. But we are far from powerless. We can do what we can to affect the outcome — we are each of us actors in the drama. And we can also stay tuned. Not to our televisions, but to our lives, and to the life of the world, as this extraordinary and critically important story continues to unfold.

Endnotes

Introduction

1 Quoted in Joseph J. Romm, *Lean and Clean Management: How to Boost Profits and Productivity by Reducing Pollution* (New York: Kodansha American, 1994), p. 28.

2 Presentation at the DeLange/Woodlands conference, Houston, Texas, March 4, 1997.

3 "In practice we all start our own research from the work of our predecessors, that is, we hardly ever start from scratch. But suppose we did start from scratch, what are the steps we should have to take? Obviously, in order to be able to posit to ourselves any problems at all, we should first have to visualize a distinct set of coherent phenomena as a worthwhile object of our analytic effort. In other words, analytic effort is of necessity preceded by a preanalytic cognitive act that supplies the raw material for the analytic effort. In this book, this preanalytic cognitive act will be called Vision. It is interesting to note that vision of this kind not only must precede historically the emergence of analytic effort in any field, but also may re-enter the history of every established science each time somebody teaches us to *see* things in a light of which the source is not to be found in the facts, methods, and results of the pre-existing state of the science." Joseph Schumpeter, *History of Economic Analysis* (London: Allen & Unwin, 1954), p. 41.

4 UNEP Press Release, *UNEP's Global Environment Outlook Report Says Progress on the Road from Rio Uneven,* January 27, 1997.

5 Ibid.

6 UNDP Press Release, *Economic Growth Has Failed for a Quarter of the World's People, Says Report Written for UN Development Programme,* July 17, 1996.

7 Ibid.

8 Ibid.

9 Remarks by President Clinton in "Address to the United Nations Special Session on Environment and Development," June 26, 1997.

10 Theo Colborn, Dianne Dumanoski, and John Peterson Myers, *Our Stolen Future* (New York: Dutton, 1996), pp. 172-175.

11 See *Reanalysis of International Data Finds Sharp Decline in Sperm Density,* Press Release of the National Institute of Environmental Health Sciences, Nov. 24, 1997. http://www.Eurekalert.org/releases/intldata-spermdecln.html

12 From *Mastery: Interviews with 30 Remarkable People* (Portland,OR:Rudra, 1997). Quoted in *The Utne Reader,* Sept./Oct. 1997, p. 37.

1: Progress Imperfect

1 The quotation is taken from the back cover of "Perspectives on Business and Global Change," *The World Business Academy Journal,* v. 10, #2, 1996.

2 See, for instance, Robert D. Kaplan, "The Coming Anarchy," *Atlantic Monthly*, February 1994, pp. 44-76.

3 David Malin Roodman and Nicholas Lenssen, *A Building Revolution: How Ecology and Health Concerns Are Transforming Construction*, Worldwatch Paper 124, March 1995, p. 5.

4 David Korten, *When Corporations Rule the World* (West Hartford, CT and San Francisco, CA: Kumarian Press and Berrett-Koehler Publishers, Inc., 1995), p. 12.

5 Korten is by no means alone in his critique of global corporate capitalism. Among his philosophical bedfellows are the neo-Luddite and deep ecologist Jerry Mander (author of *In the Absence of the Sacred: The Failure of Technology and the Survival of the Indian Nations*); the Rolling Stone journalist and cultural critic William Greider (author of the much-praised *One World, Ready or Not: The Manic Logic of Global Capitalism*); and — less probably — financier George Soros, whose *Atlantic Monthly* article "The Capitalist Threat" argued that "the untrammeled intensification of laissez-faire capitalism and the spread of market values into all areas of life is endangering our open and democratic society." (George Soros, "The Capitalist Threat," *Atlantic Monthly*, February 1997, p. 45.

6 Jonathan Rowe, "Honey, We Shrunk the Economy!," in *Yes: A Journal of Positive Futures*, Spring/Summer 1996, p. 29.

7 In this book, I use the "global *problématique* " interchangeably with "sustainability crisis" (and alternatively "unsustainability crisis"). As a writer, I find all these usages unappealing. Unfortunately, to date nothing more palatable has come along.

2: Sustainable Development and the New Humanism

1 Ken Wilber, *A Brief History of Everything* (Boston: Shambhala, 1996), p. 276.

2 World Commission on Environment and Development, *Our Common Future* (Oxford: Oxford University Press, 1987), p. 43.

3 Herman Daly, *Beyond Growth: The Economics of Sustainable Development* (Boston: Beacon Press, 1996), p. 1.

4 Ken Wilber, *Eye to Eye* (Boston: Shambhala Publications, 1996), p. 21.

5 The absence of a direct one-to-one correspondence between the image and the ideas it gives sanctuary to may seem like a shortcoming, but it is not. In the world of metaphor and symbol, which is what we are dealing with here, it is natural and indeed desirable for a single image to hold many meanings.

6 See, for instance, Ken Wilber, *Sex, Ecology, Spirituality: The Spirit of Evolution* (Boston: Shambhala Publications, 1995).

7 Toulmin's thesis is presented in Stephen Toulmin, *Cosmopolis: The Hidden Agenda of Modernity* (Chicago: The University of Chicago Press, 1990).

8 Ken Wilber, *A Brief History of Everything* (Boston: Shambhala, 1996), p. 276.

9 Presentation, DeLange/Woodlands Conference, March 4, 1997.

10 In his speeches, author and lecturer Paul Hawken likes to tell the story of the little girl who is drawing a picture in art class. The teacher asks what she's drawing. "God," she explains blithely. "But no one knows what God looks like!" the teacher cautions. "You will when I'm finished," says the child reassuringly. Ditto for sustainable development.

11 James Hillman, *Kinds of Power: A Guide to Its Intelligent Uses* (New York: Doubleday,

1995), p. 37.

12 Ibid., p. 37.

13 Ibid., p. 39.

14 Ibid., pp. 39-40.

15 Another compelling example of cognitive dissonance comes courtesy of Moonlight Tobacco, an R. J. Reynolds company, which offers Planet cigarettes, featuring a graphic of the earth under the brand name. Never mind the fact that secondhand smoke is a major cause of indoor air pollution, or the contradictions inherent in linking a carcinogen like tobacco, which grossly pollutes the human body, with the widespread longing for a pristine planetary body.

16 Just how far consumerism — "affluenza," as a recent television documentary called it — has gone in the U.S. is captured by market research by Roper Starch Worldwide into what constitutes a "necessity," as distinguished from a "luxury." Fifty-five percent of respondents deemed a microwave oven a "necessity," 36% felt that way about a remote control for a TV or VCR, and 32% absolutely had to have that second car. See "More Things Are Necessities," *The Public Pulse*, June 1997, p. 1.

17 Most of these data are drawn from the 1995 and 1996 editions of *Vital Signs: The Trends That Are Shaping Our Futures* (New York: Norton): the data on refugees comes from *Vital Signs 1996*, p. 96; on women, from *Vital Signs 1996*, p. 134; and on malnourishment, from *Vital Signs 1995*, p. 146. The figure about poverty comes from an interview with Monsanto CEO Robert Shapiro. See Joan Magretta, "Growth Through Global Sustainability: An Interview with Monsanto's CEO, Robert B. Shapiro," *Harvard Business Review*, January/February 1997, p. 80.

18 "[O]ur societies have given increasing importance these last forty years to the imperative of growth and the production of more and more goods. Fascinated by the remarkable progress of our technology, we have set at the top of our priorities the 'culture of objects.' Hence the dominant culture is one that is determined and shaped by firms. As producers of the objects, technology infrastructures, and services that are shaping the new world economy, firms tend to claim that what is good for the firm is good for the world." The Group of Lisbon, *Limits to Competition* (Cambridge, MA: The MIT Press, 1995), pp. 63-64.

19 Some of the more prominent representatives of new-humanistic thinking in the U.S. include, in the corporate community, AT&T's Brad Allenby; among academics, Tom Gladwin of New York University's Stern School of Business, David Orr of Oberlin College, and the ecological economists Robert Costanza and Herman Daly, both from the University of Maryland; and, among non-governmental organizations, Anthony Cortese, head of Massachusetts-based Second Nature, a non-profit that focuses on education for sustainability. This is only a sampling of advocates — many other people are working to propagate new-humanistic values, both domestically and elsewhere, and the numbers are growing.

3: A Short History of Corporate Environmentalism

1 Bruce Piasecki, *Corporate Environmental Strategy: The Avalanche of Change Since Bhopal* (New York: John Wiley & Sons, 1994), p. 24.

2 Joe Romm, *Lean and Clean Management: How To Boost Profits and Productivity by Reducing Pollution* (New York: Kodansha American, 1994), pp. 98-99.

3 Cover letter for Baxter International 1993 environmental report.

4 H. Dale Martin, *Environmental Planning: Balancing Environmental Commitments with*

Economic Realities, 1994 GEMI Conference Proceedings, p. 61.

5 Du Pont has also come up with a compelling argument for voluntary pollution prevention, namely that "on average, regulatory-driven work costs three times more than voluntary waste reduction — for the same environmental benefit. There is a high probability that it can cost over ten times more than voluntary measures. The cost differential arises possibly because regulatory-driven work focuses on eliminating specific chemicals and using specific technology on a specific schedule, leaving little opportunity for a more holistic approach." Ibid., p. 63.

6 Linda Greer and Christopher Van Löbel Sels, "When Pollution Prevention Meets the Bottom Line," *Environmental Science & Technology,* September 1997.

7 Noah Walley and Bradley Whitehead, "It's Not Easy Being Green," *Harvard Business Review,* May-June 1994, p. 46.

8 Joan Bavaria, "The Challenge of Going Green," *Harvard Business Review,* July-August 1994, p. 40.

9 See Joel Makower, "It Isn't Easy Being...Oh, You Know," *The Green Business Letter,* December 1996, p. 3.

10 Ibid.

11 Ibid.

12 See Carl Frankel, "The Great Divide," *Green MarketAlert,* April 1991, p. 9.

13 As quoted in Joel Makower, *Beyond the Bottom Line: Putting Social Responsibility to Work for Your Business and the World* (New York: Simon & Schuster, 1994), pp. 28-29.

14 The Group of Lisbon, *Limits to Competition* (Cambridge, MA: The MIT Press, 1995), p. 110.

15 Christopher Flavin, *The Legacy of Rio,* in Lester R. Brown et al., *State of the World 1997* (New York: W.W. Norton, 1997), p. 5.

16 Ibid., p. 4, p. 7.

17 See "Notes for Lecture" by Maurice Strong, 1995 Blue Planet Prize, Development and Implementation Award, Asahi Glass Foundation, Tokyo, Japan, November 3, 1995.

18 The International Network for Environmental Management (INEM), an organization that links up national environmental management organizations, has issued a call for an "Industrial Agenda 21" under which companies would commit to publicly setting and reporting on environmental performance targets, but little progress has been made to date.

19 Stephan Schmidheiny, *Changing Course: A Global Business Perspective on Development and the Environment* (Cambridge, MA: The MIT Press, 1992), p. 10.

20 Ibid., p. 11.

21 Paul Hawken, *The Ecology of Commerce* (New York: HarperCollins, 1993), p. 168.

22 Ibid.

4: By the Numbers

1 On a down note consistent with the point made in the previous chapter that most third-era companies are not especially interested in strategic environmental management, most of these audits are conducted for regulatory compliance. A 1994 Ernst & Young survey of Canadian companies found that 86% of audits were conducted primarily for compliance. According to the Ernst & Young survey, other

reasons for conducting audits included: 1) helping to define potential risk areas – 78%; 2) increasing management's awareness of environmental issues – 67%; 3) protecting directors from potential liabilities – 51%; and 4) measuring and tracking environmental management system performance – 48%. See "Survey of Environmental Management in Canada," Ernst and Young, 1994.

2 See McKinsey and Co., *The Corporate Response to Environmental Challenge*, The Netherlands, August 1991, p. 7.

3 American Opinion Research, *Opinion Leaders Survey*, unpublished study, Princeton, NJ, p. 35. This is an apples-and-oranges comparison because the McKinsey survey was international. Still, it gives some sense of the overarching trend.

4 For the years covered here, the law obligated manufacturing facilities with 10 or more employees to file toxic chemical release reports if they manufactured or processed more than 25,000 pounds (12,000 kg) of any of some 300 listed toxic chemicals or otherwise used more than 10,000 pounds (4,500 kg) of any reportable chemicals.

5 See Investor Responsibility Research Center, *Corporate Enviornmental Profiles Directory, 1992-97*.

6 See a survey of executives and environmental managers in "Hitting the Green Wall," Arthur D. Little, Inc., 1995.

7 INFORM, *Toxics Watch 1995*, p.76.

8 Predictably, the Nexia survey found that larger companies within its sample were likelier to have a written policy statement. Thirty-five percent of companies with annual revenues of $20-$100 million had them, compared with only 13% of companies with revenues in the $1-$5 million range. *1993 Environmental Survey of Middle Market Manufacturers*, Nexia US, Ltd..

9 Many sustainability advocates favor a world dominated by small, local enterprises. For these people, bigness – scale – is inherently a problem. But smallness, and the accompanying lack of resources, is also a problem, as we have seen in this chapter – in terms of their environmental performance, large companies are vastly superior to SMEs. This circumstance, for which there is no obvious remedy, would seem to argue for transnational corporations and against local self-reliance.

10 Personal communication, 1995.

11 Some observers have expressed concern that often this may not actually happen. As noted earlier, there is little in the ISO 14001 certification process to keep companies from cooking their environmental-management books. Nor will customers necessarily come down hard on their suppliers to compel diligent performance, or even performance at all. There are already rumors of companies agreeing, once the first certification has been obtained, to forego further certifications – and to pass the cost savings on to the customers in the form of lower prices.

12 Personal communication, 1995.

13 See The President's Council on Sustainable Development, *Sustainable America: A New Consensus for Prosperity, Opportunity, and a Healthy Environment for the Future*, p. v.

14 Joel Makower, "Beyond Regulations: Why Regulators Are Taking Bold Steps Toward Corporate Self-Enforcement," *The Green Business Letter*, April 1996, p. 1, 6-7.

5: Communications and Community

1 See "Surveys Find Consumers Distrustful of Corporate Environmental Practices," *Green MarketAlert,* March 1991, p. 4.

2 "The Green Keiretsu: An International Survey of Business Alliances and Networks for Sustainable Development," *Tomorrow* magazine, October-December 1994, p. v.

3 See Kate Victory, "Japanese Coalition Launches Green Purchasing Network, *Business and the Environment,*" March 1996, p. 9.

4 PERI is a voluntary, *ad hoc* organization whose mission is to "provide a balanced, comprehensive and understandable framework" for corporate environmental reporting. WICE and GEMI are discussed in the section on green business networks, above.

5 World Industry Council for the Environment, *Environmental Reporting: A Manager's Guide,* Paris, 1994, p. 5.

6 See SustainAbility Survey: *The 1993 Fortune 100 Survey of Corporate Environmental Reporting,* London: SustainAbility, Figure 4.

7 See Joel Makower, "Rating Eco-Reports: Room for Improvement," *Green Business Letter,* May 1997, p. 3.

8 Personal communication, 1994.

9 Responding to the persistent presence of chlorinated compounds in the Great Lakes, a usually conservative United States/Canadian International Joint Commission recommended in 1992 that the U.S. and Canada "develop timetables to sunset the use of chlorine and chlorine-containing compounds as industrial feedstocks, and the means of reducing or eliminating other uses [such as water treatment and paper bleaching] be examined." It repeated its call for a phase-out in 1994. The American Public Health Association, which represents 50,000 health-care workers, has also come out in favor of avoiding "the use of chlorine and its compounds in manufacturing processes."

10 Personal communication, 1994.

11 Personal communication, 1994.

12 Personal communication, 1997.

6: Into the Fourth Era

1 Stuart Hart, "Beyond Greening: Strategies for a Sustainable World, *Harvard Business Review,*" January/February 1997, pp. 67-68.

2 Breweries may seem like a trivial focus but they aren't, not when you consider China, where beer consumption has grown by 600% over the past ten years and is expected to increase by another 500% in the future. If that number is on target, the Chinese beer industry will consume 8.5 billion gallons of fresh water and produce roughly 170 million gallons of wastewater annually, most of which will be released untreated into waterways. By any measure, that's not small beer.

3 The President's Council on Sustainable Development, *Sustainable America: A New Consensus: A New Consensus for Prosperity, Opportunity, and a Healthy Environment for the Future,* p. 102.

4 Kate Fish, *Corporate Decision-Making, Sustainable Development, and Uncertainty,* Presentation, DeLange/Woodlands Conference, March 3, 1997.

5 George Homsy, "Feeding the World by Biotech," *Tomorrow* magazine, March/April,

1997, p. 14.

6 Stuart Hart, "Beyond Greening," p. 72. The Aracruz Cellulose case study is drawn in its entirety from Hart's article.

7 Ibid.

8 This is not to suggest that Nike is a model of social responsibility. The company has come under fierce criticism for its use of sweatshop labor in Asia.

9 See Carl Frankel, "Mission Numerical," *Tomorrow* magazine, November/Dec-ember 1996, p. 18.

10 Quoted in John Elkington and Helen Stibbard, "Socially Challenged," *Tomorrow* magazine, March/April 1997, p. 54.

11 Personal communication, 1996.

12 See Eric Payne, "A New Horizon for the Tolt Basin," *The Seattle Times,* December 6, 1993, p. B-1.

13 Peter Senge, *The Fifth Discipline: The Art & Practice of the Learning Organization* (New York: Doubleday Currency, 1990), p. 141. Organizational learning's fifth discipline is *whole-systems thinking,* yet another characteristic of fourth-era corporate environmentalism.

14 Michele Galen and Karen West, "Companies Hit the Road Less Travelled," *Business Week,* June 5, 1995, pp. 82-4.

15 Ibid.

16 "Use Advertising and Marketing More Effectively," WBCSD Special Section, *Tomorrow* magazine, July/August 1996, n pag.

17 Quoted in "Why Smart Companies Will Take Part in the Debate on Sustainable Production and Consumption," *Business and the Environment,* August 1995, p. 2.

7: Mixed Messages

1 Martin Wright, "Energy, Economics and Ethics Collide," *Tomorrow* magazine, January/February 1997, p. 28.

2 The document was called *ABB Environmental Management Programme, Initial Review.* It was cited in a press release by International Rivers Network, "NGOs Urge ABB to Quit Malaysian Dam," July 5, 1996.

3 In late 1997, the Bakun project was put on hold for financial, not environmental reasons.

4 Quoted in Martin Wright, "Green Energy or White Elephant?" *Tomorrow* magazine, January/February 1997, p. 34. The comment was outlandish enough to earn Mahathir a place on *Tomorrow*'s list of "environmental chumps" for 1997.

5 Ibid., p. 35.

6 Quoted in Martin Wright, "Energy, Economics and Ethics," p. 28.

7 Quoted in Martin Wright, "Backing Up Bakun," *Tomorrow* magazine, January/February 1997, p. 29.

8 See Carl Frankel, "Corporate Responsibility Head-Butting," *Tomorrow* magazine, May/June 1997, p. 27.

9 Personal communication, 1994.

10 Cliff Gromer, "New Age of the Electric Car," *Popular Mechanics,* February 1994, p. 38.

11 Dan McCosh, "We Drive the World's Best Electric Car," *Popular Science,* January 1994, p. 52.

12 Personal communication, 1994.

13 Personal communication, 1995.

14 Personal communication, Paul Zajac, American Automobile Manufacturers Association, 1997.

15 These data come from a table entitled "U.S. Retail Sales of Sport Utility Vehicles, 1986-1996," with the credited sources being the American Automobile Manufacturers Association and Ward's Automotive Reports, from an unpublished document developed by the American Automobile Manufacturer's Association.

16 Vince Bielski, "Fuel Deficiency," from *Sierra* magazine and the Sierra Club website. See http://www.sierraclub.org/sierra/

17 Personal communication, 1997.

18 Quoted in Bielski, "Fuel Deficiency."

19 Responding to widespread criticism, Ford and Chrysler announced in early 1998 that they would refine popular models of their sport utility vehicles so they would produce no more air pollution than cars. See Keith Bradsher, "Ford, Chrysler to Cut Emissions of Sport Utility Vehicles, Minivans," *New York Times,* Jan. 6, 1998.

20 Keith Bradsher, "Car Makers Voice Complaints about Limiting Gas Emissions," *New York Times,* October 3, 1997, p. D 2.

21 Joan Magretta, "Growth Through Global Sustainability: An Interview with Monsanto's CEO, Robert B. Shapiro, " *Harvard Business Review,* January/February 1997, pp. 79-88.

22 Quoted in Carl Frankel, "Monsanto Breaks the Mold," *Tomorrow* magazine, May/June 1996, p. 63.

23 See Carl Frankel, "Consumers Rate Environmental Performance," *Green MarketAlert,* February 1992, pp. 5-6.

24 The following case study is drawn from excellent reportage by Kate Victory in the trade newsletter *Business and the Environment.* See Kate Victory, "Pharmaceutical Firms Get Mixed Market Signals on CFC-Free Inhalers," *Business and the Environment,* October 1996, pp. 2-5.

25 Ibid., p. 2.

26 Ibid., p. 3.

27 Ibid.

28 Ibid.

29 Personal communication, 1995.

30 Stephen Engelberg, "Business Leaves the Lobby and Sits at Congress's Table, " *New York Times,* March 31, 1997, A 1, A 26. The Dole bill was not enacted, although efforts continue to enact similar legislation.

31 Faye Rice, "Hands off the EPA! Did We Really Say That?, " *Fortune Magazine,* September 18, 1995, p. 22.

32 Quoted in Carl Frankel and Martin Wright, "The Business Dilemma," *Tomorrow* magazine, January/February 1997, p. 36.

33 Personal communication, 1996.

34 See the Global Climate Information Project website, at http://www.climatefacts.org

35 See Joby Warrick, "Trade Groups Move to Blunt UN Push for Pollutant Treaty," *Washington Post,* September 10, 1997, p. A 2.

36 The efforts of the Global Climate Coalition have been detailed in Ross Gelbspan, *The Heat Is On: The High Stakes Battle over Earth's Threatened Climate* (New York: Addison-Wesley Publishing Company, 1997).

37 See American Forest and Paper Association, *Sustainable Forestry Initiative,* Washington, DC, 1994.

38 Personal communication, 1995.

39 Ibid.

40 What this told Holmes, clever soul that he was, was that someone known to the dog had perpetrated the crime in question.

41 Richard A. Denison, "It's Time to Take Another Look at Plastics Recycling, " *EDF Letter,* v. 24, # 6, November 1993.

42 Personal communication, 1995.

43 The travails of these sustainability champions are discussed in greater detail in Carl Frankel, "Twilight of the Champions," *Tomorrow* magazine, September/October 1997, pp. 28-30.

44 *Utne Reader,* July/August 1990, inside cover and p. 1.

45 In point of fact, Dow's secrets are safe with CEAC members, who are required to sign confidentiality agreements.

46 Personal communication, 1997.

47 I use this example not to argue that Monsanto's vision of sustainable development is the correct one — I am undecided on that question — but to make the more limited point that individuals within corporations can be effective change agents. If Monsanto's Shapiro can steer his company toward a version of "sustainability" with large quotations marks, then in principle there is nothing to keep another executive from guiding his or her company toward a less troublesome version of sustainable development.

48 The work of Richard Grossman and Ward Morehouse in the Massachusetts-based Program on Corporations, Law & Democracy is representative of this sort of effort. Grossman and Morehouse argue that a sovereign people should be able to revoke corporate charters (or otherwise place strict limits on corporate behavior) when that conduct is detrimental to the general welfare, and that statutes on the books in many states make it legally appropriate to do so.

8: Across the Great Divide

1 Donella Meadows, "The Global Citizen: The Importance of Accurate Feedback," *Valley News,* August 17, 1991 as quoted in Joe Romm, *Lean and Clean Management: How to Boost Profits and Productivity by Reducing Pollution* (New York: Kodansha American, 1994), p. 45.

2 Personal communication, 1994.

3 Ibid.

4 The Management Institute for Environment and Business merged with the World Resources Institute in late 1996.

5 Michael E. Porter and Claas van der Linde, "Green and Competitive: Ending the Stalemate," *Harvard Business Review,* September/October 1995, pp. 120-121.

6 Executive summary, Motherwear eco-audit, performed by Green Audit during June and July of 1994.

7 MCC itself hesitates to use the term DFE in describing this project. They prefer to

use the term to refer to specific design tools. For our purposes, however, it is useful to think of DFE as a sort of *generic, eco-conscious design process.*

8 Fiona E.S. Murray, prepared under the supervision of Professor Richard H.K. Vietor, *Xerox: Design for the Environment,* Harvard Business School case study number N9-794-022, p. 7-8.

9 Gregory Eyring (U.S. Congress, Office of Technology Assessment), *Green Products by Design: Choices for a Cleaner Environment* (Washingto,n D.C.: U.S. Government Printing Office, 1992), p. 35.

10 In a similar vein, in 1997 The Pew Charitable Trusts launched the Chemical Strategies Partnership, a two-year program intended to develop a new model for manufacturer-supplier relationships that would promote reduced chemical usage. See Kate Victory, "Project May Offer New Model for Supplier Relationships," *Business and the Environment,* August 1997, pp. 2-4.

11 Daryl Ditz, Janet Ranganathan, and R. Darryl Banks, eds., *Green Ledgers: Case Studies in Corporate Environmental Accounting* (Washington, D.C.: World Resources Institute, 1995), p. 1.

12 See press release, *Value of the World's Ecosystem Services,* National Science Foundation, May 14, 1997.

13 Personal communication, 1994.

9: Whitecaps, Green Consumers, and the Infrastructure-Building Blues

1 There may be less to these numbers than meets the eye. They are compiled for the U.S. EPA's WasteWi$e program, which allows companies to include in their totals all products that contain any recycled content, even ones with levels as low as 1%. McDonald's includes much of the steel it purchases in its computations, because it contains recycled content. That doesn't raise any red flags for Bob Langert, McDonald's chief environmental officer, who contends that "the fact that most steel contains recycled content only makes a case for buying more steel." But there is also merit in the argument that the non-extraordinary nature of many of these purchases takes the starch out of the WasteWi$e totals.

2 The Clinton Administration has been much more proactive in the area of providing regulatory relief. The U.S. EPA is pursuing a number of initiatives whose collective aim is to make environmental regulations more user-friendly. The centerpiece of the EPA campaign is the Common Sense Initiative (CSI), which proposes to reinvent the currently byzantine environmental regulatory system. Six industries have been selected as testbeds for CSI: automotive assembly, computers and electronics, iron and steel, metal finishing, petroleum refining, and printing. Working with representatives from industry, state and local governments, and environmental-advocacy groups, EPA hopes to fashion a new and more straightforward regulatory framework that protects the environment while making it easier for business to comply. CSI hasn't attracted much media attention, but it is a considered, intelligent effort to create a regulatory life-form that is more beneficent than command-and-control. Another significant program is Project XL, under which companies receive the flexibility to adopt alternative strategies to the current system of regulation, on the condition that they produce environmental results that go beyond compliance. For instance, in a recent agreement with the EPA, executives for Weyerhaeuser, a major forest products company, agreed on such

measures as reducing water usage to 10 million gallons (38 million litres) a day (40% of the industry norm) at the company's Flint River, GA, pulp mill, reducing wastewater from the bleach plant by 50% (thereby significantly reducing emissions of chlorine compounds and pollutants), getting ISO 14001 certification for the plant, and taking various steps to enhance the wildlife in 300,000 acres (121,000 ha) of Weyerhaeuser's forest land. The *quid* for those *quos*: special permission to make process control changes that will allow the company to make manufactured product changes more quickly and at less than current cost.

The EPA is also exploring other ways to encourage companies to seek ISO 14001 certification such as preferred status in bidding for government contracts and a presumption of due diligence in criminal actions. State and local governments are also actively encouraging companies to be more environmentally responsible. For instance, Seattle's EnviroStars program awards companies anywhere from two to five stars, depending on the extent of their commitment to hazardous waste reduction. And the San Francisco Bay Area's Green Business Program encourages public support and patronage of companies with a demonstrated commitment to the environment.

3 Executive Order 12873 — Federal Acquisition, Recycling and Waste Prevention.

4 *Product Alert 1996 Round-Up*, Marketing Intelligence Service, Ltd., Naples, NY: p. 34.

5 Cited in Joel Makower, "The New Green Gospel: What the Latest Research Tells Us About Consumer Concern and Action on the Environment," *The Green Business Letter*, May 1996, p. 6.

6 For instance, a survey published in *USA Today* on January 30, 1997 (p. A 1) indicates that 61% of Americans are "sympathetic to environmental concerns" and 9% are "active environmentalists." And in an April 1995 *USA Today*/CNN/Gallup poll, 63% of Americans describe themselves as environmentalists.

7 See Joel Makower, "'Green Gauge' Tracks Public's Ups, Downs on the Environment," *The Green Business Letter*, December 1996, p. 4.

8 The Hartman Group, *The Hartman Report — Food and the Environment: A Consumer's Perspective, Phase 1*, Summer 1996, p. 27.

9 Ibid.

10 Ibid.

11 Ibid., p. 13.

12 M. Jimmie Killingworth and Jacqueline S. Palmer, "Liberal and Pragmatic Trends in the Discourse of Green Consumerism," in James G. Cantrill and Christine L. Oravec, eds., *The Symbolic Earth: Discourse and Our Creation of the Environment* (Lexington, KY: The University of Kentucky Press, 1996), p. 224.

13 From this perspective, "green consumerism" is an oxymoron: one can embrace the green ideology *or* the consumerist ideology, but not both at the same time.

14 M. Jimmie Killingworth and Jacqueline S. Palmer, ibid, p. 227.

15 Kate Victory, "U.S. DOE Urged to Adopt Refrigerator Efficiency Standards," *Business and the Environment*, October 1996, p. 133.

16 Corporate social responsibility is another tie-breaker. In a 1997 study sponsored by Cone Communications, a Boston-based strategic cause-marketing firm, roughly three-quarters of the respondents indicated that, with price and quality being equal, they would be likely to change to a product associated with a good cause. The fact that the poll was funded by an organization with a clear interest in pro-cause marketing findings is reason for pause. Still, as one commentator noted,

"The stud[y] suggests that at a time when consumers' perceptions of differences between products are diminishing, and high quality and low price are an expectation of consumers, cause marketing increasingly is becoming a 'tie-breaker' in purchase decisions." See "Cause Marketing," *The Public Pulse*, Roper-Starch International, May 1997, pp. 1-3.

17 "For starters, 99% of U.S. schools have some kind of environmental program or class, and 80% of educators say their programs will grow in the next few years, according to a 1994 ERA survey." Joel Makower, "The New Green Gospel: What the Latest Research Tells Us About Consumer Concern and Action on the Environment," *The Green Business Letter*, May 1996, p. 7.

18 Dr. David M. Eisenberg et al., "Unconventional Medicine in the United States: Prevalence, Cost and Patterns of U.S.," *New England Journal of Medicine*, January 28, 1993, pp. 246-282.

19 See Joel Makower, "A More Balanced Life," *The Green Business Letter*, September 1995, p. 8.

20 See Ken Mergentine and Monica Emerich, "Widening Market Carries Organic Sales to $2.8 Billion in 1995," *Natural Foods Merchandiser*, June 1996, pp. 36-38. Also see, Karen Raterman, "Contradictions Propel Industry Growth," *Natural Foods Merchandiser*, June 1997, pp. 1, 26.

21 See Seventh Generation press release, *Green Product Market Will Hit $30 Billion by 2005*, November 4, 1996.

22 See "Widening Market Carries Organic Sales."

23 Marc Luyckx, "The State of the Future," *Yes! A Journal of Positive Futures*, Winter 1997, p. 16.

24 Paul H. Ray, "The Rise of Integral Culture," *Noetic Sciences Review*, Spring 1996.

10: The Data Game

1 *The International Thesaurus of Quotations* (New York: Crowell, 1970), p. 624.

2 Quoted in James Hillman, *The Soul's Code: In Search of Character and Calling* (New York: Random House, 1996), p. 96.

3 Wyndham Lewis, in *The Art of Being Ruled*, (1926) [from *The Columbia Dictionary of Quotations*, New York: Columbia University Press, 1993.]

4 Personal communication, 1995.

5 "The Many Uses of Risk Assessment, " *Rachel's Environment & Health Weekly*, # 420, December 15, 1994.

6 Ibid.

7 Ibid.

8 Ibid.

9 Ibid.

10 Ibid.

11 In a 1987 landmark study, the EPA ranked the risk posed by some 31 areas of environmental concern, as perceived by scientific experts and the public respectively. The study then examined the EPA's own priorities, and found that they were more closely aligned with those of the public than with those of the scientists. This revelation gave a great boost to the "good science" movement — indeed, to both its pro-science and anti-environmentalist factions.

12 Roger D. Wynne, "The Emperor's New Eco-Logos?: A Critical Review of the

Scientific Certification Systems Environmental Report Card and the Green Seal Certification Mark Programs," *Virginia Environmental Law Journal*, Fall 1994, p. 87.

13 Ibid., pp. 87-88.

14 The organization has been criticized for failing to practice what it preaches with regard to the consensus-building process, but for the purposes of this discussion, which is to contrast faith-in-consensus with faith-in-science, that is irrelevant.

15 See Richard A. Denison, *Comments of the Environmental Defense Fund on Scientific Certification Systems' Life-cycle Inventory and the Environmental Report Card* (May 5, 1992), Environmental Defense Fund, Washington, DC.

16 Wynne, "The Emperor's New Eco-Logos," p. 140.

17 Ibid., p. 75.

18 Ibid., p. 78.

19 To measure performance across companies, there must be consensus on two points: 1) what environmental burdens will be measured; and 2) what those burdens will be measured against. In other words, both common numerators and common denominators are required. Unfortunately, we are not close to having either one. The Investor Responsibility Research Center is attempting to address this problem by developing a suite of "sustainability indicators" that in its final incarnation could include such measures as energy efficiency (energy/unit revenue), water withdrawal (tons-of-water/ton-of-product or per-unit revenue), and hazardous waste generation (pounds/unit production value). Another interested party is CERES, the coalition of environmentally-concerned groups that sponsors the 10-point CERES Principles. The organization is considering tightening the requirements for its CERES Report, moving from requiring simply a statement of various environmental outputs to normalizing those figures against a common denominator such as sales or units produced. In so doing, it is following the lead of companies like Polaroid, whose Toxic Use and Waste Reduction Program (TUWR) index measures environmental performance against product units produced. CERES recently launched a multi-year Global Reporting Initiative, the purpose of which is to use a multi-stakeholder framework to build a consensus on standards for corporate environmental reporting.

20 It's not quite that simple, actually: the numbers will be "normalized" against a single baseline.

21 The development of community sustainability indexes is being nurtured by two parallel developments. The first of these is the growing realization that traditional measures such as the Gross Domestic Product are woefully inadequate — that, in the words of maverick economist Hazel Henderson, "[t]rying to run a complex society on a single indicator like the Gross National Product is literally like trying to fly a 747 with only one gauge on the instrument panel ... imagine if your doctor, when giving you a checkup, did no more than check your blood pressure," (Hazel Henderson, *Paradigms in Progress*, Indianapolis: Knowledge Systems, 1991, p. 128). Second, the movement is benefiting from the active support of the public sector and the multilateral development community. The United Nations has launched an Urban Indicators Program to develop indicators for all "major aspects of human settlements activity," (United Nations Centre for Human Settlements, The Global Urban Observatory, *Urban Indicators Programme, Phase Two: 1996-2001 [DRAFT]*, p. 6). In addition, the United Nations Development Programme has devised a Human Development Index that ranks countries based on a combination of pur-

chasing power, educational levels, and life expectancy. The U.S. President's Council on Sustainable Development has come out for a continued federal effort to "develop national indicators of progress toward sustainable development," (The President's Council on Sustainable Development, *Sustainable America: A New Consensus*, p. 66). The World Bank has developed a Wealth Accounting System that indexes countries according to four kinds of assets: 1) produced assets, such as factories and infrastructure; 2) human resources; 3) natural, i.e., environmental capital; and 4) social capital (families, communities, etc.). Cumulatively, enough momentum is building to create the impression that community — as well as national — sustainability indicators are an irresistable "emergent."

22 See The Body Shop/*Our Agenda*, p. 18 and p. 3 respectively.

23 See *The Body Shop Approach to Ethical Auditing*, 1996, p. 1.

24 Neil Postman, *Technopoly: The Surrender of Culture to Technology* (New York, Alfred A. Knopf, 1992), p. 13.

25 Quoted in Hazel Henderson, *Building a Win-Win World* (San Francisco: Berrett-Koehler, 1996), p. 224.

11: From Here to Sustainability

1 Personal communication, 1995.

2 Carcinogenicity refers to a substance's cancer-causing potential, teratogenicity to its capacity to cause malformations in embryos, and mutagenicity to its potential to increase the frequency of mutations in organisms.

3 Personal communication, 1995.

4 Ibid.

5 Günter Pauli, "Zero Emissions: The New Industrial Clusters," *Ecodecision Magazine*, Spring 1995, p. 26.

6 These figures come from Paul Hawken who cites the International Labor Organization as his source. Personal communication, 1997.

7 Personal communication, September 22, 1995.

8 Paula DiPerna, "More than money: How microcredit is challenging the world's macro-poverty," *The Earth Times*, February 16-28, p. 7. The bulk of the facts cited in my discussion of micro-credit are drawn from DiPerna's excellent article.

9 Karl-Henrik Robèrt, *Simplicity Without Reduction: Thinking Upstream Toward the Sustainable Society*, unpublished paper, 1995, n pag.

10 Ibid.

11 Ibid.

12 Ibid.

13 Ibid.

14 Ibid.

15 Ibid.

16 RMI Homepage, *Frequently Asked Questions About Hypercars*, pp. 7-8. In fact, Toyota did start offering the Prius, a hybrid-electric, in Japan in late 1997.

17 Quoted in Carl Frankel, "We've Been Wrong Before," *Tomorrow* magazine, July/August 1996, p. 22.

18 United States Department of Agriculture, *Industrial Uses of Agricultural Materials: Situation and Outlook Report*, p. 5.

19 Speech by John Browne, Group Chief Executive, British Petroleum (BP America), Stanford University, May 19, 1997.

Resource Guide:

Business and Sustainable Development

The following list of resources may be useful to readers interested in learning more about business and sustainable development. It is *not* a bibliography. Nor does it purport to be a comprehensive listing of materials on the subject — it is provided solely as a convenience for the reader. While most of the works focus primarily (if not exclusively) on business and sustainability, I have included several other works that focus on critically important related issues, e.g., the health of the planet and ecological economics. While the great majority of books are pro-business or neutral, in the interests of balance I have included several that are anti-corporate. Collectively, these works can be said to comprise a short — or not-so-short — course in business and sustainable development.

Periodical Publications

Electronic

The New Bottom Line. Biweekly syndicated column on business/sustainability strategies and policies, written by Gil Friend, president of the eco-consultancy Gil Friend & Associates. Tel: 510-548-7904. Fax: 510-849-2341. E-mail: . nbl-info@eco-ops.com Website: http://www.eco-ops.com

Sustainable Business Network. Monthly magazine disgesting business/sustainability news items. Site also provides green resources, jobs, other information. Address: http://www.envirolink.org/sbn

Tomorrow magazine website. Provides corporate environmental reports, sector-by-sector industry analyses, other information. Address: http://www.tomorrow-web.com

Print

Business and the Environment. Monthly newsletter covering global business/sustainability developments. Cutter Information Corp., 37 Broadway, Arlington, MA

02174. Tel: 617-641-5125. Fax: 617-648-1950. E-mail: bate@igc.apc.org

Corporate Environmental Strategy. Published quarterly by PRI Publishing, 333 Main Street, Metuchen, NJ 08840. Tel: 908-548-5827. Fax: 908-548-2268. E-mail: AHC_CES@rpi.edu

Environmental Quality Management. Published quarterly by John H. Wiley & Sons, 605 Third Avenue, New York, NY 10158. Tel: 212-850-6479. E-mail: SUBINFO@wiley.com Editorial inquiries: icohen@wiley.com

The Green Business Letter. Monthly newsletter providing regular updates on leading-edge corporate environmental practices and strategies, mostly in the U.S. Tilden Press Inc., 1519 Connecticut Ave. NW, Washington D.C. 20036. Tel: 202-332-1700. E-mail: gbl@greenbiz.com Website: http://www.greenbiz.com

Tomorrow magazine. Glossy Stockholm-based publication focusing exclusively on the business/sustainability domain, currently published six times a year. Tomorrow Publishing, Halsingegatan 9, 113 23 Stockholm, Sweden. Tel: 46- 8-33-5290. Fax: 46- 8-32-9333. E-mail: info@tomorrow.se

Magazine Articles

Hart, Stuart, "Beyond Greening: Strategies for a Sustainable World," *Harvard Business Review,* January/February 1997

Magretta, Joan, "Growth Through Global Sustainability: An Interview with Monsanto's CEO, Robert B. Shapiro," *Harvard Business Review,* January/February 1997

Walley, Noah and Whitehead, Bradley, "It's Not Easy Being Green," *Harvard Business Review,* May/June 1994

Books (Business and Sustainable Development)

Allenby, Braden R. and Richards, Deanna J., eds., *The Greening of Industrial Ecosystems* (Washington, D.C.: National Academy Press, 1994)

Cairncross, Frances, *Green, Inc.: A Guide to Business and the Environment* (Washington, D.C.: Island Press, 1995)

Callenbach, Ernest; Capra, Fritjof; Goldman, Lenore; Lutz, Rüdiger and Marburg, Sandra, *EcoManagement: The Elmwood Guide to Ecological Auditing and Sustainable Business* (San Francisco: Berrett-Koehler, 1993)

Capra, Fritjof and Pauli, Gunter, eds., *Steering Business Toward Sustainability* (Tokyo: United Nations University, 1995)

Coddington, Walter, *Environmental Marketing* (New York: McGraw-Hill, 1994)

Ditz, Daryl; Ranganathan, Janet; and Banks, R. Darryl, eds., *Green Ledgers: Case Studies in Corporate Environmental Accounting* (Washington, D.C.: World Resources Institute, 1995)

Epstein, Marc J., *Measuring Corporate Environmental Performance: Best Practices for Costing and Managing an Effective Environmental Strategy* (Chicago: Irwin, 1996)

Fischer, Kurt and Schot, Johan, eds., *Environmental Strategies for Industry: International Perspectives on Research Needs and Policy Implications* (Washington, D.C.: Island Press, 1993)

Frause, Bob and Colehour, Julie, *The Environmental Marketing Imperative: Strategies for Transforming Environmental Commitment into a Competitive Advantage* (Chicago: Probus, 1994)

Fussler, Claude with James, Peter, *Driving Eco Innovation: A Breakthrough Discipline for Innovation and Sustainability* (London: Pitman, 1996)

Gelbspan, Ross, *The Heat Is On: The High-Stakes Battle over Earth's Threatened Climate* (New York: Addison-Wesley, 1997)

Greer, Jed and Bruno, Kenny, *Greenwash: The Reality Behind Corporate Environmentalism* (Malaysia and New York: Third World Network and Apex Press, 1996)

Groenewegen, Peter; Fischer, Kurt; Jenkins, Edith G. and Schot, Johan, eds., *The Greening of Industry Resource Guide and Bibliography* (Washington, D.C.: Island Press, 1996)

Hawken, Paul; Lovins, Amory; and Lovins, Hunter, *Natural Capitalism: The Next Industrial Revolution* (Boston: Little Brown). The scheduled publication date is 1998.

Hawken, Paul, *The Ecology of Commerce* (New York: HarperCollins, 1993)

Hoffman, Andrew J., *From Heresy to Dogma: An Institutional History of Corporate Environmentalism* (San Francisco: New Lexington, 1997)

Hoffman, W. Michael; Frederick, Robert; and Petry, Edward S., Jr., eds., *The Corporation, Ethics, and the Environment* (Westport, CT: Quorum, 1990)

Kolluru, Rao V., ed., *Environmental Strategies Handbook: A Guide to Effective Policies and Practices* (New York: McGraw-Hill, 1994)

Ledgerwood, Grant; Street, Elizabeth; and Therivel, Riki, *Implementing an Environmental Audit: How to Gain a Competitive Advantage Using Quality and Environmental Responsibility* (Burr Ridge, IL: Irwin, 1994)

Leggett, Jeremy, ed., *Climate Change and the Financial Sector: The Emerging Threat — The Solar Solution* (Munich: Gerling Akademie Verlag, 1996)

Long, Frederick J. and Arnold, Matthew B., *The Power of Environmental Partnerships* (Orlando, FL: Harcourt Brace, 1995)

Makower, Joel, *Beyond the Bottom Line: Putting Social Responsibility to Work for Your Business and the World* (New York: Simon & Schuster, 1994)

Makower, Joel, *The E Factor: The Bottom-Line Approach to Environmentally Responsible Business* (New York: Times Books, 1993)

Marcus, Philip A. and Willig, John T., eds., *Moving Ahead with ISO 14000: Improving Environmental Management and Advancing Sustainable Development* (New York: John Wiley & Sons, 1997)

Pennell, Allison A.; Choi, Patricia E.; and Molinaro Jr., Lawrence, eds., *Business and the Environment: A Resource Guide* (Washington, D.C.: Island Press, 1992)

Piasecki, Bruce, *Corporate Environmental Strategy: The Avalanche of Change Since Bhopal* (New York: John Wiley & Sons, 1994)

Plant, Christopher and Plant, Judith, eds., *Green Business: Hope or Hoax? Toward an Authentic Strategy for Restoring the Earth* (Gabriola Island, B.C.: New Society Publishers, 1991)

Ray, Michael and Rinzler, Alan, for the World Business Academy, *The New Paradigm in Business: Emerging Strategies for Leadership and Organizational Change* (New York: Tarcher/Perigee, 1993)

Reder, Alan, *In Pursuit of Principle and Profit: Business Success Through Social Responsibility* (New York: Tarcher/Putnam, 1994)

Romm, Joseph J., *Lean and Clean Management: How To Boost Profits and Productivity by Reducing Pollution* (New York: Kodansha American, 1994)

Rubenstein, Daniel Blake, *Environmental Accounting for the Sustainable Corporation* (Westport, CT: Quorum, 1994)

Schmidheiny, Stephan and Zorraquín, Federico J. L., with the World Business Council on Sustainable Development, *Financing Change: The Financial Community, Eco-Efficiency, and Sustainable Development* (Cambridge, MA: MIT Press, 1996)

Schmidheiny, Stephan, *Changing Course: A Global Business Perspective on Development and the Environment* (Cambridge, MA: The MIT Press, 1992)

Shrivastava, Paul, *Greening Business: Profiting the Corporation and the Environment* (Cincinnati: Thomson Executive Press, 1996)

Smart, Bruce, *Beyond Compliance: A New Industry View of the Environment* (Washington, D.C.: World Resources Institute, 1992)

Stauber, John and Rampton, Sheldon, *Toxic Sludge Is Good for You! Lies, Damn Lies and the Public Relations Industry* (Monroe, ME: Common Courage Press, 1995)

Sullivan, Thomas F. P., ed., *The Greening of American Business: Making Bottom-Line Sense of Environmental Responsibility* (Rockville, MD: Government Institutes Inc., 1992)

Tibor, Tom with Feldman, Ira, *ISO 14000: A Guide to the New Environmental Management Standards* (Chicago: Irwin, 1996)

Wasik, John F., *Green Marketing and Management: A Global Perspective* (Cambridge, MA: Blackwell, 1996)

Books and Reports (Related Topics)

Brown, Lester R. et. al., *State of the World* (New York: W.W. Norton). Annual publication.

Brown, Lester R.; Lenssen, Nicholas; and Kane, Hal, *Vital Signs: The Trends That Are Shaping Our Future* (New York: W.W. Norton). Annual publication.

Daly, Herman E. and Cobb Jr. John B., *For the Common Good: Redirecting the Economy Toward Community, the Environment and a Sustainable Future* (Boston: Beacon Press, 1989)

Daly, Herman, *Beyond Growth: The Economics of Sustainable Development* (Boston: Beacon Press, 1996)

Gore, Al, *Earth in the Balance: Ecology and the Human Spirit* (New York: Houghton Mifflin, 1992)

Greider, William, *One World, Ready or Not: The Manic Logic of Global Capitalism* (New York: Simon & Schuster, 1997)

Henderson, Hazel, *Building a Win-Win World* (San Francisco: Berrett-Koehler, 1996)

Henderson, Hazel, *Paradigms in Progress: Life Beyond Economics* (Indianapolis: Knowledge Systems, 1991)

Korten, David, *When Corporations Rule the World* (West Hartford, CT and San Francisco, CA: Kumarian Press and Berrett-Koehler Publishers Inc., 1995)

Marien, Michael, ed., *Environmental Issues and Sustainable Futures* (Bethesda, MD: World Future Society, 1996)

Rich, Bruce, *Mortgaging the Earth: The World Bank, Environmental Impoverishment, and the Crisis of Development* (Boston: Beacon Press, 1994)

Senge, Peter M., *The Fifth Discipline: The Art & Practice of the Learning Organization* (New York: Currency Doubleday, 1994)

The Group of Lisbon, *Limits to Competition* (Cambridge, MA: The MIT Press, 1995)

The President's Council on Sustainable Development, *Sustainable America: A New Consensus for Prosperity, Opportunity and a Healthy Environment for the Future*, 1996

Index

Numbers following the letter 'n' refer to footnotes, with chapter numbers in square brackets, if needed.

CONSCIENTIOUS COMMERCE

*In Earth's Company: Business, Environment
and the Challenge of Sustainability*
is the first in New Society Publisher's
CONSCIENTIOUS COMMERCE
series of books.

This series aims to appeal equally to both corporate
executives seeking to bring their companies into the
21st century, and to environmental activists wanting to
know more about the ways in which business is
responding to the challenges of sustainability.

For more information about other titles in NSP's
CONSCIENTIOUS COMMERCE series, call 1-800-567-6772,
or check out our web site at:
www.newsociety.com

NEW SOCIETY PUBLISHERS